TOP MAN

TOP MAN

GEOFF TWENTYMAN

MY STORY

WITH NEIL PALMER

pitch

First published by Pitch Publishing, 2024

Pitch Publishing
9 Donnington Park,
85 Birdham Road,
Chichester,
West Sussex,
PO20 7AJ
www.pitchpublishing.co.uk
info@pitchpublishing.co.uk

A CIP catalogue record is available for this book from the British Library.

ISBN 978 1 80150 704 2

MIX
Paper | Supporting responsible forestry
FSC® C013056

Printed and bound in the UK on FSC® certified paper in line with our continuing commitment to ethical business practices, sustainability and the environment.

Typesetting and origination by Pitch Publishing

Printed and bound in Great Britain by TJ Books, Padstow

Contents

Dedicated to Dave Palmer

10 April 1961 to 2 March 2011

Taken from us far too soon

Acknowledgements

FROM MY teenage years I've always enjoyed reading sports autobiographies. It has been a surreal privilege to have written my own. Writing an account of my life has been a compelling and at times obsessive experience. When I embarked on the journey, I didn't envisage that I'd find the whole process so enjoyable.

My biggest and most fundamental thanks go to Jane Camillin at Pitch Publishing. Thank you so much for embracing my story and bringing it alive in words and pictures.

Neil Palmer has played a key role in formatting the manuscript and photos for onward transmission to the team at Pitch. Neil was always there to answer my questions and resolve any issues. He's a patient man, and I lost count of how many 'final' amendments I made.

Keith Brookman was also invaluable with his Bristol Rovers information. My daughter Hannah and her husband Jon were great champions of the project and gave me huge support and encouragement throughout.

The title of the book was my catchphrase when I addressed people at the end of a chat on the radio. I don't know when it started and how it prevailed, but 'Top Man' seems the right title.

Thanks to Ivan Butler and Dean Rockett for their invaluable expertise and knowledge in editing and proofreading my words, sentences and chapters. Also thanks to Duncan Olner for his skills behind the lens in creating the cover photograph. It's true, the camera never lies! Graham Hales did a sterling job in sorting the photographs from the ages. Pitch are a Top Team.

Huge thanks to you if you watched me play football or listened to me on the radio, and a massive thank you for reading this book.

Geoff Twentyman

Introduction

IT'S 2.40PM on Saturday, 29 April 2023. I'm presenting *Saturday Sport* on BBC Radio Bristol at a City home game for the final time. After 30 years at the Beeb, I've decided to ease back from working full-time. I'm delivering a live link. I hear my name mentioned over the PA system. Our City summariser, Gary Owers, nudges me and points at the big screen in the far corner of Ashton Gate. There's a picture of City owner Steve Lansdown and me. Warm applause reverberates around the stadium. The PA announcer asks me to stand up, if I can.

Somewhat embarrassed, I stand up to acknowledge the applause. The noise increases and reaches quite a crescendo. People are standing up to my right, in the Dolman opposite, behind me, in the lower tier of the Lansdown Stand down below, and more people are standing to my left. The South Stand to my far right has joined in the applause. The ground as one is applauding me.

An incredible moment. One I'll never forget.

Flashback 36 years to 1 January 1987. My first-ever Bristol derby in a Rovers shirt. Over 23,000 fans inside Ashton Gate. An intense rivalry. High emotions. If it was a boxing match it would have been stopped after 35 minutes, such was City's dominance.

Injury time, 0-0. Rovers have a free kick just inside our half. I'm standing over it. Option one: pass it back to our keeper Timmy

Carter (RIP Tim x) to run down the clock and take an undeserved point. Option two: stick it in the mixer, have some fun. Option two selected. From my 45-yard 'whoosh', City defender David Moyes wins the header, Gary Smart walks on to it and hits the shot of his life. It arrows towards Keith Waugh's right-hand corner. Unstoppable. City nil, Rovers one. Daylight robbery.

This was proper football. High-octane emotions. No place for coming second. An incredible experience, one I'll never forget. I certainly didn't envisage then that 36 years later I'd receive a standing ovation from the home supporters.

There have been some amazing experiences and exceptional people along my journey, and throughout this book I'll share them all, as well as my thoughts on managing people. For a considerable amount of my working life, I was in charge of individuals and groups. I didn't get everything right. As I journeyed through the years I drew on my experiences, some that may not have been overly significant when they occurred but resonated later in life. So, if you manage people, my thoughts and experiences might be useful, or at least thought-provoking.

This is my tale. I hope you enjoy it.

Chapter 1

Values

AS A youngster growing up on Merseyside, the neighbours thought I only had two forms of clothing: football kits or my school uniform. They rarely saw me in 'normal' clothes. By the age of 12 I had the best part of 20 shirts. The iconic red shirt of Liverpool was my pride and joy, but I also had the red and black stripes of Manchester City's away kit, the red shirt with white sleeves of Arsenal, and the wonderful Crystal Palace shirt, with its red and blue diagonal stripes. I always hoped to wear a 'real' shirt and follow in my dad's illustrious footsteps – he played for Liverpool after starting his career at Carlisle United in the 1950s.

As a kid I used to play Subbuteo in the lounge. As I flicked the players around the pitch, I used to commentate aloud: 'Smith to Lawler, inside to Strong, on to Hunt, who races through and smashes it past the keeper at the Kop end. It's Liverpool 4 Manchester United 0 ...'

I was blessed to follow in the great man's footsteps and then enjoy a 30-year career behind a microphone with the BBC in Bristol.

The circuitous journey started at Broad Green Hospital in Liverpool on 10 March 1959. We lived in Huyton with Roby. I was the third Twentyman sibling. I was always known as 'Geoffrey' or 'Geoff Jnr', as Dad was Geoff. My sister Susan is six years my senior and Margaret is three years older than me. My brother Billy is seven years my junior.

And, of course, there was Mum, Pat. She and Dad were two incredible people and wonderful parents. They instilled values such as kindness, compassion, understanding, honesty and integrity into all of us Twentymans. Mum was the driver; she was the glue that kept everything together. She always seemed to have a part-time job. She oversaw the pic'n'mix counter at Woolworths in Maghull. She did it with such pride. Even on her days off she'd drop in to make sure everything was well! That was a lesson in itself. Whatever you do, do it to the best of your ability.

Although I hate to use the term disciplinarian, she made sure we always stayed on the right track. I learned so much from her, not only in terms of how to be a decent human being but how to treat other people. Mum taught me practical things such as sewing, ironing and cooking. Even today I mend and sew things, especially for the grandchildren. If a costume or bit of clothing needs a needle and thread, the little people will say, 'Pops will mend it.' That's a legacy from Mum that I'm really proud of.

Dad was old-school with his morals and finances. You always told the truth regardless of the implications. He worked on the principle that if you couldn't afford something, then you had to save up and buy it when you could. I learned the value of money through Dad. As a kid I used to practise bowling a leather cricket ball against the back of the house. The target area was the brick below the lounge window. One time I got it very wrong, and the delivery was too high. Rather than hitting the wall it went clean through the window. Seconds later Dad was peering through the perfectly formed circular hole, with the cricket ball in his hand. If it wasn't so serious, it would have been hilarious. There was no case for the defence. Guilty as charged. Dad didn't shout, but calmly told me that I'd have to pay for the new pane out of my hard-earned pocket money. It was an expensive lesson, but it was good in establishing an appreciation of values and understanding how life worked.

Dad also told me to shake hands with a firm grip and look the person in the eyes when meeting them. That's something I've continued to do. Apparently, Bristol's former world boxing champion Lee Haskins wouldn't shake hands with me in the build-up to a fight to protect his hands!

Mum and Dad were both from Cumbria. Dad was raised on a farm out in the sticks at Brampton. He used to tell us about his ferrets and life as a country bumpkin. He was Cumberland wrestling champion back in the day. Mum was from Carlisle, the daughter of a steam train driver. They met at a dance and married at a church on Warwick Road, which, ironically, was just down the road from Brunton Park, the home of Carlisle United.

We lived a somewhat nomadic lifestyle in my early years. It was the back end of Dad's playing days and we went from Liverpool to Ballymena in Northern Ireland and then to Carlisle via Hartlepool. Pre-school years were in Ballymena. There was a building site at the bottom of the road where we lived and, as you can imagine, it was a source of great excitement to yours truly. When I look back, I was front and centre to a health and safety nightmare and a child protection issue – how times have changed! I used to toddle down to the site with a tin mug and a packed lunch. I'd get stuck in and 'help' the builders. I loved going to the site, and the bricklayers used to love having me there.

I still carry a scar on my lower lip from falling on a pile of bricks on that site! What was far worse, I picked up the industrial language. Much to Mum's horror, her first-born son repeated all sorts of profanities in his cute little Irish accent, which led to me not being allowed out socially until this 'phase' had passed. 'F' bombs were awkward and inappropriate from someone so young.

The next phase of my formative years took us to Hartlepool. Dad became manager of Hartlepool Football Club, but not for long. Memories are vague, to be honest, but I remember going to the ground, which was a shabby place in a state of disrepair. I recall Mum coming home from a hospital appointment elated to tell me I was going to have a new brother or sister. Then, with Mum pregnant, Dad was sacked. The chairman/owner, a Mr Orr, had lined up a certain Brian Clough as the next manager at Victoria Park.

So, for the family of five – soon to be six – it was back to Carlisle. Dad secured a job with the Cumberland Egg Marketing Board. It was a cracking job. He used to drive a lorry around the county, collecting eggs from farms. At the same time, he had spells as manager of non-league clubs Penrith and Morecambe. I used to go as often as I was allowed, and loved sneaking into the dressing room to savour the smells, the atmosphere, the buzz, the banter – it was brilliant.

My recollections from living in Carlisle are hazy. I recall starting school there and hating it. I used to get really upset when Mum dropped me off. I went to watch my first-ever professional game of football in Carlisle. It was an evening game at Brunton Park. I didn't know it at the time, but the main stand was built from the fee that Carlisle received from Liverpool when Dad was transferred to Anfield.

The game was nondescript. The brightest memory was a man in a blue-and-white top hat and tails running on to the pitch before the game and putting 'Olga' the fox on the centre spot. 'Olga' was a stuffed version of Basil Brush. 'Twinkletoes' was the guy who delivered and collected the fox. An incredible ritual, not as emotional as 'You'll Never Walk Alone' at Anfield, but it obviously affected me enough to remember it! By the way, 'Olga' is an anagram of goal. Away from stuffed foxes, I remember the roar of the crowd, the bright floodlights and the smell of Bovril permeating around the ground.

In 1967, as an eight-year-old, I remember the excitement when Dad came in from work to the terraced home in the cobbled East Norfolk Street, Denton Holme, Carlisle and told us he was going on a car journey to Liverpool. He'd had a call from a man called Bill Shankly. Shankly, who'd managed Dad at Carlisle, was manager of Liverpool Football Club. The chief scout, Norman Low, had moved to America, so Shankly wanted to talk with Dad.

It went well, as Dad was offered the opportunity to join the revered Liverpool boot room. The chief scout, with a modest national 'network', oversaw finding talent in the lower divisions that might make the first team at Anfield. The Liverpool squad had aged and needed to be rebuilt.

Dad was, in my opinion, a football genius. To find players in the lower leagues and Scotland to help Liverpool dominate England and Europe was staggering. His eagle eye and astute brain uncovered the likes of Phil Neal, Ian Rush and Alan Hansen. Imagine nowadays going to Chester, paying your admission fee and watching from behind the goal among the home fans as an unknown teenager knocks goals in for fun. Liverpool manager Bob Paisley never saw Ian Rush play before he signed him. Dad assured him he'd be good enough when Liverpool had to move quickly to seal a deal after Man City had publicly revealed their interest.

Dad spotted Phil Neal when he went to Northampton to watch an opposing player. Neal's basic skills and attributes stood out during the warm-up. Dad's attention switched during the game. He knew the player he'd travelled to watch wasn't ever going to play for Liverpool, but the Northampton No.2 piqued his interest. A few more viewings, £50,000 later, and Liverpool signed a player who went on to be the club's most decorated player. Like I say, a football genius.

So, the nomadic life was back on and the Twentymans returned to Liverpool. We moved into a house owned by the football club, 299 Northway, Maghull, which was halfway between Liverpool and Southport. It was a lovely three-bedroomed semi-detached abode with gardens front and back. Maghull was a popular suburb with footballers from both of the city's clubs. Liverpool legend Tommy Smith lived next door. Captain Ron Yeats was up the road. My mates and I used to occasionally pluck up the courage to knock on his front door and ask for his autograph. He was massive, absolutely huge, but was always welcoming and hospitable. Steve Heighway and the late Larry Lloyd were nearby too.

With Dad's new job at Anfield and the incredible importance of football on Merseyside, I soon became football mad and a huge Liverpool fan. Playing it, talking about it, reading about it – football was the focal point of my life. As kids we played football from dawn to night. We played in the local park. It wasn't always on grass – there was a tarmacked area with a big wall where an electric generator was housed. The wall was brilliant as you could practise all the basic skills on your own – striking it with both feet, control and other skills. Invariably, I played with older lads, which was very good for my development. My love of football grew and grew.

I had a group of mates who played on our self-maintained 'Wembley' at the Peafields in Lydiate, which was the suburb next to Maghull. We used a lawn mower to cut the grass so we could put our own markings down using sand. It was a slightly larger than standard five-a-side pitch. One of the lads even produced handwritten programmes to add to the matchday vibe. Saturday mornings were matchday and we loved it. Dave Rowlands, Andy Mac, Dave Bricklebank and co. were great lads.

My football ability was coming along nicely, and my reputation was growing, but the real football talent in the Twentyman household at the time was my sister, Margaret. Three years older than me, she was a real tomboy. If a young Margaret was about today, she'd have played in the Women's Super League. Sadly, back then a girl playing football was viewed as an oddity, an exception to the norm. Margaret was strong and skilful. She didn't just hold her own but many a time she'd be the best player. In her late teens she was a real star in the making, then something happened! With no prior hint or warning, one day she came down the stairs in a dress and had make-up on. The tomboy had gone. A feminine lady had appeared, and our star player was lost to the game of football forever.

Brother Billy was also talented and played for local non-league side Marine before suffering cruciate ligament injuries – not once but twice – after which he called it a day. He's now well known on Merseyside as a successful barber.

Due to Liverpool FC being part of my everyday life, I never really had an idol as such. Well, let's be candid at this juncture, I only ever had one idol: Roger Hunt, or 'Sir Roger Hunt', was that footballing god. The Liverpool and England forward was the epitome of all things that were wonderful in the game. He scored goal after goal with a clinical no-nonsense style. He was modest and, of course, was part of the 1966 World Cup-winning team. Wow.

Typhoo Tea did football cards back in the day, which came with every box of tea. I collected them religiously and, if you collected a certain number, you could get a bigger version. I saved and saved and badgered Mum to buy more tea until I got my large version of Roger Hunt. Dad got the great man to sign it for me and it took its rightful position on the wall above my bed. There were no other Liverpool pictures, just that one.

Moving swiftly forward to my 50th birthday, and incredibly my mates organised a game of golf for me with Roger Hunt. It was an extraordinary experience. We played at Portal Golf Club in the north-west of England. Roger, who agreed to do it because he knew Dad, brought his former team-mate Tommy Lawrence along, and I invited a great friend and huge LFC fan Les Gaskell. The sun shone, the sky was blue, and it was humbling to play with someone who achieved so much but was modest to the core. I'll never ever forget standing on the fairway watching Roger about to play a shot and thinking, *That's Roger Hunt, that man helped England to be the champions of the world. I'm blessed to be here today.*

We had a great game that went down to the final putt on the final green. Roger and I lost the match but that was insignificant, it was a truly remarkable day. We had a beer and a bite to eat afterwards, and Tommy, who was also tremendous company, had brought some Liverpool magazines that featured my dad. I got the guys to sign them, and Roger's signature was the same as the one on my Typhoo Tea poster all those years earlier!

Roger and I kept in touch and chatted every Christmas. His passing was extremely sad, but it was a release from a life gripped and ruined by dementia and Alzheimer's. I still send his wife Rowan a Christmas card. I'm blessed to have had Roger Hunt in my life as both a man and a boy.

Working for Liverpool was Dad's job. There was no fascination for me, it was simply what he did. However, my schoolmates were bordering on obsessive. The recurring question was, 'Who are we signing next?' The unwritten rule in the house was to never ask who Dad was watching.

To be fair there were a few amazing experiences. When I was about eight or nine, Dad asked me if I wanted to accompany him to Melwood, Liverpool's training ground, as he needed to collect something. The oblong-shaped building had a corridor that ran all the way around the changing rooms, which were in the central area. At either end there were offices, a few small rooms. Dad left me to wait at one corner of the corridor. I was there minding my own business when in the opposite corner I heard a strong Scottish accent ending a conversation as he appeared to be leaving an office. I couldn't see anything as it was all around the corner, out of sight. Then I heard the noise of steel tips on the heels of someone's shoes 'clipping' along the floor. Again, it was audible, not visible, but whoever it was, was coming my way.

The clipping sound got louder, still out of sight. Then, incredibly, at the opposite end of the corridor, he was walking towards me. I wanted to run away but I couldn't move. He had cropped hair and a huge smile on his face. He was in a suit, collar and tie, with his hands in his pocket trousers. Clippety clop, clippety clop, he was coming my way. A tsunami of charisma filled the corridor. He walked past the double doors to the car park and the training pitches. He was definitely coming my way. My mouth was dry, my heart was thumping … I dread to think what my pulse rate was.

Then he came straight towards me. He stopped, and in a deep Scottish accent Bill Shankly said, 'You must be Geoff's son.' I tried to say yes but nothing came out of my arid-dry mouth. I nodded so vigorously that my head nearly fell off my shoulders. Then he ran his hand through my mop of black hair and said, 'That's a fine head of hair you've got, son.' He smiled, put his hands in his pockets and walked off.

It was the most ridiculous, innocuous exchange but was spell-binding and captivating. I remember meeting Bill Shankly for the first time 50-plus years ago like it was yesterday. It's etched deep in my memory and my soul.

This kind of experience and day-to-day life meant everything was football or football-related for the young Geoffrey Twentyman, but there was also school to contend with. The best thing about school for me was the inter-school football matches. I was a striker back in the day. My priority was to make Northway Primary School the dominant force in the town. Time in the classroom seemed to get in the way of football.

In my final year at primary school, I sat the 11 Plus exam. This determined what type of secondary education you'd receive. If you passed it was grammar school, if you failed then you'd be set for a comprehensive school education.

A few months after sitting the exam, the all-important letter dropped on the porch floor. I picked it up. There it was, a brown envelope addressed to 'The Parents or Guardian of Geoffrey Twentyman, 299 Northway, Maghull, Liverpool L31 0BN'; it had Lancashire Education Department printed on it in black letters.

I knew what it was but had no idea what the next few minutes were about to reveal.

Nervously I took the envelope to Mum. She opened it and looked at it for what seemed like an eternity. She then looked at me and said, 'You've passed.'

I replied, 'Have I really?'

'Yes,' she said, but quickly added, 'it says you've passed but I'm going to have to ring them and check, just in case they've sent the wrong letter.'

Later that morning she rang the school for clarity and was told I'd passed the exam with a very good mark. Hilarious! Thanks for the vote of confidence Mum X.

A few weeks later Maghull Grammar School sent through the list of uniform and sports kit that had to be acquired for the forthcoming September. I went through it with Mum. It was going well: navy blazer, cap (eh?), grey trousers, white shirts, tie, etc., then the unimaginable, the unthinkable! Rugby shirt, navy; rugby shirt, white; rugby shorts, navy; rugby socks, navy. Eventually she concluded the list of rugby items. I asked her about the football kit. What colour was the football kit? To my absolute horror she explained that there was no football kit as rugby was the principal grammar school sport. Oh, my days, this was a hammer blow. If only they really had sent the wrong letter. Comprehensive schools played football.

So that was me off to Maghull Grammar School. In fairness, I enjoyed it, except for the older boys throwing your cap on the sports hall roof. The threat of having your head stuck down the toilet and the chain pulled was an urban myth, thankfully.

It was very formal; the teachers wore gowns and mortar-board hats. You had to walk on the left of the corridor. They believed in high behavioural standards. Mr Garratt, the deputy head, struck the fear of god into you from 50 paces. The cane was dished out for serious offences or repeated indiscretions. I had the ignominy, or notoriety, of receiving the first detention in my form! Miss Clarke, the history teacher, punished me for my continued talking after she'd (allegedly) called silence in the classroom.

Part of the introduction at Maghull Grammar included a one-to-one meeting with the headmaster. Mr Williams was a small-framed, fragile man. He seemed to be ancient. The idea of the chat was to establish some form of career plan. As if at 11 you knew what you wanted to be. Having said that, I actually did.

Going to the head's office was a daunting prospect. He was some kind of modern-day deity. His office was sacrosanct. I was nervous about this meeting, so in preparation I had a chat with Dad.

'I'm going to tell him I want to be a footballer.'

Dad was unimpressed. 'You can't tell the head of a grammar school that you want to be a footballer. Tell him you want to be a physiotherapist.'

'What's that?' I asked.

Dad explained, 'It's somebody who deals with injuries and fitness.'

So, the day before my meeting I kept repeating the word 'physiotherapist, physiotherapist' to ensure I didn't get this long word wrong.

I sat outside Mr Williams's office for what seemed an age but then my name was called out and I entered a huge, plush, wooden-panelled room. After asking how I'd settled in at the school, Mr Williams came to the point and asked what I wanted to be when I left school.

'I want to be a physiotherapist, sir,' I said, proudly pushing my chest out as I said this unfamiliar word.

Mr Williams looked at me and said, 'Oh … that must be an enormous disappointment to your father, Twentyman. I'd have thought you wanted to be a footballer like he was.' Wow, my aspirations to be a physiotherapist were laid to rest and I had the chief's backing to pursue a proper career.

Dad laughed when I got home and told him. It still makes me chuckle, in hindsight. The moral of the story is that you're better off saying what's in your heart and to always chase your dreams.

Incredibly, a former teacher at Maghull Grammar, Jill Dodds (aka Miss Dodds), who'd also moved to Bristol decades earlier, contacted me when I left the BBC. She'd been at the Bristol rugby game when a presentation was made to me at half-time. She contacted me and we met up for a coffee some 50 years after she taught me history. It was amazing to see her and reminisce.

So, I was chosen to don the No.15 jersey for Maghull Grammar School. I opted for full-back as I was a huge fan of the late JPR Williams, who was a courageous, front-foot full-back for Wales when they dominated the Five Nations. I used to love watching the rugby on *Grandstand* and marvelled at the imperious tones of Bill McLaren.

I still wince as I vividly remember my first game. The opposition launched a high kick. It was my job to catch it. I did my worst-ever JPR impression. As it dropped out of the sky, I could hear the cavalry coming my way as the opposing forwards chased the kick. As I was about to catch the ball and call for a mark, the oppo hit me like a juggernaut. Bang. Bosh. All I remember was the cheering as they'd gone through for a try behind me. I sat, crestfallen, legs apart, with blood gushing out of my nose.

The teacher ran by and asked if I was okay. I replied, somewhat embarrassed, 'Sir, was that not a foul?'

He replied, 'Twentyman, this is a proper sport you are playing now, son.'

So that was my introduction to the oval ball, and although it's a sport I love today, back then rugby was more a case of survival for me, and I have the utmost admiration for everyone who plays it.

After three years of rugby the good news for this boy was that, due to a government change in its education policy, the school turned from a grammar to a comprehensive. The standards in teaching and discipline at Old Hall High dropped but football became the main sport. It was a fair trade-off as far as I was concerned.

By my early teens, a combination of playing for Kirkstone Dynamos in the Bootle and Litherland Sunday League, regular school team football and practising every spare minute I had, meant my football was developing well. The Bootle and Litherland Sunday League was a high standard but it was tough! There was a combination of talented footballers and streetwise nutters. The England international Connor Coady's dad, Andy, played for us. He was more the former than the latter. Our home games were played in Bootle, but we often played at Buckley Hill in Litherland. The multitude of pitches were in a wind tunnel. Rolls-Royce could have tested their aeroplane engines there. I have great memories of playing for Davey Wilson, even if at times it was life-threatening.

I was getting occasional recognition in the *Liverpool Echo*, the city's evening newspaper, and I noticed I'd developed one of the longest names in Liverpool. I was referred to as 'Geoff Twentyman Junior, the son of the Liverpool chief scout and former player of the same name …' That rolled off the tongue, eventually.

By now I was working my way backwards and was often playing in midfield. I was selected for trials for the Lancashire representative side. Geographically, Maghull came under the authority of Lancashire as opposed to Liverpool. There was huge kudos to be included in the trials. Dad was working for LFC, and Mum couldn't take me, so an art teacher, Mr Roberts, kindly took me to Burnley for the Saturday morning selection process.

There were dozens of players there from all corners of Lancashire. There were two matches and every player had 20 minutes to highlight their skills. As they called out the teams I was named at right-back. Right-back! These were uncharted waters for me, and I struggled. The entire group gathered in a huge hall afterwards and it was no surprise that when they announced the squad I wasn't included. It was a good experience, and you have to have knock-backs to appreciate the good times.

Dad was watching three football matches or so a week as he set up a scouting network across the country, which would produce players that, in the great Shankly's words, 'would make Liverpool a bastion of invincibility'. Liverpool was an incredible football club. Despite their domination of the domestic and European game, everything was low key and understated.

One great memory I do have, and a definite benefit of being Geoff Twentyman Junior, was when I came home from school in 1977. There was a strange-shaped 'something' in the middle of the floor in the lounge. It was two or three feet high, two feet wide, covered in a green velvet bag. I walked through to the kitchen and asked Dad what it was, and he told me to take the cover off it and have a look.

I was absolutely staggered to peel back the bag and see the European Cup, what's now the Champions League trophy, in our lounge. A few weeks earlier Emlyn Hughes had lifted the massive piece of silverware after Liverpool beat Borussia Mönchengladbach in Rome. There it was in our house, gleaming and glorious. Of course, I picked it up and held it aloft. Sadly, in 1977 there were no mobile phones, no selfies, no internet. Even more sadly, we didn't take any photographs of it. Like I say, as incredible as it sounds, this was all part and parcel of Dad working for LFC.

So why was this iconic piece of football history in the Twentymans' front room? Dad had told Bob Paisley he was doing a talk at a local amateur football club that night so, in typical Liverpool fashion, Paisley suggested that he should take the trophy along to show them. That night the European Cup, the very trophy that great players such as Charlton, Best, Di Stéfano, Cruyff and Beckenbauer had all picked up was in the boot of Dad's car – thankfully it was safely locked up in the garage.

Life was never dull in the Twentyman household, that's for sure.

Chapter 2

The Liverpool Way

MY ROUTE into professional football was unconventional to say the least. An apprenticeship at the age of 16 was the norm but I did it, eventually, in a different way.

At 16, I played men's football for Maghull in the Lancashire Combination, going to places such as Nelson, Colne, Bacup, Fleetwood and Bootle. It was very tough and abrasive. You had to learn on your feet, or you'd end up on your backside.

In my mid-teens I had a real growth spurt and shot up to 6ft 2in tall and subsequently gravitated to centre-half. There's a trend here – striker when I was a kid, next stop midfielder and eventually a centre-half. I was determined never to be a keeper!

At Maghull I played alongside a footballing centre-back called Lol Armstrong. He was always very calm, read the game beautifully and never seemed hassled. I always felt he could have played at a much higher level but, as a successful businessman in later life, football was not his absolute priority. Bobby Prince was a quality centre-forward. Again, worthy of a higher level, but being a shift worker at a printers meant that he didn't venture too far from his hometown.

We trained on Tuesday and Thursday evenings. Gerry Fisher and Andy Boyd were the managerial team. They always encouraged me and were two Top Men. I developed my heading ability by literally suspending a football from the rafters in the open area between the dressing rooms. The drills included running, jumping and heading, plus standing springs.

I played three matches most weekends. Saturday morning was for the school, Saturday afternoon was for Maghull, then on a Sunday morning, after a decent Saturday night 'rehydrating', I played for Melling in the Ormskirk and District Sunday League. Melling were a great outfit. A brilliant bloke called John Clarke managed the team. We won the Liverpool Junior Cup one year when we beat The Boffin – a team of tough lads based at a pub in Kirkby in Liverpool. This was quite an achievement as we were the 'wooliebacks', a term used for people from outside of Liverpool, and The Boffin lads were hard-nosed Scousers. We matched them physically and outplayed them when we had the ball.

Although I always aspired to be a footballer, I stayed on at school and gained A-levels in English literature and French, as well as taking a sixth-form O-level in Russian. I ended up with eight O-levels.

I was doing well at Maghull, where you played for no financial reward – it was for the love of the game. Fourth Division Southport showed some interest in me. Their ground at Haig Avenue wasn't too far from home, so I made the switch and played in their reserves as a non-contract player.

Things changed significantly for me in 1977 when Southport hosted Liverpool reserves in the Liverpool Senior Cup Final. It was an annual four-team competition – Tranmere Rovers, Southport and the reserves from Liverpool and Everton. I don't know why, but the right-back position reared its ugly head, and once again and I was allocated the No.2 shirt! I was determined to fare better than I did at the Lancashire Schoolboy trials.

I chatted with Dad in the lead-up to the game and he told me that I was likely to face David Fairclough. David was very highly rated, and he enjoyed a great career at Liverpool, where he was nicknamed 'Super Sub', as he repeatedly came off the bench to score winning goals. Only a few months earlier I was in the middle of the Kop when he famously came on to score the third and defining goal against Saint-Étienne in one of Anfield's greatest-ever European nights.

Dad didn't say too much, as he was compromised. His 18-year-old lad was set to play against his employers, but his nugget of advice was crucial. David was quick, and if he got a run on you, nine times out of ten he'd skin you. The key was to get tight and prevent him from turning and running at me. It was great guidance and I thought I did well, despite us losing 5-0. David didn't contribute very much, and when I looked up to Dad from the pitch after the game, during the trophy presentation, he gave me a thumbs-up. Believe you me, a thumbs-up from Dad was praise of the highest order.

The plot from the 1977 Liverpool Senior Cup thickened. The next day, the Twentymans were sat round the table having our tea, or dinner as it's known in posher circles. It was a normal scenario, and we were having a chit-chat about what sort of day we'd all had when from nowhere Dad dropped a bombshell. Totally matter of fact, with minimal fuss, he threw me the line, 'Tom had a word with me today; they thought you did well last night. They want to sign you for the rest of the season and see what you're made of.'

It stopped me in my tracks and my knife and fork hit the plate. I was stunned. The 'Tom' that Dad referred to was Tom Saunders. Tom was a lovely man. The former head teacher was the youth development officer and was both highly respected and influential. Tom was one of the calmest men I've ever met. He and his wife Anne were a beautiful, compassionate couple.

'They' who wanted to sign me were the manager and first-team coaches, who'd been present at Haig Avenue. I'd suddenly lost my appetite, and Dad proceeded to tell me that Liverpool, one of the best teams in Europe at the time, would be phoning Southport to sort out my registration. The way Dad broke the news was brilliant. It was extremely low key, he told me calmly and it came with no pressure or expectation.

It was incredible; I had stood on the Kop and now I was going to be involved with the club, even if it was only until the end of the season. Life was slightly surreal. Some days I'd go to school during the day to study French, English literature and Russian, then play at Anfield in the evening, then go back to school the next day.

I remember Dad telling me off for signing autographs after one reserve game – he reminded me I hadn't made it yet and was a long way from doing so. Feet attached firmly to the ground with six-inch nails.

Despite donning the red shirt, I didn't ease back on the education. I hadn't pinned my entire hopes on a career in football, so I explored the possibility of becoming a PE teacher. I went to Chester College for an interview for a place to study a Batchelor of Education in physical education. I had to complete a physical test, which was to see how many lengths of the gym I could run in 15 minutes. There were six of us doing the test. The others went off like bullets at the start, but I decided to pace myself. I caught them one by one, and I completed the most lengths by some distance.

Afterwards, the instructor commented that he could tell I was with a professional club due to the way I completed the challenge. At the short interview afterwards, they knew I was on Liverpool's books and offered me a place there and then, without stipulating any minimum grades – I think they wanted me in the college football team! Two A-levels, any grades, and I was in!

Back at Anfield the reserves were a great bunch of lads. We were coached by Roy Evans, who went on to manage the first team. Bob Paisley was the first-team manager after succeeding Bill Shankly, who retired in 1974. The reserves played in the Central League, which was incredibly competitive. It was for the northern-based clubs, and you played at venues such as Maine Road, Old Trafford, Goodison and, of course, Anfield. There was huge kudos to winning the Central League title as it was a gauge as to what and who was coming through the ranks. The title was important to Liverpool. Winning the First Division, the European Cup, the FA Cup or the Central League had everyone at the club working towards being the best of the best.

I have so many memories, none more so than going out for my first game at Anfield and warming up in front of the Kop. It was empty, but it was still incredible. The huge terrace behind the goal was a sacred place that I'd stood on for years. As far as pre-match preparation goes it was quite different to today where players are regimented and work in specific groups. Back then we just kicked a few balls to each other, did some stretches and threw in a few sprints for good measure.

It was surreal for me when the legend that's Ian Callaghan, who went on to be Liverpool's record appearance-maker with an extraordinary 857 outings for the club, said, 'Come on Geoff, let's ping some balls to each other.' As if I wasn't nervous enough about making my debut for Liverpool ressies, I now had to exchange 25-yard passes with Ian Callaghan, *the* Ian Callaghan! He was returning from injury, and the first team had FA Cup and European Cup finals on the horizon. They'd already won the First Division championship.

So, from 25 yards he drilled a pass my way. The ball travelled like an Exocet missile; it fizzed millimetres above the Anfield turf. It was so perfect that it probably had the manufacturer's name facing me when it landed on my foot. I managed to take the pace off it, and the ball dropped at my feet. The return pass wasn't such a thing of beauty, but it landed nicely in his vicinity.

I saw Ian at Anfield a few years ago and he was fantastically friendly. I'm sure he didn't recall warming up with me ahead of a reserves fixture with Sheffield United, but for me it was a memorable experience. It was a joy to be among players like Ian and another great player, Alec Lindsay. What he did with his left foot was breathtaking.

The players treated me incredibly well and they knew I was there on merit and not because of who my dad was. We won the Central League after a 5-2 win at home to Huddersfield Town. It was Liverpool's eighth Central League title in ten years – you can imagine what it meant to the club.

Sammy Lee was the standout player in the group. Colin Irwin and Max Thompson were excellent centre-backs. They were both supportive and welcoming, despite me playing in their position. Brian 'Polly' Kettle was captain and the studious Trevor Birch, who ended up as CEO at various clubs and the English Football League, was a centre-forward.

After the Huddersfield win, we'd returned to the home dressing room. The door opened and in walked Bob Paisley with the entire first-team squad behind him. Emlyn Hughes, Kevin Keegan, Ray Clemence, Ian Callaghan, Phil Neal, Tommy Smith, Steve Heighway, etc. filed in and congratulated us. Keegan, a real superstar at the time, said 'Well done Geoff,' as he shook my hand. It was top class, especially as they were about to depart for London to play in the FA Cup Final on the Saturday and then on to Rome for the European Cup Final against Borussia Mönchengladbach.

It really was the Liverpool way. There was a togetherness throughout the club, and nobody was bigger than Liverpool FC. It kept you grounded. They not only tried to improve you as footballers, but the way they went about their business made you a better human being. I went back to school the next day with my head spinning, still reliving an unforgettable night at Anfield.

As a non-contract player at Liverpool, I was eligible to play for the Liverpool County FA Under-18s side. This was a combination of amateur players from the professional and non-league clubs who played in a national knockout cup competition. We were decent and made it to the final, which was at Anfield against Surrey. John Aldridge was in the squad and came off the bench to score the winner at Durham in the semi-final.

Aldo played for a non-league club called Cheshire Lines. On ability he should have started every game, but I remember the manager favoured the players from Liverpool and Everton. When the team for the final was named in the home dressing room at Anfield, Aldo was on the bench. He literally burst into tears, walked away from the ground and didn't take part in the final. We won 3-0, so the selection was never questioned.

John enjoyed many bigger and better experiences at Anfield in the ensuing years, but I'll always remember his disappointment that day. Others who made the grade from the group included Dave Bamber and Colin Russell.

So, when the big day arrived, and I was to find out if I was going to be offered a professional contract with Liverpool, they did it properly. Typically, they treated me with the utmost respect. The main man, Bob Paisley, was going to deliver the news, be it good or bad.

I entered his office. My heart was pounding. Regardless of the impending outcome it seemed a privilege to be in the actual office where Shankly and now Paisley had masterminded Liverpool's rise and domination of domestic and European football. Bob always gave you a sense of calm, like your favourite uncle. There were various stories about Bob Paisley – forgetting names was a recurring tale – but the one that fascinated me was whether he wore slippers in his office or not. Maybe it was true, but it could have been an urban myth.

He was sat behind his desk in his shirt, tie and cardigan, and for a split second I looked under his desk at the floor and there it was! He was wearing slippers. He *did* wear slippers in his office!

'So, Geoffrey, how do you think you've done?' he asked.

I replied, 'Okay, Boss, but probably not well enough, to be honest.' I knew deep down that I wasn't good enough. Liverpool had such strength in depth, and they were a great side. After all, they'd recently been crowned champions of England and of Europe.

He took a while and then said, 'Your dad tells me that you're thinking about being a PE teacher.'

'Yes, that's right,' I replied.

Again, after a pause that felt like an eternity, he said, 'Well, to be honest, I think you'll make a better PE teacher than footballer …' He delivered the sledgehammer in a totally inoffensive way.

I responded, 'Thanks, Boss, I appreciate that.' I literally thanked him for telling me I'd make a better PE teacher than footballer! He was such an amazing man.

He then stood up, shook my hand and wished me all the best. I shook his hand (firmly), thanked him and the club for the opportunity and wished him well. That was it. The way I'd been released was class from him and the football club. They could have told Dad to tell me, but they didn't. There was no cold letter of rejection signed by someone I didn't know. The main man, the Top Man, did it.

I called this chapter 'The Liverpool Way' and that's what I wanted to convey. They were class in everything they did, and still are. Even the unpopular, tough aspects such as, in my case, releasing players. It was the first-team manager who told me and, as tough as it was, it meant a great deal. I'll share an amazing, more recent experience with LFC later in the book. It's another example of an incredibly classy club.

My time at Liverpool made a fundamental impression on me. Regardless of where I played afterwards, I was never nervous. To me there was only one thing bigger than playing for Liverpool reserves and that was playing in the Liverpool first team. So, whether it was a league debut, a Wembley appearance, a Bristol derby or a game to win a league title, it never fazed me. I put that down to playing in the reserves at a club who were the best in Europe. Through that experience I gained a self-belief and a confidence that always stood me in good stead.

The big question now, though, was what was next for me? Was I really going to be a better PE teacher than footballer? Only time would tell.

Managing people – treat people with respect

Always treat people with respect. Even in tough situations when you might be the bearer of bad news, it's important to think of the recipient. What can you do to ease a difficult situation?

When I was 18 and Liverpool decided not to offer me a professional contract, they treated me with total respect. The manager told me in his office in a one-to-one meeting. Bob Paisley probably had more important things to do that day, but he deemed it important that he delivered the news in his office. Delegation is an art form, but there are occasions when you must take the responsibility yourself. Bob Paisley could have given the job to someone else, but he didn't. As disappointing for me as it was, I was treated with respect, which softened the blow. People may not agree with your decision but never leave yourself open to criticism as to how you deliver news or deal with a situation. Be respectful.

Chapter 3

You Only Live Once

WHETHER IT was a natural reaction or not, I don't know, but I lost my enthusiasm for playing football after not securing a deal at Liverpool. Furthermore, I decided that I'd had enough of 'education'. I got my two A-levels, but I decided that going to Chester to train as a PE teacher wasn't for me. I decided to get a job in the big world.

I don't really know why, but I applied to the Civil Service for the generic position of clerical officer. A pen-pusher. I didn't tell Mr Williams this was in the master plan back at Maghull Grammar.

I wasn't sure what department I was going to end up in, but I hoped it wasn't the Inland Revenue, as maths was never my strong point. I had an interview in Bootle, which seemed to go well. A week or so later a letter arrived on 'HMP Liverpool' headed paper. Her Majesty's Prison, by the way. My initial thoughts were that it was a massive wind-up, someone having some banter, but, as I read it, the letter explained that I'd been accepted for a position in the Home Office and the next step was to go beyond the walls of Liverpool prison for a chat with regards to a post in the prison's administration.

I was intrigued by the prospect of working in a prison and I couldn't wait to find out more. Prisons are fascinating places and a world within a world. I assumed a prison only had officers and inmates. Wrong! There's so much more in terms of civilian roles.

My job was effectively a modern-day personnel officer for the prison officers – not the inmates! It felt good, so I started a week or so later. Part of the induction on my first day was to be shown around the prison. The wings, which housed the inmates, were huge. Three or four landings high. It was impossible to ignore the noise and the gross smell. HMP Liverpool, a category B prison, was a big Victorian building where inmates slopped out their buckets in the morning – the individual cells didn't have toilets. Rather them than me! The prison housed a fantastic weights room and gymnasium, which I used most lunchtimes. I played five-a-side with some officers and the occasional inmate a couple of times a week.

I had no regrets about giving up on education, and a steady job while living at home with Mum and Dad meant life was pretty good.

I was selected for the prison football team – staff only, as it was a bit tricky playing away matches with inmates in the team! We won the National Prison Service Cup two years in a row. Ironically, one of the finals was at Leyhill Open Prison in South Gloucestershire, about 20 minutes' drive from Bristol. I had no inkling that the south-west of England would be my home in later life.

The job was great. I've always thrived on meeting and interacting with people. Having said that, I recall waiting to be served in a pub near Liverpool when I became aware that the guy next to me was staring at me. After a minute or so he piped up, 'Excuse me mate, but have you been on a short holiday recently?'

I thought to myself, *What a strange question*. I replied, somewhat naively, 'No, but I went to Majorca earlier in the year for a fortnight.' He shook his head and explained that in Liverpool a 'short holiday' was slang for a spell in prison. When I explained about my day job, he revealed that he'd been on the wing I walked past every morning on my way to the admin block. He'd seen me through the bars of his cell window. Apparently, inmates have exceptional memories for faces when they're doing a stretch.

Football-wise I got my mojo back and joined Formby, who played in the Cheshire League, a competition for clubs in the north-west of England. I was getting about £25 a week, which combined with my prison money meant life was good. Brian Griffiths, who was the area sales rep for the sportswear brand Patrick, managed the club. I enjoyed my time at 'The Squirrels'. I can still remember most of the squad now. Micky Quinn was a real leader on and off the pitch. A hard-as-nails Scouser with full perm but no moustache. He took great pride in his appearance and drove a Triumph Stag, which looked the business but invariably broke down. His designer gear never looked as good with engine oil all over it. Micky was a Top Man. The group included Kenny Hulme, Larry Cray, Dave Shannon, Bobby Pascoe, Tony Cahill and Ken Skupski. The assistant boss was the amiable, genial George Burns – a perfect foil for the manager, who was too intense, too often.

We were all good mates, a real band of brothers and a decent team to boot. I was selected to play for an FA representative XI against the Northern Premier League select XI at Runcorn. It was a huge honour and a clear indication that my football career was going in the right direction.

After two decent seasons at Brows Lane, I had a dilemma. Chorley, who were also in the Cheshire League, came in for me. I had a choice: I could stay playing with my mates at a ground that was 15 minutes from home or break away and travel on my own to Chorley twice a week for training. Their ground, Victory Park, was at least 45 minutes' drive from Maghull. The £50 a week was an attraction, but it crystallised down to one highly significant factor: at 21 years of age this was my last chance to have a crack at becoming a professional footballer. If I did well at Chorley then maybe, just maybe, someone would take a punt on me. Maybe.

I strongly believe that in life you must be true to yourself. You only live once so you must take your chances if and when they arise.

Chorley were keen – they must have been as they paid a transfer fee of a few thousand pounds. Everyone at Formby was great, as they understood I was trying to make my way up the football ladder. I know most of the lads would have done the same thing given the opportunity. Chorley had a great set-up, playing at Victory Park, with a great fanbase, and they had ambitions to progress into the Northern Premier League. They were a club on the up.

I was signed by a great bloke called Les Rigby. Les was a big guy and a larger-than-life football character, very likeable, very personable. Strangely enough I never got to assess or experience his football acumen as I didn't play for him! He and chairman Jim Tolson had a huge difference of opinion, hopefully not over signing me, and as always happens in these situations the man with the money has the final say. Les was sacked.

Les wasn't out of football for long. He joined Morecambe and we played them early in the season at Victory Park. Chorley won

1-0 and yours truly scored a headed goal. Typical of Les Rigby, he marched on to the pitch at the final whistle, walked straight towards me and shook my hand and said, 'Well played, big man, that's exactly why I signed you.' Les was a Top Man, and I'm disappointed that I never played for him.

His replacement was Peter Wragg, a Mancunian and a thoroughly likeable guy. 'Wraggy' wasn't a football genius when it came to tactics, but he knew a good player when he saw one and his training was very tough, with the emphasis on running. Forrest Gump would have had the time of his life.

I was the fittest that I'd ever been. I played alongside a centre-back called Ray Lugg. Ray was in the twilight of his career. He'd played loads of league games for the likes of Middlesbrough, Plymouth, Crewe and Bury, and was part of the Watford side that knocked my beloved Liverpool out of the FA Cup in 1970. 'Luggy' was a Top Man who gave me huge confidence and belief. The overriding memory of the Geordie was his pre-match ritual. Before every game, at around 2.50pm, he'd nudge me, reach into his kit bag and pull out a half-bottle of Scotch. He'd take a decent swig and then offer me the bottle. I'd decline, and he'd drop the bottle back into his bag. He did this before every game! For the record, I refused every time. Ray was a fantastic person – he sent me a good luck telegram to Deepdale on the day I made my league debut – class from a classy guy.

My first season at Chorley went well and we won promotion to the Northern Premier League. The second campaign was absolutely ridiculous. I scored 24 goals from centre-half. Now, I know a lot of you Preston North End and Bristol Rovers fans who have kindly bought this book will have to read that line again and again but, yes, it was 24 goals for Geoff Twentyman from centre-half. It was fantasy football before the expression became a thing. I scored headers, took penalties (probably scored a dozen) and free kicks, and everything seemed to go for me. I went up for set pieces and, if I didn't make the first contact, the ball would drop at my feet and I'd smash it home.

The prolific season brought inevitable interest and speculation from league clubs. The *Sunday People* used to run a transfer rumour column. Apparently, Blackburn, Barnsley and Preston were watching me. I remember being chuffed when Dad came home one Monday and told me Liverpool captain Graeme Souness had stopped him at Anfield and said, 'I see a few clubs are looking at your lad, Geoff.' Dad said it was very good, but he had concerns as I played in contact lenses.

I never quite understood his worries, but amazingly Graeme's best mate was an optician in Liverpool. 'Don't worry, Geoff, I'll put you in touch with Jonny Dexter. He'll look after your lad.' Never has a truer word been spoken. Jonny was brilliant and he supplied me with lenses and specs at trade price for decades.

Someone I befriended back in the Northern Premier League days was a certain Neil Warnock, who was the manager of Burton Albion. I scored a penalty in a win at their place. We had a chat afterwards and we've kept in touch from a distance ever since. The penalty was a comedy moment. The home keeper was giving it the 'big one' as I was placing the ball on the spot. He was on his line shouting that he knew where I was going to put it and he was going to save it. I walked towards him, offered him my hand and bet him a pint that I'd score. To be fair, he was waiting for me at the bar afterwards.

As I say, Neil and I have been friends for decades. When I was at Radio Bristol and he was manager of Cardiff City, I rang him for an interview ahead of a Severnside derby against Bristol City. I left him a message; he rang me back. He apologised for not being able to do the chat live as he was picking his wife up from hospital when the show was on. She'd had a mastectomy. Despite the personal crisis he made time for me. We recorded a chat, which I played in the programme later that day.

Another time I tried to get him on my Monday night Bristol City programme *The Sound of the City* on the eve of a game with Rotherham, where he was in charge. The media department at Rotherham struggled to get hold of him as he had Mondays off. Then on the Tuesday evening he rang me from his mobile phone when I was on air – he was on the team coach on the way to Ashton Gate for the game. I'm not sure how many local radio stations get the opposition manager on their show live from the team bus en route to the ground! Class from Neil.

Off the pitch, I left the job at HMP Liverpool. Although I enjoyed it, I moved to Girobank, based in Bootle on Merseyside. It was another admin role, but they paid more than the Civil Service. Girobank was part of a group that included British Telecom and the Post Office. They had a national football representative side, which I was flattered and thrilled to be selected for. There were some excellent players who played a decent standard of semi-pro football across the country. In 1982 we went to Belgium for a European tournament, which we won. It was top-notch: first-class train to London, a few days' preparation at Bisham Abbey, before we headed to Bruges for the tournament.

Back on English grass, the newly crowned European champions had a game at Deepdale, the home of Preston North End. I hoped Gordon Lee, the Preston manager, might be present, as according to newspaper speculation they were one of the parties in for me. I didn't play well. I probably tried too hard and felt downbeat afterwards.

It wasn't the first bad game I'd ever had but I feared it might have ended Preston's interest.

Then a few days later, on a Friday evening, I was at my future in-laws' home when I received a call on their house phone – this was pre-mobile phone days. 'Hi, Geoff, it's Gordon Lee, the manager of Preston North End,' the voice said in a strong Black Country accent. He explained that the club had been watching me for a while and wanted to sign me. One of my beliefs is 'you only live once', and this was the opportunity I'd wanted since I was a kid. There were no agents back then. Gordon waited for me to get over the initial excitement and then offered me a two-year deal on a basic wage of £200 a week plus £30 per appearance and a bonus of £150 a win and £75 for a draw. No signing-on fee, that was it. Without any hesitation I accepted his offer.

Preston had agreed a transfer fee with Chorley. Being a footballer made me marginally better off financially compared to having a full-time job and part-time football money. I couldn't believe it. At 24 years of age I was going to be a professional footballer. My former head teacher may have had a wry smile if he heard the news. This 'late developer' thought that if I could sustain a ten-year career, then it was the right decision. Mum and Dad were chuffed, really delighted for me.

The next day, the club secretary, a lovely man called Derek Allen, drove from Preston to our house with the contract to sign. The decision to join Chorley and make those motorway journeys on my own to train twice a week had paid off. It was certainly a lesson in life regarding never giving up and following a dream. Everyone at Girobank was thrilled for me. They were brilliant and didn't make me work my full notice as they knew I needed to start my new career as soon as possible.

It was all very exciting, but I knew the hard work was about to begin.

Chapter 4

An Ambition Fulfilled

PRESTON NORTH End Football Club will always have a special place in my heart. They not only took a punt on me in 1983 and gave me my chance to be a professional footballer, but they also treated me with fairness and decency when I left Deepdale. I'll always be grateful for that.

So here I was, 24 years old and joining a football club with a rich history. A founder member of the Football League. A club that had won First Division titles and FA Cups. A club where the great Tom Finney and the revered Bill Shankly had plied their trade.

I felt proud and excited. My first day at PNE was non-working. It was an opportunity to familiarise myself with the club and the people at Deepdale. It was certainly a more enjoyable and relaxed initiation than walking the wings of HMP Liverpool. The local BBC reporter Dave Jones dropped in to record a chat for Radio Lancashire. This was the first of many in my life – both sides of the microphone.

When I left the ground a group of fans had gathered, as word had spread that the 'new signing from Chorley' was present. It was very flattering to sign autographs. Signatures were the

1980s version of a selfie. Dad gave mild approval to me signing autographs but reminded me that I hadn't yet played a single game as a professional footballer. Being late into the pro game and having worked for a living meant I always really valued my football career and took nothing for granted.

So, to my first working day. It was a training day. I went in on a Bank Holiday as I hadn't quite left Girobank. The lads were very welcoming. There were no big-time Charlies, no real banter merchants and everything was low key. The first thing I noticed on the training ground was the speed and fitness levels. Don't get me wrong, we trained hard at Chorley, but the full-time professionals were just quicker! It was an eye-opener. Technically, despite being in the third tier, they were talented. A different level to what I'd been used to. Gordon Lee came into his own with his man-management. He reassured me that it was his job to get me up to speed. The lads were supportive, telling me it wouldn't take long for me to match their fitness levels.

I used to change next to Steve Elliott, who was fantastic with me. Steve was a top, top professional and a fantastic human being. He was the centre-forward and was the best player. He was incredibly modest, was respected by the lads and adored by the fans. He was six months older than me and had joined Preston from Nottingham Forest, where he'd been in Brian Clough's European Cup-winning squads. I remember Stevie scored a hat-trick at Scunthorpe in the FA Cup. The opposing centre-half was a certain Ian Botham. Botham clearly made the correct decision when it came to professional sport. Steve moved on to First Division Luton for a six-figure fee after my first season at Deepdale, but he took me under his wing and was always there for this raw player from non-league.

I visited Steve in a care home in Lancashire earlier this year. He has advanced dementia and didn't know who I was, but it was special to spend a few hours with him and his wonderful wife Maggie. Steve had the same smile and twinkle in his eye that I remembered from our time at Deepdale. They've been married for more than 40 years, and Maggie tackles their adversity with total love, immense dedication and huge dignity. It broke my heart, to be honest. Steve is and always will be a Top Man.

Other players in the squad included Willie Naughton, a 6ft 2in left-winger, and the former Manchester City centre-back Tommy Booth. Despite winning titles and cups at Maine Road, Tommy was such an ordinary bloke, with a wicked sense of humour. Peter Litchfield was the keeper. He was a very good stopper but away from the club he seemed to spend a lot of his time servicing cars! Andy McAteer was a talented left-back who should have made more of his ability.

You only ever have one league debut. Mine came in slightly strange circumstances. I was still getting up to speed fitness-wise and had played a few reserve games. In the week leading up to the home game with Oxford United, Steve Elliott's dad passed away and 'Nessie' (Elliott Ness) wasn't available for selection against Jim Smith's side.

Gordon Lee had a plan. The gaffer pulled me to one side and told me I was going to play up front as a No.9. Yes, Geoff Twentyman made his Football League debut as a striker. The gaffer was obviously mindful of the 24 goals that I'd notched the season before at Chorley, so I understood the logic.

We worked on tactics and patterns of play on the Deepdale pitch. The plan was to flood the midfield, stick me up front on my own (yes, on my own, on my debut!) and let me try to get among the Oxford defence, and hopefully we'd get something from the game.

The momentous day was Saturday, 1 October 1983. I remember the excitement of getting up, trying to kill time in the morning and the 40-minute drive to Deepdale. There were always some fans between the car park and the players' entrance who wanted autographs. Dad wouldn't have approved, but I signed them. Supporters are the most important people in the game, and it was always a joy to be asked to sign a book, a programme or a photograph.

We reported at 2pm. Dress code was jacket, collar and tie. I had to be careful that I wasn't sat ready to go out to play with my shinpads on at 2.01pm. Seriously, the manager gave a team talk at the top of the hour. I was buzzing.

As I mentioned earlier with the traumatic Ian Callaghan episode, the warm-up was very much an individual thing. The players would trickle out of the dressing room in twos and threes and do their own thing. The assistant manager, Geoff Nulty, may have got involved for a few minutes, to ensure we all did the same thing at the end. The warm-up nowadays is a scheduled process, almost scientific.

We returned to the home dressing room. A few final words from Gordon Lee. The buzzer sounded, and just before 2.55 it was 'match time'. The lads rose to their feet, some shouting out meaningless things, some clapping vigorously and others randomly back-slapping. I was always calm in the dressing room – a programme reader before the game, a tea drinker at half-time.

So off we went, the walk out of the dressing room to the tunnel. The noise of the expectant crowd was a distant rumble. The volume increased a hundred-fold as we appeared in the

Deepdale sunshine. It was special, very special. No nerves, just pure adrenaline and a sense of huge pride in achieving a near-lifetime ambition.

I always waved up to Mum just before kick-off. She was a wonderful mother and a fierce supporter of my football evolution. In the true sense of the expression, 'she was always there'.

Oxford were a good side and very much on the up. My focus was their two centre-backs, Malcolm Shotton and Gary Briggs. They were both 6ft 3in and appeared to be chiselled out of granite. They were the kind of pairing where one of them flicked you up and the other one volleyed you into the crowd. Uncompromising and effective. I don't know whether they were aware that it was my debut, but they did their level best to intimidate me, which added to the contest. I got stuck into them and let them know they were in a game. They gave me a few digs, but they took some back in return. I must admit they were more streetwise than me.

We lost 2-1 but I made our goal, which felt incredible. We were two-nil down and I got up early for a high ball with either Briggs or Shotton in their penalty box and I headed it down. As I recovered my feet it was an absolute thrill to see Graham Houston hammer the ball into the back of the net from eight yards out at the Town End. I was chuffed with that involvement. Obviously it wasn't the result we wanted but I was pleased with my performance and the lads in the dressing room confirmed that as they were generous with their praise. Peer opinion is especially important in a football dressing room.

It was a big moment for me to know that I could hold my own in league football, albeit for one game. After a few media interviews I left the ground in good spirits. When I got home, Dad asked me how it went. I gave him a modest assessment, to which he said, 'No, you did better than that, son, you did really well.' I was confused, as Dad always went scouting on a Saturday to watch potential Liverpool signings.

'Thanks,' I replied, 'but how do you know?'

His reply was one I wasn't expecting. 'I was there,' he said with a proud smile.

Making my league debut was an achievement I'll always be proud of, but for both Dad and Mum to be there, admittedly on opposite sides of the ground, made it perfect. Dad went on to tell me that he rocked up and sat in the stand among the Preston fans. No one knew who he was, but he quizzed the PNE fans next to him, 'Who's the number nine? He's useful.'

They replied, 'Oh, that's our new signing from Chorley, Geoff Twentyman. He looks good, doesn't he?'

This was brilliant from Dad, to be fair – helping to embellish my reputation and influence fan opinion on day one! I was proud that he was in the stands that day. I hope he derived as much pleasure from being there as I did from later knowing he was part of my big day.

I won't be describing every game in this book in such detail, but you only ever make your Football League debut once. It was a huge privilege and is a day that I'll never forget.

I played 38 games in my first season, but this 24-goal centre-half signed from Chorley scored only once – a header from a corner in a home win over Plymouth.

In the December of my first season, after a dip in results, Gordon Lee was sacked. This was a new experience for me but one I got used to at Preston, as we had five managers in my three seasons at Deepdale. I was gutted about Gordon. He was a decent guy who'd taken a chance on me. I'll always be grateful for that.

It was extremely sad news when he passed away in 2022. He didn't do much coaching, and empowered his assistant, Geoff Nulty, on the training ground. Geoff had played at Burnley, Everton and Newcastle. His coaching wasn't great, and his man-management was worse. He never found out what made you tick as an individual. I don't think I learned anything from him. I always felt he struggled to transition from playing to coaching, as he still wanted to be a player.

Gordon's replacement was the former Republic of Ireland goalkeeper and Preston legend Alan Kelly, who stepped up from his role of coach/reserve team manager. 'Kell' was a typical genial Irishman. He was a great guy and was incredibly likeable and engaging. Alan had scouted me from Chorley, something I'll always be grateful for.

Sadly, the demands of management changed Alan. Results weren't great and the pressure got to him. After games I was often the focus of his frustrations and criticism. Repeatedly the defeat would be my fault and all too often he'd remind me that his grandmother could defend better than me. It was tough. It was the first time in my career that I'd been the focal point of strong criticism. He had a point on occasions, but I dispute that his grandmother was a better defender. His grandfather maybe, but not his grandmother!

In all seriousness, I think he felt a sense of ownership with me, as he'd scouted me from non-league, and I was therefore an easy target. Looking back on it I should have challenged him or gone to see him for a one-to-one chat. I guess being inexperienced stopped me from doing so. I learned from it and later in my career stood up for myself and the collective group at Bristol Rovers on more than one occasion.

The strange thing was that Alan always picked me for the following game. Then criticised me, then picked me. In all, I played 52 games in the 1984/85 season. Looking back, if I was so poor, then Alan should have dropped me. If I was making so many mistakes, he should have identified why I was making the errors and corrected them on the training ground. The lads were great and very supportive. They told me to take no notice, which was easier said than done.

Results didn't improve, and Alan was sacked in April 1985. It was good to see him a few months later, when he was more like his old self. Alan was a brilliant keeper, but I'm not convinced that he had the overall knowledge of the outfield game to succeed as a manager. But I'm chuffed that his legendary status at Deepdale prevails, as one of the grandstands is named after him. Kudos to Kell. Like I said, I'll always be thankful to him for spotting me at Chorley.

Senior pro Tommy Booth was elevated to the role of manager. Tommy brought in the former Manchester United, Manchester City and Everton legend Brian Kidd as his assistant. Tommy was the quieter of the two, but when he spoke it was 100 per cent football knowledge. Big Tom was calm and considered. 'Kiddo' was an excellent coach, was feisty and could motivate. I had a year left on my contract, but it was extended to two years under Tommy.

The results weren't good, and the club continued to struggle on and off the pitch. Tommy couldn't halt the slide and we were relegated in the May of 1985 to the Fourth Division, along with Swansea and Cambridge United.

The 1985/86 season started amid a wave of positivity and enthusiasm. Preston were billed as one of the favourites for promotion. This was to be the season of the club's renaissance.

However, the early omens weren't good as we lost 4-2 at home to Peterborough on the opening day of the campaign.

Working with Tommy and Brian was enjoyable, but results were poor. Tommy was sacked in January 1986 as the club plummeted down the table. It was a mystery to understand why Big Tom didn't succeed. He played under two incredible football luminaries in Joe Mercer and Malcolm Allison in a fantastic era at Manchester City. His football knowledge was obvious, but he couldn't seem to translate it on to the training ground. The top players don't always make the best managers.

Brian succeeded Big Tom. I hope you're keeping up regarding the number of managers I had in three seasons! Kiddo, number four, had the unenviable task of turning things round. He was absolute quality in terms of coaching and man-management; he could make the hairs on the back of your neck stand up. I learned so much from Brian. You always had to give 100 per cent. I know that's a given but looking back at it too many players at Preston didn't. They were too comfortable, too familiar with their surroundings.

You certainly knew Brian was in charge, and he had an explosive spark on occasions! We played Lou Macari's Swindon Town at the County Ground. They were a team on the up and they battered us. They were passing the ball around for fun and we couldn't get near them. Late in the game, the Swindon right-back Chris Ramsey had the ball, put his foot on it and pretended to tie up his boot laces – he was clearly taking the mickey out of us. He loved it, as the crowd cheered his dubious antics. The whistle went for full time, and I noticed Kiddo had raced from the dugout straight down the tunnel. I entered the tunnel and saw Brian waiting, back to the wall, scanning to his left as the players headed towards the dressing rooms. Then in an instant Brian went straight for Ramsey. He grabbed him by the throat and with one arm pinned him against the wall and said to him, 'Don't you ever, ever take the piss out of your fellow pros again, as the day will come when you're in a team that's struggling!'

It was quite a thing to witness. He did it because he was a winner and he cared. He was annoyed at the lack of respect shown by a fellow professional as he felt respect should be a mutual thing. He was probably annoyed and frustrated by our performance as well. When it came to morals, integrity, application and being a decent and honest human being, Brian Kidd reaffirmed what Mum and Dad had taught me.

Despite the pre-season optimism, the club was struggling on and off the pitch. There was an apathy around Deepdale, an all-too-easy acceptance of where the club was. It was a very sad situation, especially for the loyal fans who stuck with the club. There was no thick and thin, it was only threadbare thin. I remember the floodlights were condemned and we couldn't use them as they were deemed dangerous, so we played Scunthorpe on a midweek afternoon. Fair play to the 2,000 or so supporters who turned up to watch us lose.

Things came to a head for Brian at a home game with Leyton Orient. Kiddo named the team at 2pm as normal. He delivered his pre-match chat, then left the home dressing room. We prepared as normal, and then at 2.15 the chairman, with one of the senior pros, Jonathan Clarke, entered the dressing room. The chairman told us that Jonathan was to oversee team affairs for the rest of the day. All very strange, but all very PNE.

I rang Brian that night to find out what had happened. He told me that the night before the game, Harry McNally, the manager of Wigan Athletic, had telephoned him to tell him that the Preston chairman had offered him the Preston manager's job. Harry declined as Preston had a certain Brian Kidd as their manager. McNally was assured that if he wanted the job there would be a vacancy. Harry McNally was a great guy and was clearly very decent and honourable.

So, Kiddo turned up for the Leyton Orient game knowing that his job had been offered to Harry McNally. He showed the players that he was in charge by naming the team at 2pm. He then went up to the boardroom and called the chairman out across the busy room, telling him to stick his job where the sun didn't shine, or words to that effect. Brian left the boardroom, got in his car and drove home.

The actions of Messrs Kidd and McNally taught me so much about honesty and integrity and standing up for yourself.

I bumped into Brian some years later when I was at Rovers, and he was assistant to Sir Alex Ferguson. I was in Manchester for a Professional Footballers' Association (PFA) meeting. I was on the management committee of the players' union. I was checking into the hotel on the Saturday evening ahead of the next day's meeting. Manchester United were staying there overnight ahead of a home game with Everton. Brian and I reminisced about our Deepdale days and caught up on other topics. I wished him well and assured him they'd have no problems beating Merseyside's third-best team.

The next morning I went down to breakfast and there was Brian once again. Without hesitation he invited me to join him and 'the boss'. He nodded over to the far corner of the restaurant where, sitting on his own in a small roped-off area, was the great man himself, Sir Alex Ferguson.

Kiddo introduced me: 'Boss, this is Geoff Twentyman.'

As I anxiously sat down, Sir Alex said, 'Your father was a brilliant football scout wasn't he, Geoff? He found some amazing players for Liverpool.' I was buzzing that he knew all about Dad. Incredible.

It was a wonderful experience, the best breakfast I've ever had. Sir Alex was warm, friendly, interested and interesting. Because Brian introduced me, I was 'in'. No hairdryer, no frosty reception, just total trust and warmth.

Kiddo explained our connection to Sir Alex and told him that I was at Bristol Rovers and on the PFA management committee. Sir Alex was a big union guy back in the day, in the shipyards of Glasgow. He asked me if there were any players in Bristol that he should be looking at. It was a remarkable experience to spend time in his company.

Back at Deepdale things weren't good. I'd suffered an abductor muscle injury, which was like a hernia. The club specialist struggled to diagnose the issue. Luckily for me, Paul Walsh at Liverpool had the same injury and symptoms. He told Dad what he'd been diagnosed with. So effectively I advised my specialist about the problem and the remedial action. Surgery corrected it. What's the expression? It's not what you know ... I missed the last two months or so of the campaign, and my contract was due to expire at the end of the season. Meanwhile, Preston were without a manager.

The season ended with Preston second from bottom of the lowest tier. Back then it meant applying for re-election. There was no automatic promotion or relegation with the top tier of non-league football. The other clubs voted to determine who stayed in the Football League or if a club from the non-league ranks was to be promoted.

I was one of eight players whose contract expired at the end of the 1985/86 season. The club held an end-of-season black-tie dinner under a marquee on the pitch at Deepdale. A 3G monstrosity was due to be laid, so hosting the event on the hallowed turf wasn't an issue. I was having a good time when the secretary, Derek Allen, sidled up to me and asked to have a word. 'I'm really sorry, Twents, but the chairman has told me to inform you that you won't be getting a new contract, and you're being released by the club.'

Derek was a fantastic bloke and he looked grey and ashen as he delivered the *coup de grâce*. He also had a dodgy ticker, which concerned me greatly. Blimey, the poor guy had to tell all eight of us we were being released. I was annoyed. Not at the club's decision but the fact that Derek had been charged with delivering the news. He was highly stressed, and this shouldn't have been his job.

This wasn't a great situation. I was married with a first child on the way and had missed the end of the season through injury. I have to say Preston were brilliant with me. Every footballer's contract runs to June of a given year. If you're released and don't get a new club, then your old club must pay you an extra month's money. So, effectively, you're paid until the end of July. As I was technically injured, Preston told me they'd continue to pay me until I was deemed fit. This was a fantastic gesture on their part and something I'll always remember. It's part of the reason I'll always respect and admire the club. I'm delighted they've enjoyed much better times since I left and that Deepdale is now a wonderful stadium.

My time at Preston was a turbulent one. There was relegation and five managers in three seasons. I made 121 appearances, which, including the injury, was a good return. The highlights included the league debut, scoring in a League Cup win at Blackpool, beating Burnley at home in the league, scoring against Bristol Rovers (!) and chipping Joe Corrigan to score in a 6-1 defeat at Norwich in the League Cup.

PNE treated me with honesty and respect, whereas they could have put me on the football scrapheap. I loved every minute playing for them, and I know I wasn't great every minute of every game, but they gave me my chance, something for which I'll be forever grateful.

I was enjoying being a professional footballer. Now I had to believe that there was something new waiting around the corner for me.

Managing people – actions speak louder than words

It's a fundamental of managing people, regardless of the industry. If you say something, back it up with your actions. I was Alan Kelly's fall guy at Preston North End. If he really believed what he said, he should have dropped me. It's a huge contradiction to consistently deliver a tongue-lashing in front of players but then retain that person in the team. It's not good for anyone … the manager's credibility or the individual's welfare. Life is more sophisticated these days, and shouting and hollering are taboo. The top bosses diagnose the problem, offer a solution and everyone benefits.

Chapter 5

As Good as Gould

WE ALL have people that have played a hugely significant role in our lives. Bobby Gould is one such person for me.

I didn't know this when I took his telephone call in 1986. 'Geoff, it's Bobby Gould. I wonder if you fancy playing for Bristol Rovers?'

Call it fate, call it good fortune, call it what you will. Bobby had bumped into Brian Kidd on holiday. 'BG' needed an experienced centre-half, a good professional and one that wouldn't be overly expensive. Kiddo told him yours truly was his man.

I knew the name straight away. Bobby Gould was a 'name'. I knew Rovers played in blue and white quarters, I knew their home was Eastville (hold that thought) and Bristol seemed a beautiful city. Bobby offered me a two-year deal on £275 a week with £25-per-game appearance money. There were also win bonuses available and the club agreed to pay my removals expenses. That was the extent of the 'deal'.

The move was a no-brainer. I was married with a first child on the way. I had a good gut feeling about Bob and the move just seemed right. I was desperate to maintain a career as a footballer. I was determined to improve and be a better version of the one who'd played at Deepdale. Luckily for me I was the only player of the eight released by Preston months earlier who was signed up by a league club.

A few days after Bobby rang me, I was in my local pub near Ormskirk in Lancashire. A group of football fans were in the bar and one of the lads asked where I'd be playing the following season.

'Bristol Rovers,' I said.

'Ah, okay, is that the team in red, or blue and white quarters?' he queried. I confirmed it was the latter and the football geek told me that he'd read an article that week and he told me that Rovers were set to play at a non-league ground the following season. He wasn't 100 per cent sure, but Twerton Park, the home of Bath City, rang a bell. Bob hadn't mentioned this minor detail! I said with minimal conviction that Eastville was where I'd be based.

This was still the pre-mobile phone era, so I phoned BG the following morning. 'Oh yes, I forgot to mention that,' he said sheepishly, but swiftly added, 'but don't worry, it's one of the best non-league grounds in the country.'

Rovers had recently moved from Eastville in Bristol to Twerton Park for financial reasons. 'One of the best non-league grounds in the country' suggested grandeur. I had the image of a new-build, state-of-the-art ground. The reality was, no, it wasn't, it was far from it. The first time I saw Twerton Park was on a wet, dank afternoon. The water was cascading over the guttering along the roof of the popular side terrace. It needed some TLC and a serious makeover. Little did I realise, despite its lack of beauty, that I'd fall in love with the place.

Two and a half thousand diehard fans were there, and I remember thinking that I'd moved my life three hours from home for this. Little did I realise that it would provide me with some truly amazing footballing experiences. Little did I realise that the wonderful city of Bristol would become a fantastic place to live, a place I'd call home. And little did I realise that Bobby Gould's phone call would have such a fundamentally amazing effect on my life.

Thank you, BG, thank goodness you bumped into Brian Kidd on holiday. Two Top Men.

Another Top Man who entered my life back then was a Rovers legend called Harold Jarman. 'H' was a skilful winger who thrilled the crowds at Eastville in the 60s and 70s and was the reserve team boss when I arrived.

Before I put pen to paper on the contract, I had to play a game to prove my fitness. This made total sense as I'd missed the back end of my final season at Preston with the abductor injury. I was confident that the injury was fully healed. So, if you want to prove your fitness, you want a steady game, don't you? Nothing too taxing. Nothing that's going to make you look absolutely useless.

'Yes Bob, I'll be there in good time. I'm really looking forward to it,' I lied. It was Arsenal reserves at Highbury on a Saturday afternoon.

I got the train from Liverpool to London, then the tube to Highbury. A commissionaire in full regalia greeted me at the famous marbled entrance. The bust of Herbert Chapman sat stoically in the reception hallway. It was an incredible place, with heated floors in the dressing room.

I was with a very young Rovers reserve side, which included Steve Yates, who'd become my defensive partner in a couple of years' time. Arsenal were Arsenal. One touch, two touch, clinical football. We got thumped 6-1. Despite the mauling, I thought I did okay.

Harold came over to me after the game and reassured me, 'You did well today, Geoff. I'll be telling Bobby that in the morning.'

It's another key moment in my life. Had Harold not seen it that way, I wouldn't be writing this book. I went back to Liverpool and slept well that night.

BG rang me the next morning and confirmed what Harold had said. I was in. I next saw Harold two days later, on the Monday. Rovers wanted to register me for the midweek League Cup tie at Reading. It was either before fax machines were invented or Rovers couldn't afford one, but Harold drove up from Bristol with my contract and we met at Charnock Richard services near Preston so I could sign the paperwork. Harold then drove to Lytham St Annes, where the Football League was based. His parting shot before he got back on the M6 was, 'You won't ever move away, you won't ever leave Bristol.' I was dismissive, but he cited Bobby Gould, Terry Cooper and others who'd settled in the area. As if …

The club trained at Hambrook on the outskirts of Bristol. The facilities were good. I drove in and met Bobby, who took me into the changing room. We stood at the door and Bob said, 'Lads, this is new signing, Geoff Twentyman. Make him feel at home.'

I said, 'Orrrright lads,' in my thick Scouse accent.

Defender Nicky Tanner shouted in an equally thick Bristolian twang, 'It's Matty from Brookside!' *Brookside* was a popular soap opera on Channel 4 at the time. It was based in Liverpool and Matty was a prominent character in the show. That name stuck with me for the rest of my time at Rovers. Even Gerry Francis, who succeeded BG, would name the team and I was always 'Matty'. Gerry and I are still in regular contact, and it feels odd that he now calls me Geoff.

It was a young dressing room, but it had a good feel to it. The other experience came from Vaughan Jones and player/coach Kenny Hibbitt, the Wolves legend. What a guy Kenny was, and is. He was still a brilliant player, a full-on trainer and a calming influence. 'Hibby' was invaluable in the dressing room and on the grass.

There were some incredible people around the club, such as Vi Harris, who was the tea lady in the kitchen – and yes, she did facilitate Nigel Martyn's trial at Rovers from St Blazey! Roy Dolling, a giant of a man, was the physio. Every time you went to see him with a knock or an injury he had a stereotypical diagnosis: 'You've got a bit of a knee …' 'You've got a bit of an ankle …'

I'll never forget the day when Big Roy literally saved Ian Alexander's life at Twerton Park. Jock went up for a header in an FA Cup tie against Fisher Athletic and clattered his head on the ground as he landed awkwardly. No one was aware, but Jock played with his false teeth in. The dental plate became dislodged on impact and was stuck in his throat. It was horrific. Jock's eyes rolled and his pupils disappeared. His eyes were totally white and he was very close to losing his life. His body seemed to go into some form of fit as he struggled, trying to break free from the people who were battling to keep him, clamp-like, as still as possible. It was clearly a race against time. Incredibly, Big Roy remained composed and managed to dislodge the false teeth with a special tool he kept in his medical bag. He'd performed this very same act on another Rovers player, Aidan McCaffery, some years previously. The incident happened in front of the dugouts, but had it been on the opposite side of the pitch it could have been a tragic outcome. Every second was crucial.

Big Royston also worked with the keepers and was responsible for finding and nurturing some incredible young local talent. Kit man Ray Kendall also did a sensational job. Not only was he brilliant with the kit but, as the club was ground-sharing, on matchdays he had to transport everything from the matchday kit, to pictures and sandwiches for the boardroom. Crockery, glassware, cutlery, toilet rolls, absolutely everything went by road to Twerton Park. After the game he'd load it all back in his van and make the return journey some 12 miles or so to the training ground at Hambrook, where he'd unload the van. As I say, he was brilliant at his job, but we once travelled to York, and on the morning of the match we went to a local park for a light training session and to practise some set pieces. Ray was mortified that he hadn't packed any footballs on to the bus. Gerry decided to practise regardless. It was one of the most surreal experiences of my career – practising corners and free kicks without a ball. The lads hammered Ray.

I don't think I've ever met anyone as upbeat and positive as Ray. He was very well spoken and was always immaculately dressed. He had some great expressions. For example, Friday was 'POETS' day. 'Piss off early, tomorrow's Saturday.' Ray was some guy.

I made my debut for the club at Elm Park against Reading in the Littlewoods Cup in September 1986. It was painful for a couple of reasons. We played in the most horrendous kit that I ever wore. As a kid this would have got nowhere near my incredible collection. Orange and yellow quarters, orange shorts and yellow-and-orange socks. We resembled a dozen or so Battenberg cakes. The Reading fans laughed as we ran out to warm up. The other pain was inflicted by home striker Trevor Senior, whose career was on the up at the time. We lost 4-0 and Senior grabbed a hat-trick.

He was one of those annoying strikers who didn't do much outside the penalty box but was deadly in the red zone.

On the way back to Bristol I was sat on the coach staring out of the window, going through the game in my head, when a wonderful man called Dennis Dunford, the chairman, came and sat alongside me. He was the archetypal old-school chairman: he had stature, presence and a measured calmness about him. He enquired how I was settling in, as I was in digs and my family was still up north. He empathised and said it must be tough, especially with a baby on the way. He then added, 'You played well tonight.' I don't know how much he knew about football, but it was a real boost and something I've never forgotten.

My league debut came three days later at York City. Thank goodness we ditched the 'Battenberg' kit for the blue and white quarters. Rovers lined up as follows: Carter, Scales, Tanner, Jones, Twentyman, Hibbitt, Francis, Penrice, Morgan, Mehew and Micallef. I was up against a centre-forward called Keith Walwyn. Keith, who was a big, mobile target man, very sadly passed away at the age of just 47. We lost 1-0 and I was booked for illegally apprehending Walwyn!

I found my feet early on, both on and off the pitch. I loved the dressing room. It's a place where banter is king, and I like to think the Scouser in me helped with that. It wasn't long before Bobby pulled me to one side and told me the lads had held a meeting and they wanted me to be captain. I was surprised and flattered in equal measure. I'd never captained a team before, well not since Northway Primary School. Peer approval is important, and it was good to know the lads respected and rated me.

I was enjoying Bobby's management style. He had a wealth of experience and knowledge. He treated me with respect and trust throughout the time we worked together. There were also some hilarious moments. The reserves lost at home to West Ham. The Hammers were in the top flight at the time. Bobby watched the game and West Ham had played the West Ham way – quick one-touch, two-touch football, and movement around the pitch like the Red Arrows. BG came in the next day and called the group together: 'Right, we're going to play like West Ham!' We all looked at each other in amazement and total disbelief. We trained and tried one- and two-touch football and the movement. The ball went here, there and everywhere that it shouldn't. The Red Arrows couldn't get off the runway. We were clearly struggling. Bobby suddenly stopped the session and shouted, 'Right, that's it, we're going back to playing like Bristol Rovers.'

He could be measured and he could be unpredictable, as one afternoon at Chester proved. Before I continue, I must tell you that Bobby loved our right-back John Scales. Forget BG's actual sons, Richard and Jonathan, we all thought he had a third son and that was John Scales. 'Scalesy' was a great lad. He had the lot. Well, almost the lot. He was blonde, good-looking, six feet tall, a great athlete and could play. He went on to play for Wimbledon, Liverpool and Spurs and made three England appearances.

So, back to Sealand Road and we're losing at half-time. Bobby was fuming, absolutely raging. His veins were protruding out of his neck and forehead. His fists were clenched. He was about to deliver an absolute major bollocking. John Scales was having a stinker and decided he had a problem with his boots – blaming his studs. Back in the day you wore black boots, either Puma or Adidas, maybe Nike were a thing. John wore Lotto, which were a little-known Italian boot. Oblivious to the mood in the dressing room and rather than face the absolute shoeing like the rest of us,

John decided to change his studs. He wandered aimlessly into the 'bathroom' part of the dressing room where the studs and pliers were located.

Then Bobby saw him, and his rage intensified. He was apoplectic. BG picked up the tray with a dozen or more real cups and an oversized teapot on it. He hurled it against the wall, shouting, 'Lotto, Lotto! Who on earth wears fucking Lotto!' We sat there in semi-disbelief. This was a five-star bollocking. Fire and brimstone were still coming out of BG's nostrils. Scalesy continued changing his studs, but my biggest concern was the tea running down the dressing room wall. And the teacups smashed into a million pieces. I was a regular three or four cups of tea at half-time kind of guy. Not today I wasn't. We lost 3-1, by the way.

Another story that involves Bobby and John should carry the headline 'Bobby saved my career but I saved his life'. We were playing Chester at Twerton Park. Graham Barrow played in midfield for the visitors. Big Graham was 6ft 2in, a unit of a human being. He was combative and adored a tackle. He was a good lad and, as a former Chorley player, I knew him well. We were playing down the hill at Twerton Park. 'Son of Bobby', for some reason, was playing left-back. Scalesy was racing forward with the ball, and as he got to the halfway line he started to overrun the ball. Graham Barrow sensed some easy pickings and knew his prey was there for the taking. The big man set off in full flight towards the ball. I winced at what was about to unfold. Scalesy didn't slow down one iota. Big Graham absolutely smashed him into orbit, somersaults, the lot, before he crashed into the mud.

BG, who was absolutely seething because his 'lad' had been flattened, jumped out of the dugout. I knew I had to get to where BG was going before BG arrived. I instinctively ran as fast as

I could and got to my snarling manager just as he was about to confront Graham Barrow. To be fair, BG may have slowed down as he got closer! I wrapped my arms around Bob and pulled him away. I have no doubt I saved someone's life with my swift intervention. That life was *not* Graham Barrow's.

As you'll have picked up from this chapter, Bobby was a massive influence both on and off the pitch. I was commuting from Liverpool, and my wife was expecting our first child. I stayed in digs in Eastville with a dear couple called Mr and Mrs Lewis. Richard Dryden, an apprentice, was there too. The house was usually very cold, the food was barely edible, and they had an annoying little dog. Apart from that it was utopia.

Sunday, 14 December 1986. The impending arrival was a few days overdue. Rovers played Newport County at Twerton Park. Back then there weren't many Sunday games, but Bath City had played on the Saturday, so we were scheduled the next day. The pitch was like a mudbath, and we drew 2-2. As I was about to get in the communal bath, BG said, 'Don't be in there too long.'

'Has she had it?' I asked instinctively. Bob told me she'd gone into labour that morning, but he had no further news.

Now, here's what being from a footballing family is all about. My mum had phoned BG in the morning to tell him that my wife had gone into labour. Bob immediately said, 'I'll send him home straight away.'

Mum instructed Bob quite clearly, 'No, tell him after the game.' Comedy from my mum as she took any decision to play or not to play out of my hands.

Within minutes I was in my pale blue Vauxhall Astra and heading to Fazakerley Hospital in Liverpool. The car was panting when I arrived. I got there in time, and a baby boy, Mark, was born an hour or so later.

Mum called it right! A short time after the blood, guts and excitement, a nurse came into the room and told me there was a telephone call for me in the sister's office. This was very, very strange. As far as I was aware no one, except my parents, knew where I was. 'Hello?' I said, to which a voice responded, 'Geoff, it's Bob. I'm just checking everything is okay.' This was highly impressive man-management. Bob congratulated me and made sure mother and baby were well. He'd rung my parents' home to find out where I was.

The man-management got even better. This was Sunday around 10.30pm. Rovers were set to play Bristol City on the Tuesday at Ashton Gate in the Freight Rover Trophy. Bob asked how I felt about Tuesday. I told him that ideally I'd like the midweek off but would be fine to play at the weekend. Without hesitation, Bob said, 'Right, here's the story. You picked up a strain against Newport today and I'll see you Friday. Congratulations, do what you have to do this week.' Rovers lost 3-0 at Ashton Gate on the Tuesday. That was an incredible bit of man-management. After that I gave Bob everything I could both on and off the pitch.

So, to the last scheduled game of my first season. We had to avoid defeat at Newport to make sure we weren't embroiled in a strange relegation play-off system, which included teams from the division below. On the Thursday before the game BG held a meeting in the boardroom at the training ground. With a huge portrait of the club president, the Duke of Beaufort, looking down on us, Bob rolled out a Subbuteo pitch. He had the 11 players in his hands and, as he explained the formation, he positioned them accordingly. Goalkeeper. Back four. Sweeper behind the back four.

Sweeper behind the sweeper … I sensed the apprehension among the players. I could tell they wanted me to say something as I was captain. I could feel the eyes of my team-mates on me.

I took a deep breath and piped up, 'Bob, we have seven players engaged in defence, how are we ever going to attack?'

Bob replied, 'Good point,' and took away the sweeper behind the sweeper. He asked, 'What do you think now?'

I looked at the formation and said, 'To be honest, Bob, I think we should have a back four, four in midfield, two up top, and have a real go at them.'

Bob removed the existing sweeper and went 4-4-2. Phil Purnell scored the only goal as we won 1-0, and the huge band of travelling Gasheads celebrated gleefully. It was classic Bob, but great management. He had a wacky idea but listened to his players and wasn't afraid to change his mind regarding the formation.

At the end of the season I was absolutely stoked to be awarded 'Player of the Season' by the fans. I played 47 games, and it was a huge honour, one I'm still very proud of as there's no better endorsement than that of the supporters. The presentation evening was a basic affair in a nightclub in Bristol called Bibas. It wasn't a glitzy occasion like they are nowadays, with big screens, bright lights and a celebrity host. I didn't even know it was an awards event. I just thought it was an end-of-season get-together with the fans. I was dumbstruck when they stopped the music, one of the supporters' club committee, Ron Hicks, called me on stage for what seemed like a chat about my first season and then made the announcement and presented me with the award. I was chuffed.

Not long afterwards I took an early morning call from BG to tell me he was leaving to join Wimbledon. I was his captain and he wanted to tell me first and make sure I didn't hear it from anyone else or through the media. Class from BG.

Fast forward to when I was at the Beeb. One summer I presented a series for *Points West*, the regional TV programme, where I played the best golf holes in the west with a sporting guest. It was a tough gig, but someone had to do it. I invited Bob to play the 11th hole at The Kendleshire in South Gloucestershire, about ten miles out of Bristol. It's a beauty of a golf hole. It's a par three, the green oasis is 170 yards away off the competition tees. Miss the island green and you're in the water. Bob was up for the feature but warned me that he hadn't played for a while and was rusty.

I hit first and knocked it on to the green. Bob, who's a leftie, then teed it up. Splash. He went again. Sploosh. Next one, splash. He put four or five into the drink, maybe six. Eventually he made the green, two-putted and walked off with a pretty high score. The measure of the man is that when he walked to the green, he said to me, the producer and the cameraman, 'Make sure you show every shot, don't edit any of them out.' He wasn't bothered at all. It made a brilliant montage of his shots, reactions and splashes. To be fair, it was a very solid two-putt. Insisting that we showed every shot was a measure of the man.

To this day, when I look back at people and events that shaped my life, Bobby is right up there. We keep in touch as he remains in Portishead in North Somerset with his lovely wife Marjorie. BG will always be a Top Man.

Managing people - go the extra mile and reap the benefits

In exceptional circumstances do whatever it takes to make your staff feel valued. Bobby Gould did this hours after my first child was born. It was rare to play on a Sunday and, without me knowing it, Bob suggested that I missed the Newport County game when Mum told him that my ex-wife had gone into labour. Mum made the decision for me to play the game. Later that night BG's management skills came into their own. Bob found out where Mark had been born and he telephoned me via the landline at the hospital very late in the day. He put my needs ahead of his own and gave me a few days off, which meant I missed a game against Bristol City to be with my new son. Bob made me feel valued. He could have left ringing me to the next day and demanded I played in the week. But he didn't. I gave Bob everything I had on and off the pitch after that.

Chapter 6

It's Never Too Late to Learn

I HAVE one regret about playing for Gerry Francis. That regret? I wish I'd played for him earlier in my career. Gerry was a brilliant coach. He was the first manager who taught me how to play the game. Since playing under Gerry Francis, I've had a more comprehensive understanding of the game. I watch football in a different way to how I did previously. I'm more analytical in dissecting the action, more forensic.

Gerry, who's eight years older than me, improved every player in the Rovers squad. His brain could compute a game into finite detail. Gerry, or 'Gel' as we called him, didn't miss a thing. As well as being an outstanding coach he was an analyst, before analysts became a thing. I think Terry Venables and Dave Sexton were big influences on Gerry's coaching philosophies.

It's a strange time when there's a change of manager at a football club. The new guy comes in and you feel vulnerable. It doesn't matter how well you've done or how many games you've played, it's like going back to the start on the Monopoly board.

Gerry Francis had an outstanding pedigree as a player. He captained England in the 70s. To be fair, he did mention that a few times, but kudos to him! Gel had played at Rovers previously and was in the team at York when I made my league debut; however, he left after a few games of my inaugural season in the quarters. I didn't know him, but I remember playing against him at Deepdale when he was player/manager of Exeter. He was tenacious, competitive, aggressive, and possessed a deep desire to win, although that day was a home victory.

In training, when we played a small-sided game, if Gerry's side was losing it went on and on and on. A game scheduled for 20 minutes would go on for an hour or more until Gerry's side won.

From day one it was obvious he had an elite football brain. He told us that he was going to improve us all, which as a player you immediately bought into. He used a whiteboard to explain the basic 4-4-2 formation and the system that he was going to employ. Gerry also emphasised the importance of corners and free kicks at both ends of the pitch. He warned us that we'd work extremely hard on fitness, patterns of play and set pieces. Understanding and repetition were fundamental to his methodology.

Gerry got us exceptionally fit. Box-to-box runs were his trademark. We'd split into two groups. Group one would set off in a line across the edge of one of the 18-yard boxes and would run to the opposite 18-yard box and back. Then the second group went. Once they were back, off the first group went again. Variations such as double runs or 18-yard box and back, halfway line and back, 18-yard box and back were tough, tough runs. It was against the stopwatch so there was no slouching. Fitness levels were impressive. Tuesdays, when there was no midweek game, were horrendous. Despite the physical challenge, the lads all dug deep and did the hard yards, but I must admit I much preferred a midweek game.

Gerry pulled a masterstroke in promoting Kenny Hibbitt to assistant manager. Kenny was the good cop, Gerry the bad cop. The managerial team oozed class, experience, knowledge and professionalism.

Incredibly, Gerry used to drive in daily from his home in Bagshot, initially to Hambrook and then to the Cadbury's chocolate factory in Keynsham where we moved to. Gerry's commute was over 90 miles each way. His office was a Portakabin, while the players changed in rickety old wooden changing rooms. I also remember him having one of the first-ever mobile telephones. It was the size of a house brick!

It was brilliant to play for Gerry and Kenny. Ken was still playing in midfield, and I was absolutely gutted when he broke his leg against Sunderland. Even by 1980s standards it was a terrible tackle by Gordon Armstrong. It was late, as the Sunderland player left the sole of his foot in, so after Kenny cleared a ball upfield his follow-through meant his lower leg whacked into Armstrong's studs. Shinpads had little effect. It was sad that Kenny's illustrious career ended in such a dreadful way.

When Gerry arrived I don't think he fancied me as a player. He made Vaughan Jones team captain, which was a fair shout, as 'Joner' was vastly experienced and a natural leader. Plus, he and Gerry had played together for Rovers previously. Gerry asked me to be club captain, which I was delighted to accept. A club captain is a kind of ambassadorial role, dealing with all sorts of club business, including connecting with the fanbase and the media. I enjoyed the role and the responsibility it brought.

My thoughts that Gerry wasn't sure about me were reaffirmed when I wasn't selected for the opening game of the season. Gary

Penrice ran Rotherham a merry dance in a 3-1 win at Twerton Park. I kept my head down as I was sure my chance would come. And my chance *did* come. My first start under Gerry was in the sixth league game of the campaign, the small matter of a Bristol derby at Ashton Gate. It was an absolute humdinger of an encounter that finished 3-3. I had a decent game and enjoyed the partisan atmosphere. I played against Joe Jordan for the first time. It was a good duel, the first of a few with Joe, and the draw was a great result for Rovers.

On the Monday after the game, I experienced Gerry's super analysis for the first time. He sidled up alongside me as we walked to the training pitches and said, 'You did well on Saturday, well done. But you did get done on the third goal.'

'Did I?' I replied.

Gerry went on, 'Yes, your body shape was all wrong. The cross came in from your right and, because your body was closed to your right, you didn't know where Joe Jordan was. He'd pulled off your left shoulder and nodded the ball back across goal for David Moyes to tap in from a yard out.' He continued with a level of detail I'd never experienced before. 'What you must do is open your body up so you can see both where the ball is coming from and where the man you're marking is. So, if he moves two paces to your left, you'll see that, so you'll then move two paces to your left, so he doesn't have a run on you.'

It was a real light-bulb moment for me. I thought, *Wow. I'm being taught the art of defending.* The manager diagnosed the problem, offered a solution and we worked on the practicalities on the training ground. This ability to improve the individual applied to the goalkeeper, the defence, the midfield and the front men. It was incredible to watch, listen and improve.

Another thing I learned from Gerry was that with 80 per cent of goals there are three phases where it could be prevented. Going back to David Moyes's goal in the 3-3 draw. Phase one: the ball was crossed – why wasn't the cross cut out? Stop the cross! Stop the supply line! Phase two: Joe pulled away off my shoulder and had a free header – poor body shape, my fault. Phase three: who was marking David Moyes as he scored unopposed? Someone had switched off. I still analyse goals nowadays and it's incredible how many have at least three points where the goal could have been prevented.

I had and still have massive respect for Gerry for what he achieved as a player but more so as a manager. He was a brilliant coach and developed a style of play that delivered a championship in 1989/90.

Man-management wasn't his strength, though. He much preferred the training ground and matchday. Gerry struggled to look you in the eye during a conversation. This was important to me as Dad taught me to always look at the person you were talking with.

On a personal basis I feel closer to Gerry now I'm in my 60s than I did when I played for him. He didn't get too close to the lads; it was his way. Sometimes he had a weird practice when you went to see him in his office. If the subject was a bit prickly or difficult, he'd grab a towel that he kept under his desk and start to towel dry his hair, even though it wasn't wet! I pulled him up on it once and said to him, 'Gerry, why are you drying your hair? It's not even wet.' He put the towel down and we had a sensible conversation. Absolute comedy.

As well as improving individuals, he made some shrewd positional changes with the players he inherited. Gerry converted

Gary Penrice from midfield to striker. 'Penny' was technically so gifted. He had an outstanding football brain; his first few yards were between his ears. His touch was like velvet, and he could finish for fun. He made goalscoring look easy at times. He wasn't very tall but was good in the air. Penny wasn't the best trainer, but he more than made up for that at three o'clock on Saturday afternoons. Penny was one of the most talented players I ever played with.

Gerry moved Ian 'Jock' Alexander from a right-winger to a right full-back. Jock was an excellent defender, aggressive, read the game well and loved to rampage forward.

Gerry had made a mental note of a player he'd faced in a pre-season game a few years earlier and hunted him down when he took over. This was another masterstroke. Devon White was a strapping, old-school type of centre-forward. Dev was an absolute quality bloke on and off the pitch. He must have been a nightmare to play against as he was 6ft 3in and had a great leap. He was unorthodox and was a real competitor. Dev and Penny struck up an almost telepathic partnership. It was the archetypal big man, little man combination.

Another signing that has gone down in Rovers folklore was when Gerry pursued the recommendation from Vi, the tea lady at the training ground, regarding a goalkeeper she'd been told about when she was on holiday in Cornwall. A keeper called Nigel Martyn, who played for St Blazey, was useful, apparently. He came in on trial and looked half-decent. We did a shooting session and he was making some incredible saves. Hardly a shot went past him. I geed the lads up and said we needed to put the trialist in his place. The harder we tried, the more saves he made. Bottom corner, no problem. Top corner, nothing doing there either.

Nigel impressed in a pre-season draw with Gillingham. This is my understanding of the subsequent contract 'negotiations' between the manager (GF) and the trialist (NM) that followed:

> GF: 'You've done okay. Not bad. Do you want to be a footballer?'
>
> NM: 'Thank you, Gerry, yes, I really do.'
>
> GF: 'How much do you earn delivering sofas for the local furniture store in St Austell?'
>
> NM: '£100 a week.'
>
> GF: 'Okay, I'm prepared to pay you £110 a week, with some appearance money and win bonuses on top. It's up to you.'
>
> NM: 'Where do I sign?'

Timmy Carter moved on to Sunderland and Nigel stepped into professional football like he was born to do it. Incredible. 'Blazey' was a natural. He had presence, was agile, he was brave, composed, had a huge desire to improve and learn, he was humble and calm – he had the lot.

Nige was called up to the England Under-21 squad in his first season. Bob Twyford, the club secretary, had to throw stones up to the window of Nigel's first-floor flat to tell him about his international call-up. There was no access to the property as the shop below was closed, and there was no telephone either.

We used to room together on the occasional overnight stay. We were at York one weekend, and on the Friday night Nigel got his boots out of his kit bag and started to polish them. I was horrified on two fronts. Firstly, that he was going to polish his boots in the hotel room in the company of the senior pro and club captain. But, more significantly, I was appalled by the state of his boots. The sole was detached from the upper at the front of his right boot. The gap was massive.

In those days Rovers players were given a boot allowance. Essentially, you bought your own boots. You could go all in and blow the lot on a pair of top-of-the-range boots. Alternatively, you could buy two mid-range pairs. Some would opt for three of a more basic model.

Anyway, after I reprimanded Nigel for cleaning his boots in the club captain's room, I asked him what on earth he was going to do the next day, as his right boot was absolutely trashed. He told me he was going to wrap some masking tape around the sole and the upper!

At the time, I knew the football rep for Puma. It was his job to make sure the best players wore Puma boots. I told Nigel I'd ring him and try to sort him out some new boots and leisurewear. I made the call on the Monday: 'The keeper at our place is top drawer, he's decent, mate. He's going to play at the highest level without any doubt. He's not after money, he just needs some help with some boots, some trainers and some leisurewear – a few tracksuits and T-shirts. Like I say, not a penny, but sign him up and you've got a star on board. It's a no-brainer.' He mulled it over for a few seconds and replied, 'Geoff, I appreciate the call, but I get lots of these recommendations. Sorry, mate, but the budget is just about spent for the financial year, so it's not possible.'

My plan B was to go to see Gerry on Nigel's behalf, and we manged to sort out a pair of boots for my roomie. The following season (1989/90) Nigel became the first-ever £1m keeper when he was sold to Crystal Palace after making 101 appearances for Rovers. England caps and top-flight appearances with Palace, Leeds and Everton followed in an incredible career.

I covered a Leeds vs Bristol City League Cup tie at Elland Road some years later for BBC Radio Bristol. I met up with Nigel for a chat after the game and I mentioned to him that he was wearing Adidas boots. He smiled and told me ruefully that a few weeks after he'd signed for Palace (the first-ever £1m keeper, remember) the Puma rep contacted him to offer him a boot deal with Puma! Nigel politely declined.

Blazey was and is a Top Man. The best thing about him is this: he's the same guy now as the one who rocked up at the Hambrook training ground all those years ago. Despite all that he has achieved, he hasn't changed. Nigel Martyn is the same grounded, well-mannered, respectful and totally humble person.

Back to Gerry's coaching. He didn't just talk the talk ... he could walk the walk. In one training session we were practising set pieces. Ian Holloway was trying to clip a free kick on to Devon's head. Ollie was struggling with his delivery. Gerry moved in and pushed Ollie to one side, stretched off his quad muscle and in a padded all-in-one thermal suit, a pair of trainers and on an allotment of a training pitch proceeded to put several deliveries on to Devon's head. Kudos.

It's interesting that so many great players fail to make great managers. The key thing for me is the ability of the coach to transfer their undoubted knowledge to the players on the training ground. It must be done in a simple way, so it's understood. Gerry could do it both verbally and could demonstrate things practically when he needed to.

Ian Holloway is obviously somebody who has been prominent in my life. We've been great friends for decades. When I joined Rovers he was struggling at Brentford and had been at Torquay on loan. Gerry wanted to bring Ollie back to his spiritual home.

Rovers had no money. Gerry resolved the problem as he loaned the club the £10,000 or so to bring Ollie back to Bristol. It was a stroke of genius.

Ollie turned up in his VW Beetle on day one. His blonde feather-cut hairstyle was very distinguished. You could see he loved the club. His confidence may have been low, but he was genuinely excited at the prospect of getting his career back on track. He was a special character; his enthusiasm was infectious. I took to him straight away. Ollie soon became the heartbeat of the side; he was passionate, an exceptionally proud Bristolian and a huge Rovers fan.

Ollie started his career as a wide man, but Gerry employed him as a central midfielder. He improved rapidly under Gerry's tutelage. He was his own man and was always prepared to offer his opinions. As I often told him, there were times when he needed to be more diplomatic or even keep schtum! For example, we were 2-0 down at half-time at Torquay in the Freight Rover Trophy. Gerry was absolutely fuming. He had a face like he was sucking a lemon and was ranting about the performance. There's only one thing to do at this point: shut up, keep your head down and listen. Ollie made the cardinal mistake of saying something, or trying to say something. He uttered two syllables and Gerry fired in with, 'You can shut the fuck up or I'll put you through that fucking wall!' Absolute silence engulfed the dressing room. Gerry had a face like thunder. He didn't lose it too often but when he did it was serious! We lost the game 2-0. It was a long drive home.

Ollie's sidekick in the centre of midfield was Andy Reece. 'Reecey' is the only guy I ever saw beat Nigel Martyn from 35 yards. It was a shame it was an own goal! Andy, who hailed from Wolverhampton, was a crucial member of the squad. His long-range passing was top drawer, and he and Ollie just clicked. Reecey was the heart and soul of the group on the team-bonding nights out.

Andy was signed after he'd impressed at Dudley Town in the Midlands League. On his first day as a pro, he presented me with a problem. 'Jiff, can I have a word please?' Reecey went on to tell me, in my capacity as club captain and PFA delegate, that he'd been banned for eight weeks after a misdemeanour at Dudley. Eight weeks, two whole months. Oh, and he'd forgotten to tell Gerry, and he'd just signed his contract. There was only one thing to do, so off we went to tell Gerry. To be fair, Gerry was okay about it and the club managed to get the suspension reduced to two weeks. Phew. Reecey and I remain big friends all these years on.

Hours and hours of work on the training ground produced an organised, highly efficient team. With players such as Penny, Nigel and Ollie we were a match for most teams in the Third Division.

Gerry labelled us 'Ragbag Rovers' and made a virtue of us being the underdogs. After all, we played at Bath City's ground (the best non-league ground in the country, remember!). We trained at Fry's Chocolate factory in Keynsham, where there were a dozen pitches, but we were only allowed to use two of them. Gerry's office, and the kit and medical rooms were Portakabins. The players changed in wooden dressing rooms. But with our fantastic, passionate support, which was increasing week on week, we turned all those negatives into positives.

We had a strong second half of the season and finished eighth in the Third Division in Gerry's first season in charge. We whopped eventual champions Sunderland 4-0 at Twerton. Gary Penrice was unplayable that Wednesday night, but the occasion was marred by Kenny Hibbitt's injury.

We won five of our last seven games and lost only once, 2-1 on the final day at Brighton, who celebrated promotion at a packed Goldstone Ground. It was an amazing carnival-like atmosphere. Gerry sat us down afterwards and told us that what we'd witnessed we could experience ourselves. The target was for Bristol Rovers to emulate Brighton and their upward momentum. He was deadly serious.

I played 43 games that season and was chuffed to change Gerry's mind on me. I knew I was his go-to man when it came to head it, kick it.

I sensed things were really on the up for 'Ragbag Rovers'.

Chapter 7

The Derby: Be Strong, Be Brave

I PLAYED in 16 league and cup Bristol derbies. My record is decent. Nine wins, four defeats and three draws. I played in 11 before I tasted defeat. The younger generations of City and Rovers fans reading this will find it hard to believe.

I established a sense of the importance of derby football at a very young age. I'll never forget my first Merseyside derby. It was November 1970; I was 11 years of age. More than 53,000 were at Anfield. I was in the main stand, level with the penalty spot at the Kop end. The atmosphere was intoxicating. An intense rivalry, not a semblance of aggression, just a fervour, a desire, a passion, a respect and a deep fear of losing combined with a deep hope that this would be 'our day'.

It was 0-0 at half-time, then the unthinkable: Everton scored twice. The blonde-haired Alan Whittle scored first then big Joe Royle got the other. I cried. I literally cried. My first-ever Merseyside derby and the Blue Noses were set to triumph. The weight of the impending defeat was unbearable. The ridicule at school, in the park, the media coverage would exacerbate the agony. Shankly's famous quote of football being more important than life and death never rang truer.

Then something incredible happened. Attacking the Kop, Steve Heighway, the Liverpool left-winger, took the game by the scruff of the neck. He strode purposefully down the flank, cut inside on to his stronger right foot and hit a low drive inside the near post and into the net. 1-2. The Kop rallied, the noise was extraordinary. Minutes later, off he went again. 'Big Bamber', a university graduate who was nicknamed after Bamber Gascoigne who hosted the TV show *University Challenge*, went outside the full-back and clipped a glorious cross on the run. John Toshack outjumped the England centre-half Brian Labone and headed the ball back across the keeper, 2-2. Absolute pandemonium.

You can guess the rest. Right full-back Chris 'The Ghost' Lawler stole into the penalty box and volleyed a glorious winner as Liverpool set siege to the Everton goal. 'You'll Never Walk Alone' reverberated around Anfield. The whistle went on a famous win, and the feeling of unbridled elation was overpowering. There's something almost indefinable about winning a derby.

As I was to find out later in life, the burden of responsibility as a player on derby day is heavy, it's different, it's all-consuming, it's one of the most exhilarating experiences that football offers.

Lancashire derbies were okay. Preston versus Blackpool, Burnley or Blackburn were decent, feisty on occasions, but were nothing compared to the real deal when the two clubs come from the same town or city. These fixtures really appealed to my DNA. It was a day to be resolute, to be strong, to be uncompromising and to show what you're made of.

As an immigrant to Bristol, derby day wasn't personal, it was purely professional. For me there was no hatred, but there was a deep desire to win as I knew what it meant to the fans. There was no better feeling than looking your direct opponent in the eye on the full-time whistle and shaking hands after a derby win. That appreciation started at Anfield in 1970.

I won't go through all the derbies I played in, but I've picked a few that remain strong in the memory. As I said, incredibly, I played in 11 league and cup derbies before I tasted defeat. Rovers had a real hold on City. Gasheads had a swagger when it came to the bragging rights.

My first Bristol derby was on New Year's Day in 1987 at Ashton Gate. Oh … my … days. A proper occasion. An intense rivalry. An aggressive, high-octane atmosphere. It was a privilege to be part of it. For me, apart from my league debut, it was the highlight of my career thus far.

As soon as we walked out to inspect the pitch an hour or so before kick-off, the enormity of the occasion was palpable. It was very different to any other league fixture. The ground was three-quarters full way ahead of the 11.30 kick-off. By the time the first whistle was blown it was packed with a vibrant, volatile atmosphere.

There was no big Churchillian speech from manager Bobby Gould. As he pointed out, if you couldn't get fired up for a game like this, then you were in the wrong profession. He also told us that a local businessman had promised us a nice cash bonus if we won. Apparently, the brown envelopes would be discreetly placed in our shoes after the game … if we won.

The game was bonkers. If it had been a boxing bout the referee would have stopped the contest after 35 minutes and awarded a unanimous home victory. City dominated from the kick-off. Rovers hung on. Our keeper Timmy Carter went off with a gash to his head that needed stitches. Dave Mehew went in goal. To this day I have no idea why 'Boris' (tennis player lookalike) went in goal. City dominated and rattled the woodwork a couple of times. Thankfully Timmy Carter returned, and the backs-to-the-wall stuff continued. I remember City striker Steve Neville went through on goal and Vaughan Jones took him out from behind. Nowadays it would be a straight red but in those more 'forgiving' times it was just about a yellow!

Miraculously, with the clock showing 87 minutes gone, it remained goalless. Rovers had a free kick inside our half. I delivered all the long-distance merchandise. I had a dilemma. Do I play it back to Timmy Carter and let him run the clock down and settle for a very undeserved draw or do I put the ball into the City penalty box to see what happens?

According to City fans, Rovers were a team who 'whooshed' it. For the uninitiated this meant going route one, back to front in one kick of the ball, bypassing the midfield – you've got the idea. Incredibly, yours truly was voted by the (excellent) City fanzine at the time, *The Bounty Hunter*, as Bristol's best 'whoosher'. This was genuine kudos. Of all the footballers in Bristol, Geoff Twentyman could kick it further than anyone else. I'm not sure I'll tell the grandkids, but it made me chuckle!

I thought, *Let's have some fun*, so I put the ball in the mixer. I went three-quarters power and dropped the ball just inside the City penalty box. Centre-half David Moyes won the header under challenge from Trevor Morgan, and Rovers' Gary Smart, a part-time professional, walked on to the loose ball just outside the box and smashed it into City keeper Keith Waugh's top right-hand corner. Right in the postage stamp. The Gasheads behind his goal in the open end (now the Atyeo Stand) were delirious. It was daylight robbery. There are people in Horfield prison in Bristol for less. Oh ... my ... days.

The Gasheads were euphoric on the final whistle. BG walked us off the pitch after we acknowledged the vociferous away support. A few of us checked our shoes for the brown envelopes but there were only socks in their rightful place. It was typical Bobby, a motivational ploy, but to be honest no motivation was needed – the result was reward enough. To win a Bristol derby was something very special.

The date of 2 May 1990 is one that will be etched in Rovers folklore forever. Those who were present will never forget it. It had been an incredible season as both clubs chased automatic promotion from the Third Division. The encounter at Twerton Park was the penultimate game of the season. This is what was on the line: a home win and Rovers went top and were promoted; an away win and City were champions; a draw meant City were promoted. The media coverage was huge but imagine if they'd had social media back then, it would have been absolute carnage. The keyboard warriors would have been in overdrive.

Rovers were in good form and we'd lost only once in our previous 25 games. City striker Bob Taylor was out injured, which was a massive blow to their promotion prospects. Twerton was packed as 9,831 crammed in. The people in high places made the interesting decision for the teams to come out side by side. The idea was to promote harmony on the pitch and on the terraces. People who have never played the game make some strange decisions! I always came out last for Rovers, it was a superstition. I noticed the body language and faces of the City lads as they filed past me to line up in the tunnel – they looked fraught with fear. By contrast, we were perfectly prepared, fire in the belly but ice in the brains and the veins. We were unbeaten at home all season, which added to our self-belief.

Rovers played well on that Wednesday night. Big Devon White was outstanding and grabbed a brace. Ollie sealed the deal from the penalty spot as it finished Rovers 3 City 0. Towards the end of the game some frustrated City fans ripped up some of the advertising boards and threw them on to the pitch. The referee, Roger Dilkes, stopped the game while the police, some of whom were on horses, restored order. City manager Joe Jordan even walked round behind the goal to try to exert some influence. As Roger and I were watching, he said to me, 'Geoff, if they think I'm going to add time on, they're having a laugh. I'm not adding on one second.'

The result meant Rovers went top, were promoted and were one win from being crowned champions. City's promotion was on hold but was confirmed 24 hours later when Notts County dropped points. It was an incredible night. We had champagne in the dressing room and a few beers in the supporters' lounge. In keeping with traditions, we celebrated afterwards at Chasers nightclub in Kingswood, which is a Rovers heartland.

I rehydrated extensively, as you can imagine. Incredibly, I remember talking football with a diehard City fan at the bar for most of the night. He was obviously gutted by the result but was gracious in defeat, and talking to him until the early hours was brilliant and a top memory for me. He introduced himself to me recently when I was out socially. He told me he had fond memories of the night – the drinking session, not the match!

I got home in the early hours and a neighbour called Gary Jones, who was a big Gashead, had taped a can of lager to my front door with a note saying 'tonight was incredible Geoff, have a drink on me'. I put it in the fridge; I had an important game on the Saturday! It was a privilege to be able to affect people's lives in such a positive way and to help to give them such joy through football.

There was an absolute humdinger of a game at Twerton Park in January 1991. It finished 3-2 to Rovers. Carl Saunders got the winner, which was the result of hours of work on the training ground. It was 2-2 and we had a corner on the left-hand side as we attacked down the slope at the Bath end of the ground. Ollie delivered it, right-footed. I made a run from level with the far post, towards the ball, along the six-yard box to just beyond the near post. I lost my marker, flicked it on, quite flat, using the pace of the cross. Carl, who was just inside the far post, nodded it in. The simple set piece took just seconds to deliver. It had been perfected on the training ground at a chocolate factory. Gerry had told us on day one about the importance of set pieces.

I lived in Yate in South Gloucestershire at the time and my local was a great boozer called the Cross Keys. Its appeal was that City and Rovers fans drank in there, but nobody overdid the football chat. After games they'd ask me how I'd got on and what the game was like, and that was it. The Keys was a kind of sanctuary where I could relax and chat about 'normal' stuff. The landlord was an incredible guy called John Peacock. He was a larger-than-life character who raised many, many thousands of pounds for charity. John was a massive City fan. After the 3-2 win, which was an early kick-off, I landed in the Keys in good spirits. Very unlike me, I gave John some good-natured stick about the result. John leaned on the bar and beckoned me towards him: 'Twents, come here, I've got something to ask you.' As I stooped in to chat, in an instant he whipped out a pair of scissors and chopped off my tie from just below the knot! The tie, with the date and score written in black marker, was pinned up behind the bar for years. Sadly, the vacant pub is rundown these days, but I guess the tie is probably still there! It was brilliant banter from JP. I walked around the pub for the rest of the night with the remnants of my tie intact. To be fair, it was no longer a tie, it was a knot. Great memories.

It wasn't all celebrations and cut-off ties. I remember the first derby I lost. In March 1991, City won 1-0 at Ashton Gate through a late Louie Donowa goal. It's weird what you pick up on, but I sensed before the game that it might not be our night. Before kick-off there was a minute's silence for Des Williams, the City chairman, who'd passed away that week. Des was a wonderful guy, a real football man. A small minority of Rovers fans broke the silence, which was dreadful. It seemed to give the game even more of an edge and really fired up the City, both on and off the pitch. Afterwards, Ollie was critical of the perpetrators during a TV interview. He was right to call them out.

We didn't play well. The better side won. Ollie had a penalty saved by City keeper Andy Leaning. In fact, Andy was ready lying on the floor waiting for Ollie's 'strike' to eventually reach him! To be fair to Ollie he didn't miss many penalties and he scored some crucial ones in the championship-winning season.

Defeat was horrible. We traipsed back to the dressing room and sat in silence. We could hear the City players singing as they celebrated in the home dressing room. Carl Saunders said to me, 'Listen to that lot,' or words to that effect, to which I reminded him that we'd had it good for a long time. We had to suck it up and remember the pain for next time.

Bob Taylor was the best City front man that I ever faced. 'Super Bob' was strong, intelligent, had great movement, had a great touch and was a good finisher. However, I don't think he ever scored against me and Steve Yates (we came as a pair). Above all else he was honest and never gave up. There's a great photo of me and Bob in which I have my hand across his mouth. It was taken at Twerton Park after I slid in and took the ball off him in the 18-yard box. He was adamant it was a penalty and had a real go at the referee. I respected Bob so I put my hand across his mouth and said, 'Shut up, mate, or you'll get sent off.' That was it. For the record, it wasn't a pen.

Another tough opponent was big Robbie Turner. He was a good lad but was very aggressive, especially in aerial challenges. I remember Kenny Hibbitt sidling up to me in the dressing room at Twerton just before kick-off: 'You're up against Robbie Turner, Geoff. Watch his elbows, expect to get split open today.' At five past three I was in the physio's room being stitched by the club doctor. Kenny was no fool. Cuts, stitches and scars are trophies of war. I went back out and played on. Robbie didn't score and we won, so a few stitches are neither here nor there. No pain, no gain.

Wayne Allison, 'The Chief', was a fantastic opponent. When I first played against him, if I'm honest, he didn't cause me too many problems. I was comfortable, as he didn't carry a real threat. Then a season or so later he really improved. He was strong, intelligent, had developed a great first touch and was brave. He made good runs to get on the ball. He'd go short then spin in behind with real intent. I imagine it was the influence of his manager Joe Jordan that improved his game. He wasn't prolific when it came to goals, but he was a very good target man and a great team player. I bumped into Big Wayner at Ashton Gate this year and it was brilliant to catch up with a real Top Man.

Playing in the Bristol derbies was a real privilege. The burden and the responsibility you carry as a team and as an individual are massive. The joy of winning is incredible and the feeling after defeat is horrendous. Thankfully, the Bristol derbies were good to me.

The last league meeting was back in 2001. The sad reality is there's a whole generation of Bristol football fans who have never experienced the fixture, which is a huge shame.

Chapter 8

The Wedding that Nearly Led to a 'Divorce'

I'LL NEVER forget where I was on 15 April 1989. I was playing in a promotion-chasing Rovers side that lost 2-1 at Brentford. The defeat paled into insignificance when the horrors of the events at Hillsborough started to unfold at half-time. A brilliant little cockney guy used to look after the dressing rooms at Griffin Park. He was a proper geezer. Always in a collar and tie, always polite, always smiling, always helpful. We came off at half-time and he was standing, in a daze, at the top of the tunnel. As I walked towards him, I asked him what was wrong. He blurted out, 'Something awful has happened at Hillsborough, people have died. It's really bad …' It was chilling. I knew Liverpool were playing Nottingham Forest in the FA Cup semi-final. There was a high probability that I knew people who'd made the journey to Sheffield.

Our second half was an eerie affair. The atmosphere was muted. Griffin Park was normally electric but even in the pre-internet and mobile phone era enough information filtered through to those present. The crowd was stunned. People had gone to Sheffield to watch their team play a football match and dozens would not return home.

Afterwards, the away dressing room was stunned. Gerry, who usually gave a brief analysis or no-nonsense rollocking, simply told us to get changed and get on the coach, which was set to leave London as soon as possible. No one really spoke on the way back to Bristol; all ears were locked on to BBC Radio 2 and the coverage from Hillsborough.

Later that evening one of the names of the victims hit me like a hammer blow. Eric Hankin. Eric was three years older than me, but we played football in the park when we were kids in Maghull on Merseyside. I can still picture him now. He'd have been 33 when he died. RIP Eric and those who perished in such a totally inhumane way. My heart aches for those poor families who had to fight for justice for decades. It was a disgrace.

A month or so earlier I was reading the programme before the game at Huddersfield. I noticed the details of the end-of-season play-offs. A date jumped out at me. If Rovers made it to the play-offs, the first leg of the semi-final was scheduled for Sunday, 21 May. The day before, on the Saturday, my only brother was getting married, and I was proud to have accepted his invitation to be his best man.

The date troubled me, so the next day I went to see Gerry to explain the potential conflict. I needed to explain, or request, that I'd need the day off training to be best man for my brother. I hasten to add that had the date been a matchday I wouldn't have asked. Billy wouldn't have expected me to be at the wedding. It was a short, positive conversation. Gerry told me not to worry about it and assured me we'd sort it out if we made the play-offs. I felt more relaxed about the situation. Our form dropped off and we won only one of our last eight games. A 0-0 draw at Bury on the final day meant we finished fifth and were set to face Fulham over two games, with the first leg at Twerton Park eight days later, on Sunday, 21 May.

On the Monday I went to see Gerry to confirm I could have the day off training. I thought it would be a formality, but he told me that I couldn't have the day off and told me that I had to train. I was staggered, as this wasn't my idea of telling me 'not to worry, we'll sort it out'. I explained the importance of Billy being my only brother. I emphasised the significance of the Hillsborough disaster and how losing someone I knew made it even more significant and important for me to be at his shoulder. Gerry insisted that I must train on the Saturday. I asked him why. He said it was vital to practise free kicks and corners. I countered his reasoning by confirming that I knew the routines as well as he did. I was pivotal at both ends of the pitch when there were free kicks and corners. But Gerry insisted I trained.

After training on the Tuesday, I went to see him to find out whether he'd changed his mind. He hadn't. On the Thursday I went for clarity. I was told I had to train on Saturday. Here were two strong-willed individuals. Gerry was flexing his muscles as the manager, the man in charge. His club captain and senior pro was resisting out of loyalty to his brother. That loyalty had been strengthened after the events in Sheffield on 15 April.

So, to the Friday. We trained as normal. I went to see Gerry afterwards and asked whether he'd changed his mind. I assured him that I'd travel home soon after the reception and sleep in my own bed. I offered to take kit with me so I could train on the Saturday morning, which I did. I must admit, having played every game of the regular season, I thought he'd relent. Wrong. Gerry gave me a stark warning: 'If you don't train tomorrow, you won't play on Sunday.'

I did what I felt I had to do on the Saturday. I didn't drink a drop of alcohol, even to toast the happy couple. I drove back from Merseyside and was in my own bed by 11pm. On the Sunday, I reported for the game. Gerry announced the team: I wasn't picked. He named the substitutes: I wasn't included. As was his prerogative, Gerry left me out as promised. He took a huge gamble. He dropped the man he'd picked 54 times in 54 matches of the regular season.

I wished the lads all the best and left the dressing room. Rovers won 1-0, courtesy of a Gary Penrice goal. After the game, our secretary Bob Twyford gave me an envelope. I was about to put it in my jacket pocket, as I assumed it was an invitation to an end-of-season awards evening, but Bob suggested I should read it as a matter of some urgency. So, I did. It was a letter on official Bristol Rovers headed notepaper, signed by vice-chairman Geoff Dunford. Essentially, it told me I was suspended on full pay until further notice due to disobeying the manager's instructions, and that I was in breach of my contract. I wasn't allowed to attend games, I wasn't to attend training, I wasn't permitted to speak with the media, and I was *not* to represent the football club on any official business. I looked at Bob and thought, *Shit, this is serious.* I put the letter back in my pocket and drove home.

A few hours later a car pulled up outside my house. It was team-mates Gary Penrice and Phil Purnell. Two Top Men. They'd dropped by to make sure I was okay. More importantly, they wanted to let me know that the lads were all behind me and each of them would have done the same thing had they been in my position. Penny lightened the mood by telling me how the lads held a mock wedding on the training ground before Saturday's training session. Bride, groom, best man (obviously) and the Wedding March. Gerry went absolutely nuts, apparently.

The situation gained traction very quickly. It was headline news in the *Bristol Evening Post*. Local radio and TV were all over it. Gerry was quoted in the press, stating that I'd let the football club down. It caught the attention of the national newspapers too. Some journalists from one of the nationals doorstepped my parents' house on Merseyside to try to get their opinion on the situation. My mum gave them short shrift. I dread to think what the coverage would be like if the same situation arose today. There would be radio phone-in debates and social media would go into overdrive.

I heard Gerry was particularly hacked off when a columnist for one of the red tops wrote a damning editorial condemning a football manager for suspending one of his players, who was from Liverpool, who asked for a day off training to be best man for his only brother, just weeks after the Hillsborough disaster. Ouch.

Rovers hammered Fulham 4-0 at Craven Cottage to set up a two-legged final against Port Vale. The first leg finished all square at Twerton Park, so it was a winner-takes-all game at Vale Park. The second leg was on a Saturday. A neighbour took me to Wembley to watch England versus Poland to take my mind off the Rovers/Port Vale game. Incredibly, Wembley didn't display the latest scores or results of any other matches on their scoreboard. How did we exist without mobile phones? It was agony not having any information from the Potteries. England won 3-0 and, as we walked back to the car, all I could think about was the lads, the supporters, the second leg, Vale Park, had we/they been promoted?

I was desperate to find out. I saw a police officer directing the traffic just outside Wembley. I made my way across the lanes of traffic and asked him if he knew the results from the play-offs.

He told me he didn't know the results, but he knew who'd been promoted. 'Bristol Rovers or Port Vale?' I asked nervously. 'Port Vale, definitely Port Vale,' was his response. I asked him if he was sure. He was certain, he assured me.

I was enveloped by the strangest set of emotions – upset, abject disappointment, frustration and anger. I was absolutely devastated for the lads; my mates had been delivered an absolute hammer blow. I was gutted for the fans, as the Gasheads had been fundamental in their team enjoying such a successful season. But I thought quite clearly that Gerry had an absolute mare. I was annoyed that he'd cut off his nose to spite his face. He'd suspended a player who he'd picked for every game for the biggest matches of the season. Yes, he'd proved he was in charge, but at what cost?

The club paid for an end-of-season trip to Majorca for the lads. I remained suspended so wasn't included. There was also an open-top bus tour, which I wasn't part of. I have no regrets about what I did. It may have put my football career on the line but at the time my brother and I were very close. Hillsborough had a profound effect on me and still does, to be candid. Loyalty doesn't cost a penny. It's important in life to be true to yourself.

Despite Gerry and I not seeing eye to eye about the wedding, we never had a cross word. Our voices were never raised, there was never a swear word. He gave me an icy glare a few times. It was just a profound disagreement.

After five weeks in the wilderness, still officially suspended, with no contact from the club, I received a call from one of the directors, Ron Craig. He told me that Gerry would be at the training ground the following afternoon and wanted to see me. I drove to Fry's thinking that this would be the last time that I'd make the 25-minute journey.

I walked into Gerry's Portakabin and the first thing he did was offer me his hand to shake, and he said, 'I think this has gone on long enough, don't you?' I instinctively shook his hand and agreed the point. We chatted and explained our respective courses of action. We agreed to put it behind us, but Gerry did warn me that the board of directors was set to meet to discuss my situation.

I had a bad gut feeling about what the board might come up with. A few days later I received a letter sent by recorded delivery to my home address. In their infinite wisdom the board of directors had decided that they were going to fine me a week's wages for 'breach of contract'. I'd already missed out on what would have been the four biggest games of my career, and four lots of appearance money and win bonuses, plus a trip to Magaluf, but the board of directors wanted to take further action.

I rang Gerry to see what the hell was going on. He and I had shaken hands and agreed to move on. Then a few days later the club was going to fine me a week's wages. Gerry claimed that he'd advised the club against it, but they were determined to make an example of me. I spoke with Gordon Taylor, the chief executive of the players' union, and he reassured me that the club couldn't fine me as they'd already suspended me. Logically, you can't be punished twice for the same offence.

The PFA took my case to the Football League, which ruled in my favour, confirming that I couldn't be suspended and then fined for the same breach. The fine was revoked. The board weren't happy. I was hacked off and submitted a written transfer request. I was told I could leave, but the club would require a transfer fee for me.

I reported back for pre-season and trained and played in games as normal. To be fair to Gerry, he treated me as if nothing had happened. I knew a few clubs were interested in me. Someone in the know at the club told me that Bolton and Scunthorpe had made offers for me. When I asked Gerry, he denied there had been any formal interest. Agents weren't a thing then, so it was DIY transfers. Interestingly, a non-league club, Colne Dynamos in Lancashire, who were on a crusade to get into the Football League, tried to sign me. Their millionaire owner/manager Graham White rang me to see if I was interested in a return to the north-west. I was, and he agreed to pay me way more than I was on at Rovers. White meant business and submitted a five-figure offer in writing for me.

I knew he'd made the bid but no one at Rovers mentioned it. After a day or two I went to see Gerry to see if there had been any offers for me. He told me there hadn't. The story was doing the rounds in the media in Lancashire stating that Colne had offered £15,000 for my services. Gerry simply told me that I was his first-choice centre-half. I got the impression I wasn't going anywhere. Gerry was good to his word as he picked me for every game that season and, wow, what a campaign it was.

A few years later, when I was at the BBC, Gerry returned to Rovers for a second spell in charge. We were chatting informally about various things, and the subject of family and children cropped up. By this time Gel was a dad. In the conversation he said to me that family was the most important thing there is! I don't think he realised the irony of the comment, but I let it go over my head. Suffice to say, I knew that back in 1989!

The whole wedding chapter was a defining period in my life, one that made me wiser and stronger. In football terms it was the prelude to a glorious season. Whether it was some form of divine intervention, karma or poetic justice, I don't know, but it was absolutely incredible.

Managing people – never deny your staff time off

If a member of staff asks for time off, never refuse their request. Always work on the basis that they asked to be off for a legitimate reason. Especially if it's at short notice, do everything you can to make it happen. If a member of staff has a stable personal life, they'll flourish in the workplace. Assess the implications of refusing a request. If there will be a wider fallout, then really make sure you're making the right decision. If there's an operational reason to deny a request, talk it through, but you'll always get more out of your staff if they're happy.

My example in 1989, when I was denied a day off training to be best man at my brother's wedding, is a good case in point. There's much to assess in these situations:

Was it important to me? Yes.

Was there an operational reason to deny the request? Gerry Francis said yes, but I felt no.

Why was the day off denied? The manager believed that training was essential to practise set plays.

Was there a wider fallout from not granting the day off? Yes, considerable media attention distracted the players from the play-offs. The players supported me throughout.

What was the gain for not agreeing to the day off? Impossible to define but ultimately the team lost the final.

What would have been the gain if the request had been agreed? A player who'd played in every game that season would have played in the play-offs. No internal or external disruption.

The rule of thumb judgement for me is always allow staff time off if they need it. As a manager you'll reap the benefits.

Chapter 9

Best of the Best

I DON'T know the statistics, but I can only guess that the percentage of professional footballers who win a championship medal in their career is low, very low. I feel exceptionally proud and fortunate to be in the privileged minority.

The 1989/90 season was remarkable. The previous campaign had ended in abject disappointment. Rovers, without the suspended yours truly, lost the play-off final to Port Vale. Back then there seemed to be a trend where teams that missed out on the play-offs struggled the following year, but that wasn't the case with us. It was back to business as usual. There was no self-pity. There was no reference to the defeat against Port Vale. There was no sense of putting right what had gone wrong. We trained hard, very hard. We practised the things we already knew as a sixth sense. The same pattern of play was employed. Why change something that's not broken? Try harder, make the system even better. Be even more determined.

In the summer recess Rovers brought in Pete Cawley, a centre-back from Wimbledon, but true to his word Gerry picked me for the opening game against Brentford. I played every game that season, 59 appearances in total.

It's funny what you remember from a championship-winning season. After the wedding business, I started the season on the transfer list, but I was totally committed to the blue and white quarters. We beat Brentford 1-0 on the opening day of the season in the sunshine at Twerton Park. I recall scoring a headed goal in front of the Preston fans in a 3-0 home win early in the campaign. We started well and won four of our first five matches – there was no play-off hangover.

The biggest factor was that we always seemed to be in games – even if we were losing it was rarely by more than one goal. The number of times we came from 1-0 down to win 2-1 showed we had an incredible inner belief and togetherness. There was a spell in the second half of the season when we won 2-1 six times in succession, and we were behind in every game. We only lost one of our last 22 matches. It wasn't all plain sailing, as we lost 3-2 at Rotherham on New Year's Day. But that and the 2-2 draw at Birmingham over Easter were our worst performances. I had a stinker in both games.

Gerry's success was built on a solid defence. That wasn't just the back four and the keeper. The midfield and the front men all played a part when we were out of possession. We were well drilled. I remember walking to the training pitches with Gel one morning and he asked me if I'd seen the match statistics from Saturday. As part of the match report, the *Bristol Evening Post* listed the match stats: corners, shots on target, shots off target, bookings and fouls, etc. I told Gerry I didn't read the papers. Gerry got very excited and asked me to guess how many times we'd caught the opposition offside! I told him I didn't have a clue. He was buzzing with excitement: 'Eight, eight times, Matty. We caught them offside eight times. Well done.' To

Gerry, a defence that functioned well meant a clean sheet and invariably a win.

Team spirit was key to the success, and we had a regular Wednesday night out at Chasers. It was important for morale that there was 100 per cent attendance. Andy Reece was often the entertainer-in-chief. He did this incredibly dangerous feat where he managed to scale up a lamp post, and when he got to the top he held his body in a horizontal position, parallel to the pavement, which was a long way below him. He'd then shout out in his Black Country accent, 'Corrr it's windy tonight lads. Mattaaay it's really windy mate.' Hilarious.

The Christmas night out was a must-attend occasion. Fancy dress was compulsory. Some of the outfits were sensational. We'd see the City lads out on their night out and they were dressed in their normal gear. We always seemed to be having a better time! I always felt little things like the fancy dress night out gave us an edge when it came to derby day.

Big Devon went as Wee Willie Winkie one year – he even had a candle. My efforts included Henry VIII, a cowboy and a Roman soldier. One year Ollie went as a bat. Well, he said he was a bat. All in black, a black balaclava with plastic bin bags fixed from his arms to his body as his wings. After visiting a few watering holes, we ended up in Odyssey, a popular nightclub in the centre of Bristol. As we walked into the main room the DJ announced our arrival and described the fancy dress outfits: 'And there's Wee Willie Winkie. Oh, look, Henry VIII is with us tonight.' Then he spotted someone all in black: 'And there's one of the lads all in black. I don't know who it is and what he's meant to be though.' Ollie couldn't believe it. He jumped up and down on the spot and flapped his wings, doing his best impression of a bat. The DJ was none the wiser: 'You can jump up and down as much as you like. I've no idea what you are!' You can imagine the stick Ollie got from the lads. It was priceless.

Fast forward 12 months and Ollie came out with all guns blazing. He was adorned in the most incredible fancy dress outfit I ever saw in all of our Christmas nights out. He came as a Christmas tree. It was brilliant. He was wrapped in a green fabric, which flared out in the true triangular shape of a tree. It covered his head, but his face was cut out. He had tinsel, baubles, decorations and lights, the absolute full monty. Underneath the costume he carried an eight-inch square battery that powered the lights, which had different settings. I remember the lads walking along Corn Street in the city centre and I looked back around 50 yards or so and there was a Christmas tree on the move with flashing lights illuminating the night. Absolutely brilliant from Ollie.

The season was going well until the squad was hit with a double blow before we put on our fancy dress outfits for Christmas 1989. In October, our best outfield player, Gary Penrice, joined Watford for £500,000. As if losing Penny wasn't bad enough, a month later Nigel Martyn was sold to Crystal Palace. As players we understood one of the sales but not two, even though we got £1m for our keeper. Imagine the meltdown on social media nowadays if a team vying for promotion sold its two best players during the season.

Losing Nigel was a massive blow, but Brian Parkin joined us as part of the deal. Parky was a top, top keeper. That said, his first training session was horrendous. He was a bag of nerves and struggled with the basics. He was all over the shop. Dave Mehew looked a better keeper. Brian soon settled down, though, and the biggest compliment I can pay him is that he negated the loss of

Nigel to almost zero. Parky was top drawer. For a few seasons he was one of the best keepers outside the top tier.

So that was the goalkeeping problem solved. Gerry then brought in a guy from Stoke called Carl Saunders. Apparently, when Gerry watched him, he played at full-back for Stoke reserves, but Gerry saw 'something'. That something was a striker. Carl wasn't the best trainer, but he came alive on matchdays. He had good mobility and touch plus an instinctive ability to score goals. As with Parky, Carl's performances, added to his goals, ensured the strong start to the season wasn't derailed.

We had a small squad number-wise and were lucky with injuries. Barely 20 players were used throughout the season. Ollie, Andy Reece and I were ever-presents. We played 4-4-2 home and away. We worked so hard on patterns of play and set pieces at both ends of the pitch. The usual team was Brian Parkin in goal; the back four was Ian Alexander, Steve Yates, Matty and Vaughan Jones; Dave Mehew and Phil Purnell were the wide men in midfield, with Ollie and Andy Reece in the middle; up front it was Devon White and Carl Saunders. Others who played their part were Paul Nixon, Ian Wilmott, Tony Sealy, Christian McClean, Pete Cawley, Billy Clark and Ian Hazel.

By and large the team spirit was brilliant, but it wasn't all plain sailing. The two strikers didn't speak for a long period of the season. Devon White and Carl Saunders literally didn't talk to each other. The situation came about after Devon's wife got involved in an issue that was none of her business. Carl, who was married, brought another woman to a game. It was his business and no one else's. Devon's wife challenged the woman as to whether she should be at the game and whether she should even be with Carl. On the Monday morning an irate Carl was waiting for Devon to arrive at the training ground. Carl told Devon to tell his wife to keep her nose out of his personal life. All hell let loose as the two strikers set about each other. Neither would win a boxing world title, but it was a decent scrap with genuine intent. Steve Yates, who was as quiet as a mouse, tried to intervene. His timing was terrible as he stepped in to separate the lads – he walked straight into a haymaker and his nose popped. There was blood everywhere. It was serious and hilarious in equal measure.

From that day onwards Devon and Carl never really spoke. Gerry and I tried to play the role of peace-makers, but they couldn't or wouldn't resolve their differences. Despite them falling out they were a formidable partnership. It was a strange situation for sure.

I mentioned Steve Yates, 'Yatesey', was head and shoulders the best defensive partner I ever played with. He was a terminator – quick, sensed danger before it happened, destructive, as well as being very good in the air. Steve and I first crossed paths at Highbury in the game where I had to prove my fitness in 1986. He was a teenager then; I remember his league debut at Darlington. We never really talked about the dynamics of our defensive partnership; it was all very natural. We both understood the patterns of play that Gerry Francis introduced, and our respective attributes combined well. Generally, I marked the tallest striker and attacked the aerial ball down the middle. Steve dropped off and cleaned up the mess. Some Saturdays his rubbish receptacle had to be emptied a few times!

Seriously, we worked hard on the training ground. Three times a week after training we did our own work together. Practising heading was the key – we'd throw the ball up for each other and do standing jumps in sets of ten. This improved timing and leg strength. Then we'd be 30 yards apart and clip the ball to each other to perfect timing and technique. Sit-ups were another discipline we did every day. We did four or five different types in sets of 20. It became almost obsessive but we both believed strong abdominal muscles made us stronger athletes. Right or wrong, it seemed to benefit both of us.

After Christmas we lost only three games. We were never top but were never lower than fourth. I came off the transfer list in March and signed a new contract. The campaign crystallised down to the last six games or so. After a disappointing 1-1 home draw with Crewe we went to Tranmere Rovers on a Monday night. Tranmere were three points behind us, but we had a game in hand. This was a prime opportunity to deal them a fatal blow in the promotion race.

Into the second half we were losing 1-0 (again) when we got a free kick just inside the Tranmere half. Usually, Big Dev and I would play crash ball in the opposing penalty box. But for some reason I opted to let Dev fly solo and I held my position just outside the area. Joner clipped a decent ball into the mixer. Dev was outnumbered and one of the Tranmere defenders won the header. In a split second, the ball came back to me a yard or two inside the penalty box, on my left foot, my swinger! In the millisecond that it took the ball to drop, I thought, *Drop the right shoulder, keep the ball down, hit if off the laces, hit the target.* I volleyed it off my laces, and I did keep it down by hitting the top half of the ball. Incredibly, the ball careered into the ground about ten yards from goal, then it bounced and looped up into the top right-hand corner, leaving home keeper Eric Nixon grasping at fresh air. It was either fortuitous or an absolute fluke, or somewhere between the two! It wasn't the best goal I ever scored but it was the most important one of my career. The momentum of the game shifted and, after Carl Saunders was fouled, Ollie slotted home a penalty to seal another 2-1 win.

What about the schedule? Crewe at home on the Saturday, then Tranmere away on the Monday, we then lost at Notts County on the Thursday. Two days later we beat Shrewsbury on the Saturday, courtesy of another pen from Ollie. As you read earlier, we beat City 3-0 on the Wednesday before we went to Blackpool on the final day of the season – our sixth game in 15 days. Modern players please discuss.

So, a 46-game season came down to one match, 90 minutes. After securing promotion on the Wednesday there was a deep determination to complete the job and be crowned champions. The group had an inner belief, not an arrogance, that we'd win. The only uncertainty was by how many goals.

We travelled to the north-west on the Friday afternoon. The squad was very relaxed. Evening meal, overnight stay. Brian Parkin was my roomie. He was top drawer. He didn't clean his boots in the room, made a decent brew and didn't want to watch TV into the early hours. After breakfast on the Saturday morning, we had a training session in a public park. We always used the same park in Blackpool. We called it 'dog shit park'. You had to be very careful where you walked and ran, for obvious reasons. It was a far cry from the high-performance centres that prevail in the modern game!

We headed back to the hotel for our pre-match meal, via the seafront. We stopped at some traffic lights. Amazingly, to our right, Rovers fans started to pour out of a pub. The building only looked about ten feet wide, but it was obviously a Tardis as hundreds and hundreds of Gasheads spilled out on to the pavement. Blue wigs, scarves, banners, klaxons and oversized foam cowboy hats were the order of the day as they delivered a rousing rendition of 'Good Night Irene'. It wasn't the last time we heard the Rovers anthem that amazing Saturday in Blackpool. Seeing the travelling supporters reaffirmed our determination to deliver a win, to deliver the championship.

Come three o'clock we were good value and won 3-0 with goals from Dave Mehew, Phil Purnell and Paul Nixon. The fans were extraordinary, and after the third goal there was the first of several pitch invasions from all four sides. For the last few minutes the pitch must have been five yards narrower as Gasheads lined both sides of the playing surface.

As the game edged towards its conclusion, I asked the referee to give me a few seconds' warning before he blew his whistle. The changing rooms were in the corner at Bloomfield Road back then, so it was a quick dash to my left. On cue, he said, 'Twents, off you go.' I exited stage left and, as I got to the tunnel, he blew his whistle and the party started. Thousands and thousands of delirious Gasheads ran on to the pitch in sheer delight. The players and staff went on to a balcony, which was a perfect vantage point to see the sea of blue and white and interact with the fans. The chant of 'campeones, campeones' reverberated around Bloomfield Road.

When I was a teenager, I used to go to watch Liverpool's open-top bus tours and see the players receive the adulation of the supporters. Here I was, part of a team who'd won a championship. I'd played every game, 12 months after being suspended by the club because of the wedding shenanigans. This was the very reason I took my opportunity and signed for Chorley all those years ago – that was the start of the journey in many ways.

We'd won a championship; we were the best of the best. We lost only five games and lost none at home. We conceded fewer goals than Liverpool, who won the First Division title, and we played eight games more than them. We won the Third Division title by two points. Amazingly, Rovers didn't have one player in the PFA Third Division team of the year, a team voted by fellow professionals in your league. Ollie, Yatesey and maybe Big Dev would have got the nod from me if you were allowed to vote for team-mates.

The enduring image of 5 May 1990 came 45 minutes or so after the final whistle. From the elevated balcony the view was spectacular. A mass of blue and white. Thousands and thousands of Gasheads continued to sing their heads off. They were in no rush to leave Bloomfield Road. Then, beyond the madding crowd, I spotted two people standing alone in the comparative tranquillity of the deserted grandstand to the left of the pitch. The silhouettes were familiar. There they were, Mum and Dad. They both waved, and Dad, who wasn't one to lavish praise easily, raised his thumb and nodded. Those actions were worth a million words.

This was my best day in football. To share it with Mum and Dad was incredibly special and something I'll never forget.

Chapter 10

Wembley with a Spot of Bother On the Way

AS WELL as winning the Third Division title in 1989/90 we made it to Wembley in the final of the Leyland DAF Trophy. This was the knockout competition for the two lower leagues. We lost 2-1 to Tranmere. To be honest, as disappointing as it was to lose under the famous Twin Towers, I wouldn't have swapped it for one of the two wins we enjoyed over Tranmere in the league. Being crowned champions was more important to me. Playing at Wembley was the fulfilment of a boyhood dream. But it's not a great place to lose.

The LDV Trophy in its various forms and titles was and is a strange tournament. It carries little importance in its early stages but, the further you progress and the closer you get to Wembley, the interest increases. We came out on the right side of Torquay, Exeter and Gillingham in our group. In the knockout stages Brian Parkin's ability to save penalties was incredible. We won at Brentford and at home to Walsall, both on spot kicks, where Parky (Mr Glum) nearly smiled after his heroics. I went fifth, so it was either crucial or I wasn't needed at all. Ollie used to go first. It made sense for our regular taker to start proceedings. Ollie rarely missed. Vaughan Jones was up next. Andy Reece went third, followed by Phil Purnell, before yours truly rounded things off, if needed.

At Griffin Park, I was needed. It finished 2-2 after extra time. Parky had done his stuff. It was 3-3 in the shootout but Brentford had taken all five of their kicks. Opportunity knocked. I walked towards the penalty box and referee Brian Hill stood with the ball on the palm of his right hand: 'No pressure, Geoff, score and you're through …' Tony Parks was in goal for Brentford. In 1984 he was the Tottenham hero for saving a penalty in a shootout when they won the UEFA Cup against Anderlecht. Brian was right, no pressure!

I put the ball on the spot, walked back a few paces, hitched up the right leg of my shorts. The process was simple: a few slow, deep breaths, shut out the crowd noise, don't look at the keeper. Bottom right corner was my favourite, keeper's left, firm off the instep. Keep your head down and make sure you get a good contact. Simples.

I knew as soon I hit it that I'd got plenty of my right boot on the ball. I kept my head down, which kept the ball low. When I looked up, Tony Parks had dived to his right. He was on the ground looking to his left where the ball had nestled in the opposite corner. Job done but there was further drama and excitement to come. This was box office.

The players changed and boarded the coach. Word had got to me that Paul Nixon was the worse for wear. Griffin Park was a great venue – one of my favourite away grounds. Apparently, it had a pub on every corner of the ground. Nico, who was a great lad, had been left out of the matchday squad despite enjoying a run of good form. Gerry had opted for Tony Sealy ahead of our resident Geordie. Nico decided to go for a beer or two, or three, maybe more. Pete Cawley chaperoned him as they frequented all four of the pubs during the game.

The lads had smuggled Nico on to the back seat of the coach. I walked down and told him to sit in the corner by the window and keep schtum: 'Nico, keep quiet, do *not* utter a syllable, do *not* say a word.' You might guess where this is going. It was traditional that the non-playing squad players would help the kit man Ray Kendall after the game. The squaddies would load the large wicker baskets that held the matchday kit and equipment on to the coach. Nico hadn't helped load the coach as he was having one for the road in one of West London's finest watering holes.

Word had reached Gerry, who was the last person to get on the coach. Before we left, the manager shouted down the coach, 'Nico, big thanks for helping Ray with the kit. Thank you so much!'

Nico didn't heed my guidance as he semi-staggered to his feet and responded to Gerry's sarcasm, 'It's not in my fucking contract to do the kit! I'm not the fucking kit man!'

Gerry responded, 'It's not in your contract, is it? I'll tell you what's in your contract.' He was seething and sat down in one of the front seats as a stoney silence descended on the coach as we departed Griffin Park. I thought the penalty shootout was exciting, but this episode was set to get even better.

Gerry and the London-based players had left their cars at the Holiday Inn near Heathrow. As the coach pulled in to drop them off, Gerry stood up and announced, 'Everybody off the coach *except* Paul Nixon.' I thought, *Yikes, this is not going to end well.* As club captain I deliberated as to whether I should intervene, but I opted not to as there was a duty director, Ron Craig, on board, as well as the assistant manager Kenny Hibbitt.

I must add at this point that the *Bristol Evening Post*'s Rovers correspondent Richard Payne was covering his first-ever Rovers game and was on the coach, as the local media travelled with us back in the day. This was his first-ever game! What a baptism of fire!

Everyone, except Gerry and Nico, filed off the coach and we gathered in the reception area. Minutes later the automatic doors flew open and in marched Paul Nixon. 'I've been assaulted, I want the police, I've been assaulted.' Nico demanded that the receptionist telephoned the police.

Everyone got back on the coach except for Gerry, Nico and Ron Craig, who were in a police vehicle on their way to a local police station. The whole episode was surreal. Netflix, Amazon Prime and Disney would have paid serious money for this. Kenny Hibbitt approached Richard Payne, who looked like he'd seen a ghost … no, several ghosts. Hibby told Richard that none of this needed to be reported. Bravo to Richard, who did what he had to do. The next day it was the entire front page of the *Bristol Evening Post*. The story was attributed to a certain Kevin Blackadder. We all assumed it was a fictitious name, but Kevin was for real and was a great bloke. Not that I should query the validity of surnames!

So, to the nitty gritty of the incident. I spoke with Nico the next day and he filled me in. Gerry was livid and there was a verbal exchange. Gerry grabbed Nico by the neck, pushed him backwards on to the table and shook him. Gerry then let go, having realised the seriousness of the situation. He stepped back and invited Nico to punch him. A free punch from the player with no response from the manager to level things up! Nico was an intelligent guy and declined the invitation, so Gerry went for him again and shook him on the table: 'Hit me, you bastard, hit me.' At that point Nico got off the coach and flew through the doors into reception.

No police charges were brought by any party. Nico was fined by the club for drinking during the game (quite the charge!) and Gerry was warned about his future conduct. What a night! My winning penalty kick seemed to pale into total insignificance.

Thankfully, we were at home in the next round. We beat Walsall on penalties at Twerton Park. Parky guessed right so many times that I didn't need to take a spot kick. The semi-final was against Neil Warnock's Notts County. Dave Mehew scored in the 1-0 home win in the first leg. Boris bagged 21 goals that season, 18 of which were in the league. It was an incredible return for someone who played on the right-hand side of midfield. He never scored more than one in a game, so his tally was exceptional. Boris was a better midfielder than goalkeeper.

The return leg at Meadow Lane was a tense, close affair. It was goalless, and late in the game we were defending a free kick when Phil Stant beat me in the air to score a headed goal. If there was any contact, it was minimal. The referee, Brian Hill, who was in charge at Griffin Park in the earlier round, blew for a foul and disallowed the goal. In my playing days there was no VAR, no technology and you played with the attitude that sometimes decisions went your way and sometimes they didn't. We later found this out in the final, but this one was definitely a decision that went our way.

We drew 0-0, which meant The Gas were going to play at Wembley for the first time in their history. All those times I played in the park as a kid and imagined we were playing at Wembley was to become reality. The celebrations on the final whistle were fantastic. I remember Gary Penrice (who was now a Watford player) was among the Rovers fans on the terrace at the side of the pitch. He shouted at me as I walked past. It was incredible to see him. I pleaded with a senior steward to let me go through the cordon of fluorescent orange jackets to see Penny. Eventually he agreed and we embraced and jumped up and down like two kids. A brilliant moment. I rang Mum and Dad from a payphone in the social club at Meadow Lane to tell them they were going to watch their lad play at Wembley. Mum cried tears of joy. I remember reading Dad's comments in the lead-up to the final: 'If you can't play at Wembley yourself the next best thing is to see your lad there.' That summed Dad up perfectly.

The final was scheduled for 20 May, which was 15 days after the all-conquering day at Blackpool. Gerry prepared us as well as he could. We trained at Yate Town's ground, which was a huge playing area. One big issue was the fact that we didn't have any games, so our match fitness dropped off. Gerry brought in Jerome Anderson, one of the game's biggest agents at the time. He sorted out a few commercial deals, including some boots for the players, a premium phone-line competition and a book deal. Jack Steggles penned an excellent book, to be fair to him.

Talking of money, a dark cloud hovered over the lads as we prepared for Wembley. The bonus scheme stated that the players were entitled to 30 per cent of the club's gate receipts from the final. Whoever negotiated this clause from the players' perspective was a genius. I'd like to take the credit, but it was already in place when I arrived at the club. Thirty per cent of a decent crowd at Wembley was a great windfall for the players. It was a 'bonus' and, let's be honest, we weren't on big wages.

One day in the lead-up to the game, vice-chairman Geoff Dunford rang me, in my position as club captain and PFA delegate, to 'clarify the bonus clause for Wembley'. Geoff told me the players would receive 30 per cent of the net gate receipts after the expenditure for Wembley had been deducted. He told me such things as the cost of the pre-match hotel, the players' Wembley blazers and trousers, etc., the post-match reception and overnight stay at a London hotel would be deducted from the gate receipts. Even the cost of putting in extra telephone lines to deal with the ticket demand was to be deducted from the figure. The club was adamant that the 30 per cent was a net figure as opposed to a gross one. It was time to ring my mate, Gordon Taylor. The chief executive of the players' union assured me that the clause was clear, and the players would receive 30 per cent of the club's gate receipts. The word 'net' was nowhere to be seen.

To prevent it becoming a major issue and newsworthy, I told Geoff Dunford what the PFA had advised. Geoff was adamant that the expenses would be deducted before the share-out. They were the employers, we were merely the employees. I'm not a socialist, but I do believe in standing up for what's right and against what's wrong. The players all wanted me to see this one through, for obvious reasons.

The dispute lingered beyond the final and was presented to the Football League Management Committee at its monthly meeting. My understanding is that the case was looked at for a few minutes and the committee's chair asked why this case had even been presented to them. It confirmed that the football club had to pay the players what they were owed – 30 per cent of the gate receipts that the club received from Wembley, nothing more, nothing less. The players were delighted but the directors not so.

Playing at Wembley was everything you'd expect. The drive from the hotel was exciting and seeing the Twin Towers in the distance. Arriving at the home of football was exhilarating as the route was packed with fans of both clubs. There were twice as many Gasheads as Tranmere fans, as they were due back at Wembley for a play-off final against Notts County the following weekend.

The coach drove through the massive gates into the Wembley tunnel. It was just like we used to see on TV when there was saturation coverage of the FA Cup Final. We didn't visit Wembley before the final, which was a mistake, as we had to digest the incredible wow factor on the day of the game. The dressing rooms were huge. The bathroom area had a massive, deep communal bath and several individual baths and showers. For the era it was palatial.

Walking out on to the pitch to inspect it an hour or so before kick-off was another similarity to the FA Cup. I was able to see Mum and Dad and a group of more than 30 family and friends who'd travelled from Merseyside and Bristol. They had a huge banner: 'Lancaster Road on Tour at Wembley. Good Luck Geoff.' Incredibly, there was a charity match on the Wembley pitch before the game, which meant neither side was allowed to warm up on the famous playing surface. This was ridiculous as we went through the warm-up process in the tunnel. It was far from ideal but was the same for both sides.

With just under 15 minutes to go to kick-off it was time to make the walk. It was match time. Both sides were in their traditional home kits. I was the last man out of the dressing room in keeping with my superstition. The walk down the tunnel was incredible. The sunshine was a distant sight but as we walked towards the pitch the mouth of the tunnel got bigger and bigger and more and more sunshine poured in. The noise of the crowd became louder and louder. Eventually we were in daylight and bright sunshine.

The far end of Wembley Stadium was a glorious sight to behold. The Rovers fans stretched from the halfway line on one side of the stadium, and continued behind the goal, where the mass of blue and white then went all the way to the halfway line on the other side of the ground. Half of Wembley was occupied by Gasheads. It was spine-tingling as the Rovers anthem 'Goodnight Irene' reverberated around Wembley. We lined up to meet Sir Stanley Matthews, who was the guest of honour. I remember bellowing out the National Anthem with absolute pride.

The game remains a bit of a blur. I remember some big calls and moments didn't go our way. The sight when Devon White equalised was incredible. As the ball hit the net 40,000 people leapt from their seats in unison. Half of Wembley Stadium was a vibrant sea of blue and white. Tranmere played well, to be fair, and, although some may disagree, they just about deserved their win. It was their day.

Having said that, the winning goal was a foul, as Jim Steele pushed me in the back before he headed the ball into the net. To be fair, the winner wasn't marginal, it was obvious, but like I said after the draw at Meadow Lane in the area final, some decisions go your way and others don't. Had Phil Stant's goal stood, which it probably should have, we'd have gone to extra time and the momentum would have been with the home side. Maybe, just maybe, we wouldn't have even reached Wembley.

I don't think we did ourselves justice on the big stage and I know I was below par. Once the final whistle went it was a huge anticlimax. Wembley is a terrible place to lose. I remember shaking hands with every Tranmere player and congratulating their manager, John King, who was a great man. There was a huge but respectful rivalry between the two clubs. We beat them twice in the league, but all three games were very close. As I said earlier, I wouldn't have swapped a win at Wembley for one of the league victories. Being crowned league champions by two points was more important to me. Gerry has reminded me since that a draw with Tranmere in one of the league games and we'd still have been champions on goal difference – I think we'd have missed out on top spot as Rovers and City both had a goal difference of plus 36.

We took a slow walk around the stadium to acknowledge the incredible support, with some of the lads in tears. The Rovers fans were incredible as they'd remained in the ground, and they bellowed another rendition of 'Goodnight Irene'. As we walked towards the tunnel end, where the Tranmere fans were housed, something incredible happened. The Merseysiders, despite this being their moment of glory, started to sing 'champions, champions, champions' as we approached. It was an exceptional act of sportsmanship and epitomised the rivalry between the two clubs at the time.

Tranmere returned to Wembley the following weekend but lost the play-off final. I'm sure they'd have swapped their Leyland DAF Trophy win for victory over Notts County.

A week or so later we still hadn't received our winners' medals and I asked our secretary Bob Twyford almost incessantly when I'd get my hands on the priceless bit of gold. Back then only the champions received medals. It was the ultimate reward for being the best of the best. Nowadays, any team that's promoted get medals, which is ridiculous. And on the subject of promotion, doing it through the play-offs is not the best way to go up. Being the champions, the best team in the regular season, is without doubt the most coveted way to do it. There's no discussion to be had here.

Bob told me the medals were being engraved so we'd have our names on the back, and we were to receive them at a civic reception for both clubs at the Council House, hosted by the mayor. I couldn't believe that we were going to be presented with our medals in front of the City lads. Regardless of my protestations, the evening went ahead as planned. The main room was packed with the great and the good, plus a few hangers-on. The mayor made his speech to congratulate both clubs on their promotion and he then invited the Rovers players on to a raised stage to receive their medals. Wow, this was somewhere between awkward and uncomfortable. When we were all in place on the stage, the whole room, everyone standing in front of us, broke into applause. I remember noticing Joe Jordan, the City manager, in the middle of the room and, although he clapped, he turned his back to face away from us. I don't blame him, to be honest, as that was a tough experience.

The medal is a thing of beauty. It's gold, is only a few centimetres in diameter and sits perfectly in the palm of your hand. The great thing is that it's the same medal that the Liverpool players won. The only difference: theirs say First Division while ours is Third Division. The medal comes in a classy, small, hinged red box.

As I was leaving the Council House with my bit of treasure, I nipped to the loo. I bumped into the City striker Bob Taylor. He asked me if I could do him a favour. 'Yes Bob, of course. What is it?'

He replied, almost embarrassed, 'Can I see your medal, please?' I took the box out of my jacket pocket and handed it to him. He opened it and, without saying a word, he gazed at it ruefully for several seconds, maybe longer. He closed the box and handed it back to me, nodded and said, 'Thanks Geoff, well done, mate.' We shook hands and went our separate ways.

Chapter 11

Yellow Socks and Blue Socks

THE YEAR of 1990 was an epic one. Playing in the Second Division was incredible, plus child number two arrived. Our first game in the second tier was Leicester City at Filbert Street. It was a hot and sunny day. It was a sign of things to come as Leicester played a fast, slick-passing game. I was up against David Oldfield, who set an extremely high bar in terms of the quality of striker I'd be facing this coming season. He was mobile, had great touch, made great runs and took you into places on the pitch that you didn't want to be. He'd go short then spin in behind, or go long to create space to drop into and get the ball to feet. As Gerry Francis used to coach our strikers 'keep out of the space you want to use'.

We lost 3-2. I remember afterwards feeling absolutely knackered. I'd done okay in the game, but it was 25 per cent quicker, and more intense than the level below. I remember wondering afterwards whether I could play at this new level. But it was fine, as I played every game that season. Things settled down as my match fitness kicked in and I got used to the new level. The strikers were all-round better players – stronger, quicker, better football acumen and technically better. They were also more ruthless in front of goal – give them a chance and they'd rarely miss; give them two chances and they'd score twice. In the level below, conversion rates were less than 50 per cent.

As I said, Twentyman number two arrived that year on 5 November and there were some fireworks in the Twentyman household. My wife went into labour in mid-afternoon. Our neighbours, John and Beverley Hauges, took in Mark, who was coming up to his fourth birthday, and looked after him 'for as long as you need us to'. They were a brilliant family and had three children of their own, Michael, Alex and Ellen, so I guess one more wouldn't make a difference!

On arriving at Southmead Hospital, the midwife said I could go home as nothing was going to happen for a few hours. She told me they'd ring me when things started to happen. The only phone in the house was downstairs, so as the evening became night, I put a duvet on the sofa downstairs and watched one of my favourite movies, *Top Gun,* on television. There was no phone call for hours, which seemed strange. Then around midnight I received a call from a slightly concerned nurse, who told me to get to the hospital asap. They had a problem with their phone system and hadn't been able to make any calls, otherwise they'd have called me earlier. I did a decent impression of Lando Norris and floored it to Southmead. I was there to see Hannah arrive. I picked the name. One of the Walton sextuplets was a Hannah, and it was the perfect name for a beautiful little girl.

We had Barnsley at home on the Wednesday. I didn't train on the Tuesday and reported for the game having had minimal sleep for 48 hours. I played the match on adrenaline and euphoria. Late into the game it was 1-1 when I went up for a free kick. I took my position on the edge of the Barnsley penalty box at the Bath end of the ground. The ball in was good and, as it started to drop, I got up early and stayed in the air long enough to win the flick-on. Tony Pounder pounced to drive the ball past Clive Baker in the Barnsley goal, who was a colleague on the PFA management committee. We won 2-1 and the assist was for Hannah.

* * *

It was inevitable that Gerry Francis would move on from Rovers. He'd done a brilliant job. The season after being promoted to the Second Division, we more than held our own and finished 13th, which wasn't too shabby. Oldham were crowned champions, with West Ham, Sheffield Wednesday and Notts County all promoted to the elite level. Gerry had proved that he could manage in the second tier and now wanted to work at the highest level. No one could deny him the opportunity. A return to his old stomping ground at QPR beckoned.

I was 32, and I knew the club inside out. I understood the culture of football in Bristol. Flatteringly, the media suggested that I should be the new manager of Bristol Rovers. I fancied the job, so I threw my proverbial hat in the ring and applied for the position in writing.

I'd played every game the season before, in the second tier. *Match*, the respected football magazine, did an article on the players who'd made the most consecutive appearances in the entire Football League. I was fourth on the list with 173 successive appearances. City's Rob Newman was top. Fair play to 'Biff', he'd made 260 appearances on the spin. John Humphrey of Crystal Palace was second with 209, and Leeds' keeper John Lukic was third with 198. After me on the list were Palace keeper and former roomie Nigel Martyn with 164, Neville Southall with

154 successive appearances at Everton, and Aston Villa's Dean Saunders was seventh on 151.

Overall, I felt I was entitled to a few more quid on my basic wage. I called Geoff Dunford, who agreed to see me at Dunford's Dairies, their family-based business in Longwell Green in Bristol. We met in the boardroom. Geoff, who basically ran the club, was at one end of an enormous wooden table and I was at the opposite end. Before we talked money, he asked me what I thought about the managerial situation. I thought, *Oh, hello, here we go then.* I suggested Gerry would be a tough act to follow and the person who took over needed to know the club and its unique dynamic inside out. The ball was back in Geoff's court. I assumed that he knew I'd applied for the job. I was absolutely staggered by what he said next: 'I'd do the job myself but running the dairy takes up too much of my time.' The vice-chairman told me he'd take on the manager's job but he was too busy with the day job! I had to be careful. Had I started to laugh, which was my obvious inclination, I'd have jeopardised my chances of getting an increase in my wages. So, with my best poker face, I nodded in sympathetic acknowledgement of his difficult situation! I then asked him for a rise. He agreed to an extra £100 a week. I left the dairy knowing that I wasn't going to be the next manager of Bristol Rovers. But I also knew, neither was Geoff Dunford!

The media speculation about who'd be the next manager gathered momentum. Yours truly remained a recurring name in the various articles and reports. Several weeks after Gerry's departure I was up a ladder painting some windows to the rear of the house. Keith Beech, the sports editor at BBC Radio Bristol, rang me. He enquired, 'Where are you going to be at two o'clock this afternoon?'

Me with Mum and Dad in Ballymena, Northern Ireland, early 1960s. My favourite photo with my parents.

Dressed to kill, bizarrely not in a football kit. It's the ill-fated window that came a cropper with a cricket ball.

The special ones – Mum and Dad. I think one moustache in the family was more than enough.

A tough upbringing at Kirkstone Dynamos in the Bootle and Litherland League in Liverpool. Almost, but not quite blue and white quarters.

Maghull FC – 16 years old playing men's football, nearly as tall as the church tower. Back row, left to right: Andy Boyd (trainer), Gordon Iveson, Geoff Twentyman, George Brown, John Coles, Tommy Hornby, Brian Walsh, Gerry Fisher (manager). Front row: John Yule, Dave Barraclough, Lol Armstrong, Keith Bancroft, Frank Killen, Phil Tinney.

A textbook header Chorley 1 v 0 Morecambe 1982/83.

We have conquered all of Europe. Dad and I share our haul of silverware.

I made the grade in 1983. I owe a huge debt of gratitude to Gordon Lee and Preston North End.

Preston 1984. Back row, left to right: Tommy Booth, Andy McAteer, Glen Campbell, Peter Litchfield, Paul Wilkins, Paul Welsh, Jonathan Clark. Middle row: Dennis Loze, Dave Jones, Me, Mark Jones, Dale Rudge, Peter Houghton, Andrew Murphy, Mike Farrelly. Front row: Mark Walsh, Graham Houston, Chris Hunter, Alan Kelly, Duncan Crosbie, John Kelly, Willie Naughton.

First game after Hillsborough at home to Northampton Town, 22 April 1989.

Registered Office
199 Two Mile Hill Road
Kingswood
Bristol

For the attention of G Twentyman Esq

21st May 1989

Dear Mr Twentyman

Your actions of yesterday have been considered a breach of contract by the Manager, Mr Francis. The Directors therefore have no option but to suspend you on full pay until a meeting of the Directors is convened to discuss the situation.

In the meantime please note that your attendance is not required at any training session, club fixture or any other club event until further notice.

Yours sincerely

G M H DUNFORD
On behalf of the Board.

1883
BRISTOL ROVERS
FOOTBALL CLUB PLC

Registered Office:

Telephone (0272)
510363/510828
(Secretary and Commercial)

(0272) 312327
(Match Day Office)

Stadium:
Twerton Park
Bath

Please address all correspondence to the Registered Office.

Reg. No. 51828 England
VAT Reg. No. 137 4967 35

President: His Grace
The Marquis of Worcester

Vice Presidents:
H.E.L. Brown
Dr.W.T. Cussen

A.I. Seager

Directors:
D.H.A. Dunford (Chairman)
R. Craig
G.M.H. Dunford
R.C. Redman (Vice Chairman)

Manager:

Hon. Company Secretary:

Commercial Manager:
A.J. Wood

May 1989 Mr Twentyman …

Bristol Rovers 1989/90 squad that went on to be champions despite only having one goalkeeper and selling two of their best players. Back row, left to right: Andy Reece, Paul Nixon, Ian Willmott, Steve Yates, Vaughan Jones, Ian Alexander, Phil Purnell. Middle row: Me, Christian McClean, Pete Cawley, Nigel Martyn, Devon White, Billy Clark, Ian Hazel, Marcus Browning. Front row: Roy Dolling, Gary Penrice, Dave Mehew, Des Bulpin, Gerry Francis, Kenny Hibbitt, Tony Sealy, Ian Holloway, Ray Kendall

September 1989, eyes on the prize, a headed goal against former club Preston at Twerton Park.

1990 Bristol Rovers Christmas fancy dress night out. Ian Holloway rocking the Christmas tree look. Elton John came as director Ron Craig.

Bloomfield Road, Blackpool – 5 May 1990. Division Three champions next to Paul Nixon and Andy Reece.

1990, Wembley. Left to right: Andy Reece, Phil Purnell, Devon White, Carl Saunders, Steve Yates, Brian Parkin, Me, Vaughan Jones and Gerry Francis.

I always enjoyed a joust with City's Bob Taylor. A top striker and a great guy.

With a young Hannah, a beautiful young girl who's become a beautiful woman.

Wembley, a tough venue to lose at but an amazing place to have a photograph taken with my two-and-a-half-year-old son Mark.

1993. Helping Linfield to win the Irish League was a wonderful experience. The kit man Gary Eccles was a special guy.

The Geoff Twentyman XI who played the Downs League Select team to celebrate the League's centenary in 2005. Back row, left to right: Keith Millen, Tim McSweeney, Andy Howard, Gary Owers, Alan Walsh, Me. Front row: Dave Mehew, Mark Twentyman, Chris Spittles, Tom Ryan, John Bennett, Tom Burridge.

The King and I. Twerton Park, 2009. Eric Cantona had the audience in the palm of his hand.

A round of golf with my only ever idol, Roger Hunt, in 2009. An exceptional day.

Dave Palmer. An incredible guy, my best mate died in 2011. He was only 49.

May 2019, my favourite edition of Having a Gas *with departing Rovers players Stuart Sinclair, Tom Lockyer and Chris Lines.*

Bristol's Callum Sheedy co-hosted The Scrum *with me. Sheeds is a class act and overall Topman.*

With Bristol City owner Stephen Lansdown. He never declined an interview request and never ducked a question.

With my former Preston bestie Steve Elliot and his wife Maggie in January 2024.

April 2023. One of my final studio guests was the best player I ever played with. I am proud to have been Marcus Stewart's captain when he made his league debut.

Hannah and Mark, 22 May 2023. The perfect end to an amazing final programme with my two (and soon to arrive Teddy James).

I replied, 'Up a ladder painting Georgian windows.'

'Are you sure?' he cross-examined me.

'Unless you want to come and do them for me, and I'll go for a game of golf,' I responded.

He informed me, 'Rovers have called a press conference for two o'clock. They're going to announce their new manager.'

Rovers appointed Martin Dobson. I knew the name and remembered an elegant midfielder who played for Burnley and Everton and made five England appearances. He'd done a very good job as manager of Bury but the alarm bells started to tinkle when I heard he'd been out of the game for a couple of years and had been running a fashion boutique in the north-west of England.

Day one of pre-season training was interesting. The new manager addressed the players for the first time. We were all sitting on the grass in front of Martin, his assistant Dennis Rofe, physio Roy Dolling and kit man Ray Kendall. The staff were standing. Martin stretched out his arm and pointed straight ahead: 'Geoff Twentyman, I've only been at the club for five minutes, guess what I've noticed?' Martin had actually pointed at Ian Alexander – dark hair, moustache. I was sitting there, dark hair and moustache, to Martin's right at three o'clock on the clock face. Jock looked back and didn't speak.

I sensed it was a loaded question, so I replied from Martin's right, 'I don't know, Martin, you tell me.'

Somewhat embarrassed, he swivelled to his right, realigned his focus, and said, 'Ah yes, Geoff. Well, I've been here for five minutes and I've noticed there's no team spirit, no morale, there are little groups, there are cliques. It's not good, but don't worry, I'll sort it out.' I thought for a moment, *No team spirit, really? No morale, really?*

Martin was on a roll, as he added, 'And see that man on the end of the line to my left [kit man Ray Kendall]? I'm going to make his life easier from now on because you lot are going to take your training kit home and wash it yourselves.' *Wow, that's different*, I thought. The new manager continued, 'Oh, and you'll wear yellow socks on Mondays and Thursdays, and blue socks on Tuesdays and Fridays. You'll be fined if you wear the wrong socks on the wrong day. Right, let's start training.'

As we walked to the training pitches, the lads implored me to have a word. After the morning session I went to see Martin in his office. I told him the lads weren't happy about having to launder their training kit, and the yellow socks/blue socks rule. I told him we were a very tightly knit group and team spirit was actually our biggest attribute. I enlightened him as to the football landscape in Bristol. City were the bigger club, City had bigger attendances and City paid bigger wages. Rovers were the smaller club but were exceeding expectations. Team spirit was fundamental to the recent successes.

Martin wasn't having it: 'It's all about teaching you and the players about responsibilities.'

I countered, 'Martin, I have a mortgage, I have two kids, I have bills to pay – they're actual responsibilities, not worrying about yellow socks or blue socks.'

Martin was unmoved: 'You'll probably manage one day, Geoff, and you'll do it your way. Tell the players it's blue socks tomorrow.'

The lads weren't happy. Ian Alexander rang the *Bristol Evening Post*, and the next day it was a front-page story, with a picture of Jock hand-washing his training gear in the kitchen sink. It was an inauspicious start that got worse. Martin dismantled the way we played. I'm not sure how we were supposed to play under him, to be honest. We went from being a highly spirited, well-organised, disciplined outfit to playing off the cuff.

To be fair to Martin, he gave the young Marcus Stewart his league debut in the season opener at home to Ipswich. We were 3-0 down at half-time. We were all over the place, playing without a plan and were lucky to have nil. In the second half we rolled our proverbial sleeves up and the team spirit kicked in. Marcus was brilliant and Big Dev was equally effective. The 3-3 draw felt like a win.

The results weren't good, though. The players tried but when we went a goal down there was no spirit to fight back. It was as if Martin had eroded our strongest attribute. He did something I'd never experienced before. He drove to away matches in his car as opposed to travelling on the team coach. He appeared distant. He struggled to motivate and inspire. His tactics were vague, and an air of doom and gloom soon enveloped the group.

After 11 games and just one victory, Rovers were bottom of the Second Division. The board decided enough was enough and Martin Dobson was sacked on a Friday morning. Assistant manager Dennis Rofe was put in charge for the home game against top-of-the-table Middlesbrough the next day. You can probably guess, or part guess, what happened next. In an incredible game, Rovers won 2-1. More remarkably, I scored a volley from outside the 18-yard box to win the game. It was a pure strike off the laces. Yes, it's on YouTube for those who struggle to believe this startling fact.

Three days later Rovers overturned a 3-1 deficit in the League Cup to beat Bristol City on away goals after it finished 4-2 at Ashton Gate and 5-5 on aggregate. Dennis Rofe was a breath of fresh air. He was the king of the one-liner and always made you smile, with his bouncy, effervescent approach to life and football. Dennis allowed the lads to play with a structured freedom but, more importantly, the hitherto errant spirit had returned.

I liked Dennis, he did a decent job and was deservedly appointed manager. During his time in charge, I suffered a break that led to a break, so to speak. We played Plymouth at home in the third round of the FA Cup. After 20 minutes or so I went up for an aerial duel with their centre-forward Dave Regis. I won the header, but he'd nudged me and I kind of lost my balance in mid-air and landed on the outside of my left ankle. Ouch. Searing pain engulfed my ankle. I didn't like it one bit and sensed something serious had occurred. I hobbled off but told Dennis Rofe that I'd be okay. He told me to go sit in front of the back four for five minutes while it settled down. Five minutes? Five seconds later I knew it was curtains. Next stop for me was Bath Royal United Hospital via an ambulance. It was the turning point of the game. It was 0-0 when I went off. When the ref blew his whistle for the final time it was a 5-0 home victory!

Later that afternoon the draw was made for the next round of the FA Cup. Rovers would host the winners of Crewe Alexandra and Liverpool, who were playing on the Monday evening. A minute or two after the news of the dream tie came through, a stern-faced consultant appeared with my X-rays in hand: 'I'm sorry Geoff. It's bad news, you've broken your ankle.' I was no medic, but I knew a broken ankle wouldn't heal within a month, when Liverpool (assuming they'd beat Crewe, which they did) would visit Twerton Park.

I stayed in the Glen Hospital to have a metal plate screwed into my broken ankle. I was recovering after the surgery and who should walk in to visit me but Buster Footman. The City physio thought he'd pop in to see how I was doing. Absolute class from an absolute gentleman. It's things like that you don't forget. Buster was a Top Man. Everything went well with the operation and after a few days I was sent home.

Call it fate, call it a stroke of luck, call it destiny, but Keith Beech, from BBC Radio Bristol, rang and asked if I'd summarise on their live commentary of the Liverpool tie. I'd been interviewed hundreds of times as club captain and PFA delegate. In 1991 I'd been a weekly contributor on the BBC Radio 2 flagship sports programme when Lee Chapman, of Leeds, and the Lincoln keeper Mark Wallington and I recorded a 20-minute feature with presenter John Inverdale. The 'Three Wise Men' discussed the issues of the week and it was good fun, but it wasn't as thrilling as broadcasting live at a ground. This was my first experience of headphones, lip mics and hearing talkback from base. I felt the next phase of my life started that evening when my beloved Liverpool rocked into Twerton Park and forced a 1-1 draw.

Soon after the adrenaline-filled evening, I decided to find a sports journalism course where I could get a qualification to show people that I was serious about becoming a broadcaster. I was still a pro footballer, albeit injured, but I discovered a course at what was then Bristol Polytechnic, now the University of the West of England. When my career ended, I wanted to do something that motivated me, something that I'd be excited by. I also wanted to make that transition when it was right for me. I promised my wife that she'd never read about me being released by Rovers on the back of the local newspaper. Being in control of your own destiny is very important.

For an academic year I trained in the morning and studied one or two afternoons a week. After producing a radio documentary and a 20,000-word thesis, I was awarded a diploma in Time Based Media Journalism specialising in Radio. Bingo.

Taking Liverpool to two games in the FA Cup was the highlight of Dennis's time in charge. The thing he struggled with was making the transition from assistant to manager. Whenever he tried to give out a rollocking it never had the required effect, as we all expected the punchline, the infusion of humour that was typical Dennis. In September 1992 we lost 3-0 at home to Grimsby Town. We were abject and Dennis read the riot act afterwards. Well, he tried to. He went mad, veins raised in his neck as he shouted and bawled. We were useless (true), we didn't try our arses off (not strictly true), the performance wasn't acceptable (definitely true). He was effing and jeffing. To be fair it was a good old bollocking. In isolation it was eight out of ten until Dennis went to kick a shinpad, which was in the middle of the floor, and his standing leg went from under him and he fell flat on his backside. Oh my god! And who should he be facing when he hit the deck? Yes, yours truly had to bite my lip. It was one of the funniest things I'd ever seen. Dennis got up and walked out of the dressing room, muttering under his breath. To be fair, we went to Maine Road and drew 0-0 with top-flight Man City four days later in the League Cup.

As results waned, the club brought in Malcolm Allison as a 'football consultant'.

It wasn't handled very well at all. Dennis was still officially the manager, but 'Big Mal' took the training and was given ultimate control – he picked the team. After a few uncomfortable days of Dennis still being on the training ground and Malcolm being 'in charge', the former left the club, and the latter was officially in control.

Malcolm was a hugely likeable guy and, despite being in his 60s, he was ahead of his time. Big Mal took us to the University of Bath, where he knew the director of sport, Ged Roddy, and we did plyometric work in the gym to improve reactions and muscle power. He brought in Lenny Heppell, a renowned dance instructor, to work on balance and agility. It was very clever and a real thought-provoking approach. Another 'Malcolm Allisonism' was kicking the ball off the front of your foot, off the laces. Malcolm called it the 'big bone', and whether you were striking it three feet, three yards or 30 yards, the ball had to be kicked off the big bone, the instep. This was easier said than done for some.

Malcolm had only been at the club a few days, and on the Friday he called me into his office. I'd been out of the team as I hadn't recovered from the broken ankle against Plymouth.

> MA: 'Geoff, your dad was a great football man. He found some great players. I need your help.'
>
> GT: 'Thanks Malcolm, yes, I'm immensely proud of him. Yes, I know you do.'
>
> MA: 'How do you know that I need some help?'
>
> GT: 'Well, we've got a game tomorrow, you have to pick a team and you haven't got a clue about any of these players.'

At this point Malcolm pushed a blank piece of paper and a pen across the desk and said, 'Geoff, will you pick the team for tomorrow, please?'

I agreed on the proviso that no one else knew, literally no one. For those who are wondering, no I didn't! Andy Tillson and Steve Yates were my centre-back pairing. I wasn't in my matchday 13 (two subs were the norm in 1992) but Malcolm included me as a substitute as he valued my presence and knowledge.

Despite playing well, Rovers lost 2-1 at home to Derby the next day. Malcolm said to me afterwards, 'We should have won today. I'm going to stick with the team that you picked.'

Rovers won four of their next five games and drew the other one. There were some highlights in that mini sequence. At Leicester, while we enjoyed our pre-match meal, Malcolm sat at the hotel bar and necked a bottle of red wine! His team talk was brief. Ten minutes before kick-off he got the entire group – players and staff – to stand and hold hands in a circle. He asked the group, 'What are we going to do?' Instinctively and with no prompt we replied as one, 'Win!' I did say the pre-match talk was brief. Result: Leicester City 0 Bristol Rovers 1.

Two games later Rovers beat City 4-0 at Twerton Park. The game was live on local HTV. All the goals were technically excellent strikes, three of them from at least 20 yards from goal. Marcus Stewart and John Taylor notched, as did Carl Saunders. Justin Channing scored the first from a different postcode. After the game there was euphoria in the home dressing room and Big Mal called for order.

He took centre stage as the room fell silent: 'I've only got two words to say to you lot …' The lads looked at each other quizzically, wondering what he was going to say. Then with perfect timing and a huge smile, Malcolm blurted out, 'Big bone!' He took his leave, enjoyed a cigar and wallowed in the company of the media.

Malcolm's effect wasn't sustainable, and results deteriorated. I knew my time was up as a footballer, and BBC Radio Bristol had made some positive noises about me joining their sports team. I was chuffed that I'd planned for this moment in my life by successfully securing my diploma. The BBC knew I was serious about being a journalist and wasn't merely a footballer who wanted to talk about football on the radio.

I was and remain proud of my time at Rovers, but it was time to move on. Time stands still for no sports person, eventually your number is up, and it's someone else's turn. Andy Tillson was my replacement. Tilly is a class act, an exceptional player and top professional. I was delighted that such an outstanding individual, a brilliant man, took over from me at the heart of the Rovers defence.

I didn't want to linger, just see my contract out and fester with no motivation. My plan was simple. In January 1993 I met the hierarchy at BBC Radio Bristol. The most important thing I needed clarity on from the managing editor Mike Hapgood, news editor Stephen Lamb and sports editor Keith Beech was that my strong Liverpudlian accent would be acceptable on their radio station. It seems my concerns were without foundation as they offered me a six-month contract – effectively a trial – as a sports reporter.

I arranged a chat with Dennis Dunford, the Rovers chairman, the man who was so supportive on that coach journey back from Reading after my Rovers debut seven and a half years earlier. To help negate the drop in salary, I asked the chairman whether the club would pay up the existing six months or so of my contract in a lump sum and I'd leave. Dennis was a man of huge integrity. He was compassionate and understanding. He knew the cost of everything and the value it brought. Within a few seconds he'd agreed to my request. He told me it was a mark of the club's gratitude for the service that I'd given them. He was a thoroughly decent man.

Managing people – read the room and act immediately

Managing a group of people is a skill. In the fullness of time, it's essential to get to know each person individually and what makes them tick. No two people are the same and you must treat them all as unique individuals. In group meetings or staff gatherings, you must read the mood and act accordingly. On his first day, Martin Dobson was convinced it was his way or no way. He was oblivious to the shockwave he delivered to the group when he accused us of having no team spirit and no morale. It was as if he'd fired a taser. Martin should have seen the expressions; he should have felt the mood. He should have adjusted his approach mid-meeting.

When I went to see him after the morning session he was under no illusions as to the dissatisfaction among the playing group. He still didn't act. Admitting you're wrong is an endearing quality. Compare that to Bobby Gould's team meeting before the crucial final game of the 1986/87 season when Rovers couldn't afford to lose against Newport County. Initially he was going to send the team out with a back four, a sweeper and another sweeper behind a sweeper. I felt the mood in the room as Bob delivered his tactics and I immediately expressed the squad's concerns about the inability to attack with so many players being deployed to defend. Bob switched to a 4-4-2 line-up. He read the room, he acted instinctively and the players backed him to the hilt. Rovers won 1-0. The key is to listen, to watch, read the room and act.

Chapter 12

Extra Time and a New Job

WHEN I initially joined BBC Radio Bristol I didn't work on Saturdays. I was learning the ropes from some top-drawer people. The station manager Mike Hapgood put me in the capable and caring hands of Keith Warmington and Polly Lloyd, both experienced broadcasters in their own right. They were very patient and exceptionally helpful towards me. Delivering on the radio from a written script is a skill and was something I struggled with in the formative weeks.

Keith, who to this day is a wonderful friend, was a brilliant help. A real chemistry developed between us. As my career evolved, we became well known for 'corpsing' on air. The definition of 'corpsing' is the inability to speak because you're overcome with an all-consuming fit of laughter.

Believe you me, it wasn't great when both of us were on air and neither of us could speak. I'd look to him for help, and he'd have his back to me, with his shoulders going up and down nineteen to the dozen. It's impossible to define why it happened. It's like when the schoolteacher gives the entire class a huge telling-off and someone sniggers, the sniggers turn into chuckles and the chuckles explode into full-blown laughter. It was that kind of thing except we weren't schoolchildren. We were professional broadcasters, apparently.

For years and years we were very popular. Apparently, people tuned in hoping we'd fall apart on air. We rarely disappointed. One year at the Bath and West Show at Shepton Mallet, Keith and I were billed as a form of entertainment. People queued outside the BBC marquee to get a seat. There was standing room only. People loved to listen to our tales.

I remember when Leo Devine, a new boss in charge of TV and local radio across Bristol, Somerset, Gloucestershire and Wiltshire, joined. On the first Saturday of his tenure Keith and I had a spectacular corpse on air. Again, we couldn't speak. When I tried to talk my voice was high-pitched. Keith had beads of sweat on his forehead as he gasped for air. Hilarious. On the Monday, Leo came striding to my desk. I thought, *Oh heck*. Things looked a bit iffy. He told me he'd listened to me and Keith on Saturday. This wasn't sounding good. Then he said, 'It was absolutely brilliant, the best radio I've heard in some time!' Like I say, it became a bit of cult radio, dangerous but huge fun.

Paradoxically, Keith had a wonderful way of extracting some of my football anecdotes on air. They were serious in-depth chats, sometimes about my career and other times about Dad and his amazing work at Liverpool. Keith was an exceptional broadcaster and a brilliant guy. I'm hugely grateful for the help he gave me in my formative months and for our enduring friendship. Keith is a Top Man.

Back to my early months, and as hard as Keith and Polly tried to make my delivery from scripts more natural, I struggled. Then one day Mike Hapgood came up with a brilliant idea that cracked it for me. Rather than read off a script word for word,

Mike encouraged me to do 'two ways', which was a more ad-libbed, relaxed delivery. This was much better for me, as it allowed me to be more relaxed and more natural.

I wasn't working on Saturdays, so Pete Jackson smooth-talked me into seeing out the season at Yate Town Football Club. Jeez, it was rough-and-ready football. The game was quick, physical and frenetic. I'd played a few games for 'Jacko' when I received a phone call from an agent in late March 1993. This was the first and only time I'd worked with an agent as they weren't prevalent in my Preston and Rovers playing days. I always sought contractual advice from the PFA.

The agent was representing the Belfast-based club Linfield, who needed an experienced, readily available centre-half to help them qualify for the Champions League. Linfield were top of the Irish League with five games to go. The offer was very attractive – £1,000 a game. I'd pick up my pre-paid flight ticket at Heathrow on the Friday afternoon and fly on the Belfast shuttle. I'd be met at the airport and taken to a hotel for bed, breakfast and an evening meal. After the game I'd be dropped back at the airport, then I'd do it all again on the following Friday. It was almost too good to be true.

I accepted the offer. Then an hour or so later the agent rang back to say the terms of the deal had changed. The £1,000 a game was now £750. I told him to forget it. My inkling was that the £250 was going in the agent's pocket. An hour later he rang back and told me the deal was back on! Funny that.

I wanted to tell Pete Jackson to his face what was going on, but I struggled to get hold of him. If only mobile phones were available sooner! His wife worked at the local bookmakers, so I left a message there for him to contact me as soon as possible. I'd given BBC Radio Bristol the heads-up as it was important that they had the scoop, for obvious reasons. They wanted to run the story in their news bulletin at 4pm, but I convinced them to hold it until I'd told Jacko. Time slipped by and they got twitchy, so I agreed they could run the story in the news at 5pm.

At 4.59pm, I looked out of the kitchen window and Jacko's white van appeared on my driveway. He turned off his engine and sat upright, staring into space. I knew he was listening to the radio. I could tell. Then his head dropped forward and slumped on to the steering wheel for a few minutes! I knew what station he was listening to. Pete got out of his van and trudged slowly towards my front door, by which time I'd gone out to meet him. I put the kettle on. Over a brew I apologised about how he'd found out the news, but he knew that I'd been trying to get hold of him. I told him the pounds, shillings and pence of the deal, and he fully understood. He said he'd have done the same if he'd received such an offer. I reminded him that he'd never have received such an offer, which lightened the mood. Jacko is a Top Man.

So off I went for a five-game sortie in Northern Ireland. I was paid more than at any time in my ten years as a professional in England. I admit I did it for the money as it was convenient and useful in terms of my transition into the BBC. I was told they'd started their search for a centre-half in the February. If only they'd found me sooner!

Playing for Linfield was a wonderful experience. Windsor Park, where Northern Ireland play, is their home ground. Crowds exceeded 10,000 and there was a real passion and desire to be champions and qualify for the Champions League. One Saturday, Glasgow Rangers were without a game, so six coach-loads of Rangers fans made the trip to Windsor Park to support the

Blue Men. The Irish are fantastic people and were wonderfully hospitable and welcoming. They used to call me 'Big Marrrn', and I loved every minute in the blue shirt.

The kit man, Gary Eccles, is a beautiful human being, with a heart of gold, and did everything to make me feel welcome. He loved Linfield and was so proud to work for the football club. The manager, Trevor Anderson, was a great bloke too. Cor, he was passionate. I've never seen anyone get so wound up before a game. The colour drained out of his face as kick-off approached. Trev was under huge pressure to win the league.

The guy who used to pick me up from the airport was quite a character. I was interested in the city and the Troubles that sadly prevailed. One day we were driving to the hotel from the airport, and I asked him if ever felt threatened. He pointed to the glove compartment and said, 'Open that and have a wee look, Big Marrrn.' I opened the compartment and there was a handgun, loaded, safety catch on. Ready to go if needed!

Security seemed high. Cars were stopped and checked. The Troubles had flared up. I remember travelling out of Belfast on the team coach and witnessing two groups of children at the end of two rows of terraced houses hurling bottles and stones at each other. The gable ends carried spectacular murals. The groups were 25 yards apart and were in range. This wasn't mock aggression, this was for real. I asked one of the lads what was going on. He explained that one group was Protestant and the other was Catholic. The worst thing for me was that the parents who were present encouraged and congratulated their children. Religion doesn't matter to me. But it made me sad to witness this aspect of life in Belfast, a city populated by such wonderful people.

We won our first three games and then went to local rivals Glentoran, knowing if results went our way we could clinch the title with a game to spare. The Oval was an incredible sight that day. From the halfway line on the opposite side to where the teams came out there was a sea of blue, red and white as the huge throng of Linfield supporters was packed all the way behind the goal to the left as far as the corner flag on the near side.

We went behind, then we got the game back to one-all. Late in the match I went up for a corner on the right-hand side. The flight was spot on, and I timed my leap to perfection, heading goalwards from about ten yards out. The keeper dived to his left but couldn't hold the ball and our striker Ritchie Johnson pounced and stabbed the ball into the net. The Linfield fans exploded into frenzied celebrations. It was an incredible sight. We won 2-1 and word came through that the results had gone our way. We were champions. The management team and subs ran on to the pitch to celebrate. Gary, the kit man, ran straight to me and we embraced and jumped up and down. Big Gary sobbed tears of total joy and happiness.

Leaving the pitch was a bit hairy as some of the home fans hurled huge stones at us. We were sheltered by the police as we made it down the tunnel. There was no love lost between Linfield and Glentoran. I hosted a golf trip earlier this year in Northern Ireland, and on the way back to the George Best city airport we passed the Oval, and all the memories came flooding back. The ground hadn't changed a bit.

We lost our final game the following week at Windsor, but the celebrations afterwards were spectacular. The pitch invasion was huge, with thousands and thousands on the pitch as the trophy was presented to captain Alan Dornan. I still have the season ticket number 1534 presented to me by Linfield fan Trevor Cairns from Lisburn, as a keepsake of my time with his club.

There was a reception in one of the function rooms at Windsor afterwards. After the food and speeches, the boys went into Belfast to celebrate. Believe you me, those lads could party. Around midnight we got back to the bar of my hotel and after one for the road I apologised and turned in for the night. The lightweight Englishman had had enough, but the locals were just getting a second wind.

Incredibly, after what seemed like a split second, the phone rang in my room. It was around 8am. I felt like I had an axe in my head. 'Hello,' I said tentatively. 'Big Marrrn, Big Marrrn, are you coming down for a wee drink, Big Marrrn? You're going home today; we need to have a wee drink.' Four of them were still sat in the chairs that I'd left them in when I bailed out. They were still drinking, still going strong. Champion footballers and champion drinkers! I have nothing but fond memories of and huge respect for the people of Northern Ireland and Linfield Football Club. My short time with them was a wonderful experience. Up the Blue Men.

Linfield really was the final chapter. I look back on my career with pride and satisfaction. Joining Chorley from Formby was a big decision. Leaving my mates to travel solo twice a week to train proved to be the right call. Joining Preston was a dream come true. Although I played 121 games in three seasons, I don't think Preston fans saw the best of me often enough.

Luckily for me, I got a second chance in the professional game after Bobby Gould met Brian Kidd. Moving away from my roots was a good thing. Not simply because Bristol is a wonderful city, but the move made me more independent and more determined to succeed. After proving my worth to Gerry Francis, it was a wonderful journey at Bristol Rovers. I made 296 appearances for The Gas, and I'll always be proud of my spell of going more than three seasons without missing a game. Apparently, I'm only the fifth player to achieve this in the club's history. I'm sure there will never be a sixth.

Then 1989/90 was exceptional. Winning the league was incredible, as was walking out at Wembley. I enjoyed representing the players on club issues and standing up for what was right. However, helping to give Rovers fans a team to be proud of is the most satisfying aspect of my time wearing the blue and white quarters.

I was satisfied that I'd achieved the ten-year career I'd hoped for when I joined Preston in 1983. I played 417 first-team games in those ten years. And I played against some excellent players. When I was wet behind the ears and learning my trade, the tough guys to handle included the following:

- Bobby Campbell – Bradford City. Big and strong and knew the game inside out. Bobby had a strong Irish accent and hoarse voice. Although he wasn't overly tall, he made it difficult to win a header.
- Tony Cascarino – Gillingham. A man mountain who was also picked up from non-league football. Played down the middle. Archetypal target man with a great touch.
- Billy Whitehurst – Hull City. Playing against Billy Whitehurst carried a health warning. A hulk of a guy, brutally tough but very likeable. I played at Hull for Preston and the game was one of the two featured games on *Match of the Day*, with Barry Davies on commentary duties. I had an indifferent game as I gave away a penalty in a 2-1 win. Big Billy whacked his elbow across my

face and split my eye open, which needed stitches. Another badge of honour! My mum rang me the next morning to see if I was all right as she'd seen the blood on my shirt when she watched *Match of the Day*. Bless her.

- John Fashanu – Lincoln and Millwall. A real handful. When he was in the mood, he was almost unplayable. I remember ploughing into 'Fash the Bash' at Lincoln in the first few minutes. The plan was to get my retaliation in early. I kicked him in the Achilles. He went to ground in apparent pain. The referee came straight towards me, brandishing a yellow card. I thought it was well worth it until John sprung to his feet, winked at me, and said, 'That didn't hurt!' That match was a long 87 minutes after my indiscretion.

As I learned my trade, dealing with the physical players became easier. You had to nudge them when the ball was in flight, step in front of them to intercept the ball or win the header. If the striker moved to the side to get a run on you, then you had to mirror his movement to counter the advantage. It was important to read what the opposing midfielder might do with the ball. If you saw him look towards his striker, then step in front and intercept the pass. You had to make the striker think about where you were and what you might do next. It was important to ruffle their feathers now and again, take a yellow card in the process. I call them the tricks of the trade.

The higher up the pyramid I played, the players were quicker, both physically and mentally. They were technically superior and barely missed a chance. Here are some names that spring to mind:

- Gary Nelson – Plymouth and Brighton. 'Nelse' was a hybrid striker, a cross between a winger and a centre-forward. Good mobility and pace. He wasn't great in the air, but he knew where the back of the net was. I was on the end of a great bit of banter from Nelse in 1987. At Twerton Park, I came on as a sub versus Brighton. I ran on and shouted to the other defenders that these front men were no threat, etc., etc. Nelse turned round, looking at me in disbelief: 'You can shut the fark up. If you were any farking good, you would have been on from the farking start!' Good point well made. Nelse paid me an important compliment a couple of years later. In July 1989 Rovers won a pre-season tournament in Arundel, beating Brighton in the final. As we shook hands after the game, Gary complimented me on my fitness and how I'd played. 'I used to run away from you Geoff, but I can't anymore. You're quicker and stronger, fair play, have a great season.' Looking back, at that time I was at the peak of my career. I was fit and understood the game more than ever. What Gary said was a little thing, but it meant a lot. Gary and I are still buddies, but from a distance.

- Teddy Sheringham – Millwall and Notts Forest. Teddy was top class. Quiet and respectful. At times he was like a ballet dancer on the football pitch. He had balance, poise, touch, vision, technique and was a great finisher. His anticipation more than made up for a lack of pace. I played well against Teddy in the League Cup when he'd moved to Nottingham Forest. I was chuffed when Brian Clough took him off. Even after he made the really big moves to United and Spurs and was an England star, he always remembered me and we had a chat at the PFA annual dinner. Teddy didn't forget his past. A class guy on and off the pitch.
- Johnny Byrne – York, Brighton, Millwall and Sunderland. 'Budgie' could play. Good mobility and strength meant he was always a threat. John was good with his back to goal and could run in behind. He wasn't the biggest but was good in the air. Budgie and Nelse were a strong pairing at Brighton.
- Guy Whittingham – Portsmouth. A prolific goalscorer. Guy was a great finisher who constantly ran in behind. Never gave

up and kept coming back for more. Ex-army man who made the most of his late start in the game.

- David Hirst – Sheffield Wednesday. Probably the best first touch of any striker I played against. Whatever height the ball was fired into him, he killed it dead or played it first time into a colleague's path. He possessed a radar-like awareness of his team-mates' whereabouts. Hirst had a great left peg; he could link the play and was a great finisher. Give him a quarter of a chance and it was in the back of the net.
- Steve Bull – Wolves. Season on season Steve Bull was the best. 'Bully' was a great competitor. He pulled off your shoulder into the blind spot, so you didn't know where he was. As well as being quick and powerful he was an assassin in front of goal – a great finisher. He was a top pro who took a dig and gave a dig. He never moaned to the referees, he just got on with the contest. Funnily enough, I used to play well against Bully, and it was a long time before he scored against Rovers.

I remember Bully and I contesting a long kick by the Wolves keeper at Molineaux. I won the header, but it ricocheted off his back into his path and he raced away down the middle of the pitch towards the goal at the South Bank end, where the home fans were amassed. My brain computed the immediate situation. Bully was quick, he was too far ahead of me to catch him if I let him run. He was effectively clean through. Bully rarely missed. There was only one thing to do. I took him out from behind. It was crude, uncompromising, but effective. Bully went down, the referee came running towards me. I thought I was colour blind as the red card the referee was waving at me was a yellow one! Surely he'd pulled out the wrong card. Trevor Simpson was in charge; he'd started the game as a linesman but had taken over a few minutes earlier when the referee went off injured. Trevor was a decent, likeable bloke and, as he beckoned me towards him, he told me I was lucky as my left-back could have got round on the cover, so I wasn't the last man. As the Wolves fans bellowed 'off, off, off' it was hard to hear Trevor, who only booked me. No disrespect to Vaughan Jones but Usain Bolt wouldn't have got to Steve Bull had he not been taken out by yours truly. Nowadays, I'd have been sent off for the challenge, without any doubt. The South Bank booed me every time I touched the ball after the incident. I loved it.

We always did well against Wolves and Steve Bull. During his barren spell, Richard Payne, the Rovers correspondent for the *Bristol Evening Post*, rang me ahead of a league game at Twerton Park. He wanted some bravado from me about the game, and particularly Steve Bull. I halted Richard mid-sentence and told him that there was no way I was going to make any predictions about stopping the top striker in the division from scoring. I warned Richard that I must not be quoted in any shape or form, not a single letter, not a word, not a sentence, nothing.

As I drove into Twerton Park for the game I couldn't believe my eyes. The billboards had the front page of the *Bristol Evening Post* sports supplement on them. In huge capital letters it read: 'I'LL TAME THE BULL – GEOFF'. Wow, I was raging, I was absolutely livid. I heard afterwards that Graham Turner, the Wolves manager, pinned the page on the noticeboard in the away dressing room before the game. If you believed what you read, I'd done his team talk for him. They must have thought I was an arrogant so and so. It gets worse.

Midway through the first half with the score at 0-0, Robbie Dennison, the Wolves left-winger, went down the flank attacking the Bath end down the slope and clipped a ball into the near-post area. Positionally I was spot on. As Bully ran towards the near post, I was in front of him on his right shoulder. Perfect. As the ball came in at thigh height my correct positioning meant that I was able to play the ball first. I went to volley it away, and to this day I have no idea how my left thigh got higher than my right boot. I volleyed the ball right-footed against the inside of my left thigh and the ball rebounded into the bottom corner of the goal. The difficulty factor was very high, but it was an own goal. Bully said to me, 'Unlucky Jiff, mate, that was unlucky.' Bully wasn't taking the mickey, as it wasn't in his nature. He always seemed to be a serious guy; maybe that was his desire to score and to win. His sympathy was genuine, but I was both raging and embarrassed. 'I'LL TAME THE BULL – GEOFF' was all I could think about. Later in the first half Carl Saunders equalised and it finished 1-1.

After the game I had the shortest shower in the history of living man and went in search of Richard Payne. The journos congregated on the edge of the pitch by the tunnel. Richard saw me making a beeline for him and the colour drained from his face. He looked more distressed than his first-ever Rovers game and the Gerry Francis/Paul Nixon shenanigans. I went straight for Richard and tore a strip off him. I shouldn't have done it in public as other journalists were present and, to be fair to Richard, he was and is a top bloke. We had a very good relationship as he used to ring me to pen my weekly Captain's Column in the *Bristol Evening Post*. Richard was apologetic and told me the sub-editor was responsible for the headline. Regardless, I was still livid and refused to do the weekly column for the best part of 12 months. The decision cost me money but sticking to my principles was more important. Eventually we made our peace and Richard is still a good friend and is a respected journalist with HTV West these days.

Referees are not what they used to be. To be more accurate, referees are not allowed to officiate the way they used to. When I played you could talk with referees. There was a two-way line of communication. There was banter. My best playing days were from the age of 28 through to 31. As well as being at my peak fitness levels, I understood the game more than ever. I also appreciated the need to treat the match officials with the respect they deserve. I got to know them and had civil conversations before the game. The majority were receptive to building relationships, as it made their job easier and, to be candid, from my point of view, if there was a 50/50 decision, I knew I had more chance of it going my way if I got on with the ref. It's common sense but so many people in football nowadays don't get it. Too many look upon referees and their assistants as some kind of foe. Embrace them, respect them and enjoy a positive relationship.

Some of the referees I rated and enjoyed sharing a pitch with included Roger Gifford, Keith Cooper (his son Steve has made a decent fist of football management) and Roger Dilkes. They were all super refs. My favourite was Neil Midgley. 'Midge' was brilliant. He hailed from Bolton and, as well as being a top ref, he had razor-sharp wit and banter. I remember playing at Port Vale for Rovers. I had a stinker in the first half. The striker I was allegedly marking had scored a couple and we were losing 3-0. At this point, rather than being responsible for my own performance, I vented my frustrations on the referee: 'Come on, Midge, keep up with play.' 'Come on, Midge, that was handball, didn't you see it?' 'Midge, that was a foul.'

As he blew for half-time, I tracked him to the tunnel and muttered some ridiculous dialogue, blaming him for us being three goals behind. We came out for the second half, and I jogged across to take up my position. Midge walked towards me and said, ''kin 'ell Twents, I didn't expect to see thee son. I thought Gerry would have taken thee off at half-time.' Game, set and match to the man in black. A few years later we met at a convention for the Devon and Cornwall Referees' Society. He represented the elite referees, and I was there on behalf of the PFA. We had a few beers and a good reminisce. It was very sad news when he passed away at the age of just 58 back in 2001. Neil Midgley made refereeing an art form but did it with personality. Midge was a Top Man.

So that was the football done and dusted. I now had a new career to forge. I'd worked hard to get an opportunity with the BBC, and I was determined to make it a success.

Chapter 13

Microphones and Headphones

TALK ABOUT a change in your life over a relatively short period of time. In March 1993 I was a footballer, then six months later I was the sports editor at one of the country's Big City stations.

When Keith Beech moved on to Radio Gloucestershire the role was advertised nationally. Back in the day, the Saturday edition of *The Guardian* had a media job supplement. Dozens of jobs were advertised. One week the gig at Radio Bristol was included in the vacancies. I was still learning what a sports reporter was all about, but I felt the need to apply. It was important to show ambition and commitment. Obviously, I had no chance of getting the job. I might get an interview if I was lucky.

For whatever reason, the Beeb thought I was worthy of an interview. I put on my best suit, collar and tie and headed for the interview with hope rather than expectation. A panel of four sat behind a big desk. John Conway, the head of regional and local programmes in the west; the station's managing editor, Mike Hapgood; Keith Warmington, who was the acting assistant editor; and the personnel officer, Jude Grey.

It was going pretty well, then John Conway, in his booming Northern Irish brogue, pulled out the pin and chucked in the hand grenade with his killer question. John asked how I'd get people from different socio-economic backgrounds to listen to the sports output. I wasn't sure I understood the question, but with a degree of feigned confidence I assured him that a football or rugby stadium is a clear representation of the society in which we live. A high-earning blue chip company chief executive can sit next to someone who works on a factory shop floor. They have a common bond – their sport and their team. The essence is to deliver a comprehensive sports output that appeals to everyone. He nodded in agreement and smiled, which I hoped was a good sign.

The good thing about BBC 'Boards' (interviews) is that you find out on the day whether you've been successful or not. Later that afternoon Mike Hapgood rang me. He asked if I was sitting down. I said I wasn't. He said, 'Well I'm delighted to tell you that you've got the job. Your interview was very impressive, and you were easily the best candidate.' Gulp.

The newsroom was chuffed for me, and what I had to do was pay back their support by delivering a good product, improving the sports coverage and increasing the audience. I had a few ideas.

A predecessor of mine, Rob Nothman, was a huge help at this point. I'm a great believer in the notion that 'if you don't know how to do something, find someone you trust who does and pick their brains'. 'Nothers' had interviewed me countless times when I wore the blue and white quarters. He's a great journalist and really gets radio. He'd moved on to the bright lights of the BBC in London and was very generous in passing on his thoughts and vast experience.

Commentaries are a key commodity in radio sport. Radio Bristol wasn't delivering anything like enough live matches. Commentaries were an exception, not the norm. I wanted to change this. As well as delivering more commentary matches, I wanted to make the content of the midweek programmes totally sport-based. The station relied on music to fill the programmes. I remember shadowing a midweek football programme when they were called *Soccer Specials*, but they weren't very special. A guy called Ian Fisher by and large just played music. The reporter at the game filed a preview, three reports in each half, plus a half-time round-up and a full-time report. Six reports during the game was the maximum allowed in accordance with the Football League/BBC broadcast agreement. Broadcasting commentary of the matches cost money, as the clubs had to be paid. At one point Ian played three tracks back-to-back without speaking. I challenged him on this and asked why he didn't at least give out the latest scores between the music. He assured me that people stayed listening as no other stations covered the local sport. Complacency is a highly dangerous trait. I was staggered but it made me more determined to effect change. There were plenty of people who'd give their right arm to work on a BBC local radio station. I was keen to find them.

Another idea was to have studio guests to talk sport and football. If there wasn't a match commentary, having a live guest was far more engaging than playing music. Sometimes radio production involves a fair amount of creativity and graft: identifying content, chasing people, getting numbers, making calls, digging out archive audio, sending messages, but the net gain is always worth it. Playing music made no sense to me.

Another issue I had to deal with early doors was a difficult one. The station was without an experienced sports presenter as Keith Beech was off up the M5 to Radio Gloucestershire, and Dominik Holyer had secured a gig at Sky Sports. We managed to agree a deal with 'Beechy' to do Saturday afternoons. This was all fine until one Saturday when he (presenter) and I (sports ed) didn't see eye to eye. It was Five Nations weekend in rugby. England weren't playing, so there were no local players in action. City had enjoyed a good away win. I told him to lead the headline sequence at five o'clock on the football, then do the rugby. He opted to lead on the rugby. I told him he was wrong, editorially, and wrong to ignore my instructions. As we approached six o'clock and the close of the show I instructed him to lead on football. He once again chose rugby. It was a costly move by him as he never presented the show again.

I rang Keith Warmington, the assistant editor, my line manager, that evening and told him the sequence of events. He asked me what I wanted to do about it. There was only one course of action from my perspective. Without any hesitation Keith backed me and telephoned Beechy to stand him down. The sports editor is the person in charge of the sports output. Had Beechy followed my instruction at 6pm, he'd have been fine, but to defy me twice was a step too far. Beechy did a huge amount for me in terms of getting me into the BBC, but I couldn't let that influence the situation. I was in charge and there are certain scenarios where the chain of command must never be broken. This was one such situation.

One of the big changes I brought to the station's football coverage was live interviews with the managers during the games. In 1993 this practice was unprecedented; it was groundbreaking. Russell Osman was in charge at City, while John Ward was the Rovers boss. I'd played against Russell a few times in Bristol derbies. I didn't know John, as I'd left Rovers just before he was appointed. The whole concept worked because the two men in charge trusted me implicitly due to my professional football background.

The idea was simple. At the midway point of the second half, the match commentator would throw to me during a break in play and I'd ask two or three questions depending on the state of the game. It was awesome to hear from managers as the adrenaline of the match coursed through their veins.

I remember one amazing live insert at Twerton Park when Rovers played Bradford City. The commentary team handed to me. I was getting the analysis from John Ward. While we were chatting, Rovers went on the attack, so I broke away from the chat and described the action as Rovers equalised. John gave me his excited reaction as the teams went back to the halfway line. I was back in conversation with a composed John Ward as Bradford kicked off. Rovers regained possession immediately through Worrell Sterling, at which point John Ward assumed the role of commentator as he described the action: 'Oh, hang on a minute, Geoff, we're on the attack here. Go on, Worrell, go on Worrell. He's crossed it for Marcus … GOALLLLLLL!' Pandemonium broke out. It was fabulous radio.

The fact that Russell agreed to do it was important. I guess it was strange for City fans at the time. Suddenly, a guy who used to kick lumps out of their centre-forwards was now on the radio talking about their team. From my perspective, to see and hear their manager talking with a former Rovers centre-half during a game was a glowing endorsement. It sent a positive message to the fans. It was a matter of taking small steps to be accepted by the Bristol City fans. I'll always be grateful to Russell for being so receptive and hospitable.

I had to be consistent, fair and offer decent analysis, having played the game. I had to praise and criticise both clubs on merit. I also had to offer an insight and conduct interviews from a former player's perspective. I guess some Rovers fans found it strange when they heard me praising City. I knew it was going to plan when City fans said to me, 'I quite like you on the radio, Twentypence, you're not bad for a Gashead!' Like I said, small steps.

I mentioned Russell, which reminds me of the time he signed striker Ian Baird from Hearts. I went to Ashton Gate to record a chat with the new arrival. Russell introduced me: 'This is Geoff Twentyman from BBC Radio Bristol.'

Baird replied in a flash, 'Yes, I know Geoff,' and as he continued he ran his forefinger across his eyebrow. 'I got this scar off him when I was at Middlesbrough!' They're badges of honour, Ian!

Back at base at Whiteladies Road, Bristol, I was really enjoying life with the BBC. There was so much to learn, it was a vibrant place to work and there were some outstanding presenters and brilliant people in the newsroom. Alongside the great Keith Warmington, the other heavyweights were Roger Bennett and John Turner. Roger was the classic local radio breakfast host. He knew every nook and cranny of the broadcast area. He was so knowledgeable but was incredibly modest. I remember being wowed by how he went from interviewing a politician, to a sports person, then a teacher.

I asked him how he knew so much about so many things. He just smiled and counter-claimed that he didn't know very much about anything. He was a genius behind the microphone and was incredibly supportive of me. He used to play the clarinet in the Blue Notes jazz band during the week too. I had no idea how he got up at silly o'clock, cycled in from Long Ashton, which was at least half an hour away, and then presented *Morning West*. It was dreadfully sad when Roger lost his battle with cancer, but I'll never forget the wonderful occasion that celebrated his life at St Mary Redcliffe Church in Bristol.

Keith had the perfect face for radio … I mean the perfect voice for radio. The former schoolteacher at Merrywood School in south Bristol was a brilliant drivetime and Saturday morning host. He had a very inquisitive mind and asked some great questions of his guests. He thrived in the political forum. He was versatile, had a wonderful sense of fun and was exceptionally engaging. I learned so much from my mate 'Bags'. Keith retired too soon, to be honest, but he became disillusioned after he was moved from his beloved drivetime show to do a programme from 10pm to 1am. This was a poor decision by the manager of the day, Tim Pemberton.

Keith did so much to help me in my formative months. We had so much fun, but he must have nearly got me the sack a thousand times when we completely lost it on air. Always his fault, never mine. Keith is a Top Man.

JT was an iconic figure. He was a paradox in many ways, off air he was introverted and kept himself to himself. On air he was bullish and displayed an ultra-strong personality. He used to hold people to account and for years presented a consumer programme where he solved listeners' problems. He had a high success rate and many companies sorted issues off air as they didn't fancy going on his show, knowing he'd tear them apart. Again, JT was shifted from his hugely popular mid-morning slot to do the breakfast show. JT, who was a bon viveur, was not an early morning person. He too decided to leave prematurely, which was another big loss to the station.

They don't make them like Keith, Roger and JT anymore. It was a privilege to learn so much from three titans of the broadcasting world.

The sports output was improving but had some way to go. I convinced Mike Hapgood, who ran the station, to find some money to enable us to provide football commentaries. Back then a fee was payable to the clubs. There were two rates: full match or second-half commentary. Nowadays, a season-long deal is agreed with the clubs. We started off by doing commentary of the away Bristol side, with updates from the home fixture. We didn't have a budget for both clubs, so I worked on the basis that the majority of fans went to the home games, so the captive audience was for the away fixtures.

As for rugby, well, there were a lot of Bath players in the England rugby squad. It made sense to me to have our own broadcast point at Twickenham, so we could cover the games. It didn't get much bigger than having international players on your patch, and we needed to be there. Putting in broadcast facilities was expensive, even for a temporary installation. As we were there so often it made sense to have our own permanent broadcast point. The router allowed two simultaneous, independent broadcasts so I was able to rent out the other line to another station. Eat your heart out Arthur Daley.

People told me it was very different moving from football to radio. To be honest, there are some clear similarities. On a football pitch what you do is what the spectators see. If you score an own goal against Wolves, there's no second chance. With live radio what I said is what you heard. There's no delay on BBC output, so there's no second chance if you mess up. To me, these were significant similarities.

I soon realised that being a BBC sports editor enabled me to be present at some amazing sporting events and to meet some incredible people. The first biggies were the Bristol City v Liverpool FA Cup ties in 1994. This was a massive draw and presented an opportunity for me to gauge whether our coverage had improved. Ten days or so before the game the newsroom telephone rang: 'Geoff, there's a call for you.' I asked who it was, as I often got calls in the newsroom from football fans who wanted to share their opinions and concerns on their team. 'It's Graeme Souness.'

A wow, a gasp, then silence descended on the newsroom as I casually picked up the call: 'Hi Graeme, how are you?' Souness was the manager of Liverpool. I'd got his number from Dad and had left him a voicemail to ask whether I could travel to Merseyside to preview the game for radio and TV in Bristol. We arranged the time, date and place there and then. Life before press officers was much easier.

Graeme was a family friend in many ways. He loved my mum and dad, and he came to Dad's funeral. Graeme was manager of Blackburn Rovers by then. I remember mouthing to him, 'Thanks for coming,' as I walked past him, carrying the coffin down the aisle. He mouthed back, 'Not a problem.' He was standing next to Emlyn Hughes.

After Liverpool let my dad leave Anfield, Souness rang him the next day and took him to Glasgow Rangers as his chief talent scout. Graeme wanted Dad to go back to Liverpool with him when he returned to the club as manager, but Dad remained loyal to Rangers. He should have followed Graeme.

I learned one of the most important lessons there is when I went to the Liverpool training ground to interview Graeme Souness. No one taught me this, but it was something that came to me naturally. You must ask the big questions, regardless of the circumstances. As a reporter you're in a privileged position. I had special access to Graeme Souness because of the family connection but I still had to ask him the big question. The killer question was whether he feared being sacked if they lost. Liverpool were struggling in the league and the fanbase was restless.

I knew that was going to be my last question. I looked him in the eye, took a semi-deep breath, then asked, 'Do you fear being sacked if Bristol City knock Liverpool out of the cup?' He gave me the Souness glare! The two-footed look that people have seen over the years on the pitch, in the technical area and on Sky Sports. I kept eye contact with him as it added credibility and weight to my question. He answered with typical Souness alacrity. Yes, he was aware what the implications of defeat were. He was acutely aware.

I thanked him for his time and we shook hands. It was a firm handshake from both parties. He was absolutely fine and told me to get in touch when Liverpool travelled to Bristol, and he'd do any interviews I needed. He's some guy, Graeme Souness.

The first game at Ashton Gate was abandoned due to floodlight failure, and the rearranged match ended 1-1. Then City famously won the replay at Anfield courtesy of a Brian Tinnion goal in front of the Kop. Graeme Souness was sacked the next day.

I presented our coverage, along with Phil Tottle, from Anfield. It was my first 'big' outside broadcast and I loved every minute of it. Jon Kay, who now presents on *BBC Breakfast*, travelled with me that day. He was a young news reporter at Radio Bristol and produced some incredible radio for the next day's breakfast programme. He recorded chats with fans and programme and scarf sellers. It was glorious radio and gave the audience a wonderful sense of the occasion.

'Jonkers' was highly amused when we stopped at a fish and chip shop to replenish before the drive back to Bristol. A Liverpool fan was convinced that I was Ian Rush. Same moustache, same hooter, different football ability. We drove back to Bristol and then pulled together our respective radio features for the breakfast show *Morning West*. It was about 5am when we finally left for home. Roger Bennett arrived in the studio to present *Morning West* before we left. Sometimes there were long days in local radio, but some occasions are so special that it's worth every second.

There was a takeover at Ashton Gate in 1994. A group led by Dave Russe took control. As often happens with a change in the boardroom, there's a new face in the manager's office. I was told by a credible source that Russell Osman was to be replaced by Joe Jordan. I rang Joe on his landline. I asked him if it was happening. He was evasive, as I guess my call must have seemed quite intrusive. I think Joe was surprised that I'd got his number and had the audacity to ring him. I knew City were going to announce his appointment the next day. When I put him on the spot and asked him if I would see him in Bristol the following day, Joe admitted it was all happening. It was our lead story on Radio Bristol the next morning.

Joe made me chuckle when one of my colleagues, Matt Pick, interviewed him on his return to Ashton Gate and asked him if he was looking forward to locking horns with me again. Joe said, 'Aye, I hear he's a better journalist than he was a footballer.' He gave with one hand and took away with the other!

Joe came into the studio once as a guest on *The Midweek Match* and was captivating as he talked about his time at AC Milan as well as playing for Manchester United, Leeds and Scotland. My ambition was to replace music with a studio guest – this was Utopia.

I sensed there was always a mutual respect and admiration, but Joe and I didn't always see eye to eye. He brought a player in on loan from Arsenal called Mark Flatts. He started off on the subs' bench, but he looked lively when he came on late in the game at Ashton Gate, which finished 0-0. Afterwards I asked Joe if he regretted not bringing Flatts on earlier, considering how he affected the game. Joe answered the question, but the following Thursday when I went to record a preview for the next fixture, Joe was waiting for me. He had a bee in his bonnet: 'Dinnae ever ask me about my team selections. You should nae ask me about ma substitutions.' I stood my ground and said it was my job to ask what the fans might be thinking, plus as a former player I felt it was a legitimate question. Joe wasn't having it and for about ten minutes told me I must never ask about team selections. I said I'd ask if I felt it was appropriate. It was like a prolonged rally on centre court. In the end I suggested we agreed to disagree so we could record the chat ahead of the forthcoming game.

Some of my colleagues were in awe of Joe, intimidated by him at times, but when you've done battle at three o'clock on a Saturday afternoon it's just another interview. The apple doesn't fall far from the tree – Joe has a couple of cracking lads in Andrew and Tom. I always enjoy bumping into them around Bristol and having a chat.

Boxing is something I grew to love in my time at BBC Radio Bristol. It's an incredible sport on the naked eye. It's raw and brutal, and there's nowhere to hide, no team-mate to bail you out if you're below par. You almost feel the punches as you hear them land, as the blood and sweat flies across the ring.

My first foray with the Queensberry Rules was at The Colston Hall in 1994. The concert hall, which has since been redeveloped and renamed The Beacon, was packed as 2,000 Bristolians crammed in to see Ross Hale, one of their own, challenge Andy

Holligan for the British and Commonwealth light-welterweight title. I was ringside.

The roar when Ross appeared for his ring walk was deafening. It was incredible as the partisan crowd cheered on their man from the first second of the fight. It was live on Sky Sports and, from the get-go, 'The Rooster' was all over the defending champion from Liverpool. Hale put his man on the canvas in the second round and stopped him in the fourth to win the title. The scenes of elation and celebration were incredible. The king was crowned in front of his fellow Bristolians. Mint.

Putting together a report for the breakfast show was an absolute joy. Ross Hale is a brilliant bloke, modest to the core and down to earth. Sport in Bristol, and boxing in particular, suffers as there's no decent indoor arena. Ross and others, such as Glenn Catley and Lee Haskins, who followed in his footsteps, should have defended their titles in Bristol. Home support makes an enormous difference. Instead, they all fought their big fights away from home. Ross lost his first title defence to Paul 'Scrap Iron' Ryan in Bethnal Green, London. I have no doubt that had they fought in Bristol he'd have won.

Things were going well but there was a long way to go. I suppose looking back it was fresh, new and at times, groundbreaking. How times have changed, though. In 1995, Bristol's Ed Morrison refereed the Rugby World Cup Final when South Africa beat New Zealand at Ellis Park in Johannesburg. Ed is a class guy, an absolutely brilliant bloke. He used to come on the sports shows quite often. I think the fact he's a big Rovers fan helped whenever I rang him to request a chat! On the morning of the World Cup Final, I thought it would be a good idea and a bit of a coup to get him on Radio Bristol. The day before I rang him and asked if he'd come on for a chat, and he said, 'Yes, of course. I'll only be killing time before the game.' So, the referee of the 1995 Rugby World Cup Final was live on BBC Radio Bristol a few hours before the historic game when Nelson Mandela, wearing the green-and-gold jersey with the No.7 on the back, presented the Webb Ellis Cup to Francois Pienaar. Imagine trying to get the referee of a World Cup Final on a local radio station on the morning of the game these days!

Talking of rugby, when Jack Rowell was the England head coach, the former Bath boss would do live chats with me on the morning of Five Nations matches. I'm pretty sure my professional sport background was the reason why he did the chats, plus of course no one had dared ask him before. Jack passed away earlier this year, which was terribly sad. I have fond memories of his dry sense of humour and wonderfully warm personality. Sleep easy Big Man.

Meanwhile, life was good at BBC Radio Bristol. I was enjoying the role and improving the output, then one day I received another phone call to the newsroom. It wasn't Graeme Souness.

Chapter 14

'Matty … I Need Some Advice'

BY MARCH 1996 I'd been at BBC Radio Bristol for three years. A colleague answered the general newsroom number and called across the room, 'GT, there's a call for you, line one.'

'Hello,' I enquired from my desk, which was secluded from the main body of around 50 journalists who were working on BBC Radio Bristol, and BBC *Points West*, the regional TV programme.

'Matty, it's Ollie. I need some advice.'

Ian Holloway was playing for QPR in the Premier League at the time. I always felt Ollie looked upon me as an elder brother; older (definitely), taller (beyond debate), wiser (possibly) and more sensible (debatable).

'What is it, mate?' I replied inquisitively.

'Geoff Dunford [the Bristol Rovers vice-chairman] has been in touch. He wants me to take over as the player/manager at Rovers next season. What do you think?'

'Take the job,' I replied in an instant.

'What do you mean, take the job?' he responded, totally unconvinced.

'Ollie, mate, what do you know more about than anything else in the world?' I asked in hushed tones.

'Football,' was his immediate response.

'There you go then, mate,' I elaborated. 'If you don't take the job now, they'll appoint someone else, and he might do well for a few years. In the meantime, you'll stop playing, so what will you do then? Take the job, mate, take the job.'

'Ah, okay, you're probably right. You usually are. One thing, though. If I do go for it, I'll need an assistant. Someone I know, someone I can trust ...' There was a pause for a few seconds then we both giggled. Proper giggled. Ollie took the lead. 'You wouldn't, would you?'

'I wouldn't what?' I countered.

'Be my assistant.'

'You haven't asked me.' I was playing hard to get.

'Will you be my assistant?' He went for it.

'Yes,' I replied.

'Yes?! What about your missus?'

'No, she doesn't want the job.' Banter from me. 'She'll be fine, mate, she'll be fine.'

'So, you'll leave the BBC and be my assistant?'

'Yes, mate,' I almost whispered.

'Matty, I'm going to take the job. I'll ring you later.'

So, there it was. The biggest football story at BBC Radio Bristol for some years. Rovers weren't going to renew John Ward's contract at the end of the season in May. Rovers legend Ian Holloway was going to be appointed the new player/manager of the football club and yours truly was to be his assistant. I was neck deep in the story and I couldn't tell anyone for the time being. Confidentiality was key to my future employers, but I also knew the BBC had to have first dibs on the story when the time was right. I didn't want to burn any bridges with my current employers.

Thereafter life was far from straightforward. I was the sports editor at BBC Radio Bristol and had to carry out the role as normal. Ollie and I used to meet up to devise our plan. We'd watch Rovers reserves in action at Yate Town, where they played their home games. We'd travel independently and watch the game from opposite sides of the pitch. We'd leave separately to try to avoid any suspicion.

The hardest thing for me at this stage was dealing with John Ward. John was and is a stellar guy. He was a huge help to me when I moved into broadcasting and he did the live, groundbreaking interviews with me during the games. He's a top professional, honest and trustworthy. Conducting interviews with him wasn't easy at this time as I was privy to his future before he was.

Ollie and I knew that Marcus Stewart was going to leave at the end of the season. Marcus was the star pupil. He was a truly outstanding footballer. 'Stewie' was the most natural of strikers and is the best player that I ever played with. His touch, his anticipation, his finishing, his football brain, his movement, his aerial prowess, all of it was imperious. I'm devastated by his current situation and being diagnosed with motor neurone disease. He's an inspiration to us all in dealing with the adversity. It was humbling that he sought my advice on how he should make his situation public knowledge. I'm exceptionally proud to have been his captain when he made his Football League debut in 1991. He was outstanding in a 3-3 draw with Ipswich at Twerton Park, when we fought back from being 3-0 down at half-time.

Marcus was destined for bigger and better things and the time was right for him to fly the nest. I told Ollie that I'd get in touch with Graham Roberts, as I was confident that he'd be able to help. Graham was the manager of Yeovil Town, who we covered on the radio. The former Chelsea, Spurs and Rangers defender was a brilliant guy. He was old-school and called it how he saw it. I also trusted his football judgement, so I gave him a bell:

'Graham, a mate of mine, Dave Jones, is the manager of Stockport [true]. He's looking for a striker [untrue]. Who's the best striker in non-league football?'

Without hesitation, Graham, replied, 'Barry Hayles. Tell your mate there's only one striker in non-league football, that's Barry Hayles at Stevenage.'

So, I told my mate Ian Holloway, not Dave Jones, 'Ollie, Barry Hayles is our man.'

One Saturday QPR were without a game, so Ollie went to watch Hayles in action at Bath City. He rang me after the game, while I was still presenting *Saturday Sport* on BBC Radio Bristol. I had a break from being live on air, so I took his call. 'Matty, Matty, what a player. He's got the lot; he's got the lot.' Ollie had a high opinion of Jeff Sherwood, who played centre-back for Bath City, and he said Hayles had given him a torturous afternoon.

We didn't get Barry straight away. Stevenage had finished top of the Vauxhall Conference but were denied promotion after some shenanigans, so their chairman, Victor Green, wouldn't sell him. He did a year later. Rovers spent £250,000 on Barry. He scored 36 goals in 68 appearances and two years later was sold to Premier League Fulham for over £2m. You can see why I trusted Graham Roberts's judgement.

Ollie and I met and formulated our squad as best we could. Other than that, it was a matter of keeping our heads down as things came to a head in early May.

Rovers' last game of the season was a 3-0 win at Millwall. The last-ever game at the Old Den in Cold Blow Lane, which was the most intimidating ground I ever frequented. Rovers had called a press conference at the training ground two days later, on the Monday morning.

It was time for me to tell my boss what was going on. For future happy relations I had to keep the BBC sweet, just in case. I rang Mike Hapgood, the managing editor. Mike was from football stock. His dad, Eddie Hapgood, played for Arsenal and England. Mike had given me my big chance at the BBC; he was pragmatic and studious but very likeable.

'Mike, just to let you know Rovers are holding a press conference on Monday,' was my starter for ten.

'Ah, okay, do you know what it's about?' he asked.

'Yes, they're going to announce Ian Holloway as their new player/manager.'

'Brilliant work from you, great journalism, well done. I couldn't think of anyone better to go and cover it for us. Are you able to go?'

There was a delay. This was my 'in for a penny, in for a pound' moment. 'Well, Mike …' pause, deep breath, '… there's something else. Ollie has asked me to be his assistant and I've agreed.'

Mike's response was immediate and brilliant. 'That's absolutely fantastic. Obviously we'll be really disappointed to lose you, but we know football is your core subject. This is a great opportunity for you.'

The plan was put in place with the football club's approval. Radio Bristol would break the story on the Monday morning. News of my involvement was deferred until the Tuesday morning as Ollie had to deal with members of staff who he wasn't going to retain. This is the tough part of the industry. John Ward's right-hand man, Steve Cross, was a great guy, but he was wise enough to know the score. On the Tuesday, Radio Bristol would break the news that their sports editor was leaving to be Ian Holloway's assistant manager. I worked a nominal notice while Mike Hapgood sorted a succession plan.

And breathe.

I signed a three-year contract. It was exciting, very exciting. I loved working on the radio and had a real passion for the job. Broadcasting was exhilarating, the nearest thing to playing football. As Mike Hapgood had correctly identified, football was my core subject. I firmly believe we only live once and opportunities are there to be seized. I guess the easiest decision would have been to stay at the BBC, but I knew I had to be true to myself and give it a go with my buddy. Ollie told me he wouldn't have done it, had I not agreed to be his wingman.

Although Ollie and I had played over a thousand league games between us, we didn't have a full coaching badge. The rules stipulated that someone in the first-team coaching group had to have an FA full coaching qualification. We retained Terry Connor, who had the required qualification, as reserve-team coach. We also kept Tony Gill as youth-team coach. Ray Kendall and Roy Dolling continued in their roles as kit man and physio, respectively.

Ollie delivered a stroke of genius regarding Marcus Stewart. In fact, he delivered two strokes of absolute genius. Marcus wasn't going to sign a new deal but, to prevent him from walking away for free, we needed him to sign a document confirming that he wouldn't accept the new contract offer that the club had made to him. Amazingly, Marcus said that he might sign a new deal if the club would give him a sports car as part of the agreement. Ollie told Marcus to come back and see him at ten o'clock the next morning. Ollie got on the phone and in the space of a few hours had found a sponsor who'd fund a lease deal on a new Toyota

MR2. He sourced the car and told the dealership to deliver it at nine o'clock the next day.

Marcus came into the office the next morning and was staggered when he saw his brand-new dream car outside waiting for him. He couldn't pen a new deal, but he signed the bit of paper that ensured Rovers received £1.2m when he joined Huddersfield. The car went back to the dealership. Genius from Ollie.

So, Marcus was leaving. Barry Hayles wasn't yet in the Stevenage departure lounge, so we had to get a goalscorer. Genius part two from Ollie was equally impressive. Jamie Cureton was a Bristolian who'd scored goals at Norwich but was out of favour at Carrow Road. Ollie struck a loan deal for 'Curo'. Regardless of how well Jamie did, the fee of £250,000 was set in stone. Curo was sensational on loan and bagged a load of goals. The £250,000 transfer fee was an absolute snip. Strangely, the goals dried up for a period after the permanent transfer, but Jamie got back on track and was an incredible striker. He made goalscoring look ridiculously easy. He's a class act and one of the best pros I ever worked with. Ollie also tried to sign Ade Akinbiyi from Norwich, but they wouldn't allow him to leave Carrow Road.

Ollie did most of the coaching. He/we employed similar methods to Gerry Francis. Ollie was as fit as a fiddle and led the running. He and Marcus Browning were like two Olympic middle-distance runners on occasions. The group were exceptionally fit due to Ollie being in the mix. The partnership worked well. I was a bit more measured, while Ollie wore his heart on his sleeve. I remember once, I'd got home from training and the phone rang. It was Ollie and he was livid. He was raging about the vice-chairman, Geoff Dunford. 'Dunford can have his job. I'm resigning. I'm not doing it anymore. I'm not working for him. You can have the manager's job. I've had enough. I'm resigning. He's signing players behind my back. Do you know about this signing? I'm packing it in ...'

I waited for him to pause for a millisecond so I could join the conversation. 'Ollie. Shut up for a moment. Slow down and tell me exactly what you're going on about.'

A considerably calmer Ollie recapped: 'I've had a voicemail from Jason Cundy's agent. They've agreed a loan deal. The player's up for it, so it's happening. The deal is on.' Cundy was a defender at Spurs and had previously played for Chelsea.

Whether it's from my BBC background or just me being me, I said, 'Ollie, stay calm, show no emotion but ring the agent back and get the details. Let him tell you what's going on. Let's get the facts before you resign or do something stupid.' I always feel it's important to get the facts and find out both sides of any situation.

A contrite Ollie rang me back a few minutes later. 'Matty, you were spot on. I rang the agent and he's embarrassed. He called the wrong manager. It's Bristol City who are taking Cundy on loan. He rang me by mistake; he got his Bristol clubs mixed up.' Ollie thanked me and told me that was the very reason he'd wanted me as his assistant.

Resigning from your job should always be a final act, a last resort. There's no going back so you must be sure of the facts and be certain that you won't regret it.

Sometimes, though, we didn't see eye to eye over team methods. While we were away on our pre-season tour to the Isle of Man, Ollie told me he wanted the players to do sessions with a therapist called 'Queenie'. She was a dear old lady who Ollie had worked with before. Basically, she put the players to sleep and said positive things to them. This was a new concept at the time that alarmed me as I was old-school and thought strength and belief came from within. I know this sort of practice is part of modern-day elite sport. I told Ollie if that's what he wanted to do then it was fine, but I wasn't prepared to be part of the process.

On the eve of the first game of the season, Queenie came into the training ground at Fry's. After the session on the grass all the players went down to the gym. I told Ollie that I was staying in the office. He told me he wanted me to be part of it, but I declined. He was somewhat disappointed. I'd been in the office for about 15 minutes or so when my inquisitive nature got the better of me. I tiptoed down the stairs and peered through the window into the gym. All the lads, including Andy Tillson, Peter Beadle, Jamie Cureton and Ollie, were lying on their backs with their legs stretched out. The majority had their eyes closed, and those whose eyes were open seemed to be in a trance. It was a strange sight.

Of course, we won the next day, 1-0 at home to Peterborough United. Andy Gurney scored the winner. And our decent start continued with a 0-0 draw at Preston. Our move away from Twerton Park and the return to the Memorial Ground in Bristol had been put back due to a delay in the safety certificate being issued, so the first game back in Bristol after a ten-year exile in Bath was against Stockport County, who were managed by my mate Dave Jones. On the eve of the game, Queenie was on the edge of the training ground ahead of her second session. She said to me, 'You don't believe in me, do you Geoff?' I told her it wasn't personal, but I didn't really believe in what she was delivering. The pre-Stockport session was her last one. The players never spoke about it, but I got the impression that they weren't fans of it.

As I said, Ollie and I were a good combination. Ollie was fiery at times; he was instinctive and shot from hip. There were times when his confidence was up and down, but I got used to that. I was more reserved and considered. Ollie did tell me once that I should swear more often in my team talks! I very rarely swore and told him swearing should be done to have an effect. Repeated swearing becomes meaningless.

In my role as assistant manager, I remember I had my biggest ruck with Joe Jordan. Forget Mark Flatts and querying team selections, this was right up there! It was the Gloucestershire Cup, a pre-season game at Ashton Gate. To me the fixture was a waste of time. As a player it was meaningless, the fans got worked up about it because it was City v Rovers but there was nothing tangible at stake as far as I was concerned. The league and domestic cup meetings were all that mattered.

City's Junior Bent was flying down the left wing towards the Atyeo end; he was just in front of the technical areas. Ollie set off from ten yards away to tackle Junior. I could work it out in my head in an instant that Ollie wasn't going to make a legitimate tackle. To be fair to Ollie, he got there as soon as he could, but he sent Junior into orbit. Cor, he went several feet in the air and landed flat out on the deck. From my right, Joe raced forwards to the touchline with his right arm raised and wafting an imaginary card in the air – Italian style. All hell let loose on the pitch. I was flabbergasted that a manager was trying to get a fellow manager sent off.

I walked straight towards Joe and said, 'Are you having a laugh, what are you doing trying to get a fellow manager sent off?'

Joe snarled back, 'Ahhhhhh fuck off!' I was livid and went in nose to nose, firing in some expletives of my own. It was an F-bomb fest.

A minute or so later I returned to my technical area and the game resumed after the hoo-ha settled down. Then out of the corner of my right eye I could see a bright yellow colour and heard a voice: 'Excuse me, Geoff, can I have a word?' I turned to my right and a police officer was standing there, with the words 'Match Commander' on his fluorescent jacket. He added, 'Down the tunnel, if you don't mind.'

We walked a few paces down the tunnel, and he warned me that my behaviour had been out of order. He was at the back of the stand where the Rovers fans were located when Joe and I had our disagreement, and a load of Gasheads had surged forward, shouting their support and encouragement for me! He told me it must not happen again or I'd be in serious trouble. I asked him if he'd had the same conversation with Joe. He confirmed that he had. The respective management teams had a drink in Joe's office afterwards. To be honest, Ollie had to coax me into taking part as I was still annoyed about the shenanigans. It was a strained atmosphere, so we had one drink and left.

Being back in Bristol was brilliant for the club and, of course, the fans but the grass at the Mem was too long. The ground was shared with Bristol Rugby Club, so the grass was kept long to protect the pitch when the big boys were in action. It slowed down the pace of the game for the footballers. The surface made it difficult to deliver a slick-passing game, which was our ambition.

A few months into the season I realised that I wasn't enjoying the role as much as I thought I would. Ollie took most of the training sessions, which is what I'd expected, but he allowed Terry Connor to become more influential on the training ground. Worryingly to me, the style of play shifted from what Ollie had introduced to a more basic version. Ollie liked the lads to get the ball down and play a passing game. TC seemed intent on getting the ball into the final third as quickly as possible and to play for mistakes by the opposition.

The reality was that the job didn't stimulate me. I was fortunate to be able to compare and contrast with my previous job at the BBC. A lot of former players stay in the game and naturally evolve into coaching roles, so they don't really know any different. An assistant manager is a curious role. You're betwixt and between. You don't pick the team; you don't really give out the meaningful rollockings. You don't have genuine authority or control. Effectively, you're the middleman between the players and the manager. Maybe I was impetuous, but I decided to see if I could navigate my way back to the world of microphones and headphones.

In late November I met Mike Hapgood, my previous boss at Radio Bristol, for lunch. He thought I'd got in touch to chat about me doing a weekly show on Radio Bristol, a keep your hand in kind of thing! When I put my cards on the table and told him I'd be prepared to return on a full-time basis he was shocked and delighted in equal measure. He told me there wasn't anything he could do right away, but he'd be in touch if things changed.

Things did change at Rovers after a remarkable incident on the training ground. Ollie was taking a pattern of play session. This is crucial, fundamental work when the manager delivers his style of play, laying down how he expects the team to play. It was extremely thorough and painstaking and if it's done correctly every player knows their role and what's expected from them. It was bit stop-start but the nature of the beast meant it had to be that way. Just after Ollie had delivered some information and was about to restart the session, Terry Connor stepped in and blurted out, 'No, no, we're not doing that, this is what we're going to do,' and delivered some directions that were a complete contradiction to what the manager had laid down. Wow. I remember captain Andy Tillson looking at me and, with a 'what the hell is going on here' expression on his face, raised his eyebrows and shook his head. Afterwards Ollie asked me whether I felt that Terry had undermined him on the training round. I told him he had, and that it was an extraordinary thing to witness. Ollie rang Geoff Dunford, and Terry Connor was sacked later that day.

Being a man down, Ollie brought in Phil Bater. Phil, a former Rovers full-back, is an absolutely top bloke. The three of us saw the game in similar ways. We knew we had to multi-skill and get through to the end of the season. I volunteered to look after the reserves, who played during the week. I enjoyed working with younger players and also developing them as young men.

When I reverted to this role, I uncovered something that wasn't good. One of the trainees, Simon Teague, came to see me. He was anxious and upset. I assured him that whatever he had to tell me would be treated with total confidentiality. This was courageous from one so young. Simon claimed that Tony Gill, the youth coach, was playing the same 11 players or so most weeks. He had his favourites and the players who weren't playing on Saturday mornings had no way of showcasing their ability. It was unlikely, therefore, that they'd be taken on as professionals. If this was true, it was fundamentally wrong, as every youngster should have an equal opportunity to show what they can do.

I sought information from other trainees and researched the team sheets from the youth-team games. There was indeed a flawed practice. Tony Gill took exception to our inquiry. He also left the club.

I remember talking with two of the lads, Dave Hope and Nick de-Long, who hadn't been given a proper chance to show their ability. All I could do was apologise to them and their families. It was too late to right the wrong and they weren't offered professional deals. I'm glad to say that I struck up a strong friendship with both lads and they worked for me on a soccer school that I subsequently set up. Nick went on to have a very successful career in the forces. Both men are a credit to their parents. It still hurts me that they and others didn't get a fair crack of the whip.

This was a stark lesson for Ollie and me. We should have had a closer handle on the youth set-up. We shouldn't have assumed all was well with the group that worked on the opposite side of the training ground. It still rankles that the lesson was learned at a cost to others.

The reality was that we were bereft of both a reserve-team and youth-team coach, so I agreed to get involved in both areas of the football club. I enjoyed it, and Ollie and I spoke about me taking on the role of youth development officer. I was interested, so Ollie spoke with Geoff Dunford about me being formally appointed to the role. The vice-chairman agreed to it, but he said I'd have to take a drop in my salary – £35,000 would be reduced by £5,000. I'd not long moved house, and with two children at home there was no way that I'd agree to taking a reduction in wages. In an instant, the role of youth development officer lost its appeal. I hoped my future was back at the BBC.

I kept my head down and worked more with the reserves and youth teams and less with the first-team group. I'll never forget when the reserves had away games in the same week at Norwich and Ipswich, the journeys were made separately, which made it a very long few days. I was effectively treading water, and I knew more than ever that my future was back at the BBC.

Then in May of 1997, a year or so after leaving the BBC, Mike Hapgood rang me to say there was going to be some staff movement and he wanted to meet me to talk about a return as sports editor at Radio Bristol. He shmoozed me with lunch and we agreed the terms and conditions of my return. It was a huge relief.

It was time to tell Ollie. It was a difficult and emotional conversation for us both. I told him it just hadn't turned out as I'd hoped. I told him that I'd compared the level of job satisfaction and knew I had to return to the BBC. He pulled out all the stops and told me I could revert to working with the first team and that Phil Bater would look after the reserve and youth teams. He got upset and shed a few tears. Ollie tried his best to persuade me to stay put but he knew that when my mind was made up, it was made up.

Ollie was brilliant at this point. Outstanding. He told me not to tell anyone about the BBC until he had spoken with the board of directors. I don't know what he said to the hierarchy, but he rang me to tell me that the football club was going to give me a financial settlement on the two years that remained on my contract. So, I wanted to leave but Ollie had managed to get me a 'golden handshake' of £20,000. Incredible from my mate. The club said the payment was to acknowledge their appreciation for my service as both player and assistant manager.

When I spoke with Geoff Dunford to finalise my departure, he said that if he was in charge at Radio Bristol, he'd 'take me back tomorrow'. I don't know if he knew what Ollie knew or it was just an educated guess.

I have no regrets about having a go at football management. It didn't work out, but I was true to myself, and I wasn't left wondering what might have been had I not given it a go. It was educational, and on my return to the BBC it meant I could operate not just as a former player but also someone who'd experienced the cut and thrust of life in the technical area. Ollie and I never fell out and our friendship is as strong today as it has ever been.

I'm chuffed that I talked him into taking the Rovers job when he was offered the opportunity. Imagine football without Ian Holloway over the last 30 years or so. I'll always be grateful for how he looked after me when I decided to end my time in football.

So, it was back to BBC Radio Bristol as I dusted off the microphone and headphones.

Managing people – resignation is a last resort; think outside the box

Never offer or threaten to resign unless you're one million per cent sure it's the right thing to do. In a crisis remain calm and logical, establish the facts before you make any far-reaching decisions. When Ollie rang me about Jason Cundy's impending arrival, he was raging. Ollie was apoplectic and was going to tell Geoff Dunford to stick the job where the sun doesn't shine. The agent had rung the wrong Bristol club and subsequently left a voicemail on the wrong manager's phone. Thankfully, the crisis was averted after Ollie established the facts. Never make a big decision when your brain is simmering.

When you have a problem to solve, do not always follow logic. Is there a non-conventional solution? When Marcus Stewart was out of contract, he mentioned that if the club got him a sports car he'd possibly sign a new deal. The football club couldn't afford to buy the car, so Ollie sourced a sponsor. The upshot was that Stewie didn't pen a new deal. But he signed a document that ensured Rovers received a fee of over £1m when he joined Huddersfield Town. This was clever from Ollie. Always think outside the box.

Chapter 15
Back to the Future

THERE WERE two incredibly important issues that I had to resolve on my return to the BBC. One was the considerable technological challenge of familiarising myself with the digital age and a completely different broadcast system. The other issue was John Ward. I had to go to see John Ward.

John would have worked out that I knew he wasn't going to have his contract renewed at Rovers just over 12 months earlier. When Ollie appointed me as his assistant, the penny would have dropped. Awkward. We always had a harmonious relationship in my first spell at Radio Bristol. He did live chats with me during the second half of home matches. He confided in me on certain issues that couldn't be put in the public domain. I had to go to see John as he was now the manager of Bristol City.

I walked into John's office at Ashton Gate, and he was frosty. He wasn't aggressive, he was just distant. I asked him to let me explain what had happened. I told John it was impossible for me to tell him what was going on as I had to preserve levels of confidentiality with Rovers. Joining Ollie was an opportunity that I couldn't turn down. I told him the BBC didn't even know about it until the day before it was announced. To be fair to John, he gave me the benefit of any doubt and we shook hands. He said he was looking forward to working with me again. John was an exemplary professional and is a thoroughly decent guy. We still have a mutual respect and friendship all these years on.

The technological issue was much harder to resolve. When I left for Rovers in 1996, interviews were recorded on 'Uhers', a tape recorder that used reel-to-reel quarter-inch tape. They were the size of a small suitcase, and you carried it by using its shoulder strap. To edit the audio, you'd listen back and mark the start and end of the edit points with a chinagraph yellow pencil. You literally used a razor blade to cut out the unwanted section of quarter-inch tape and joined it back together with sticky tape. The tape was played into the radio desk on a reel-to-reel machine. Once the interview had been broadcast, you removed the reel and put the next one on the machine in readiness for when it was needed. 'Carts' were also used to play out audio. These were oversized cassettes. They had to be cleaned of audio at the end of a programme. On Saturdays there were dozens of them by the end of the show. If you were out on location, at a ground, for example, and wanted to feed an interview back to be played on the show, it came back in real time. So, a ten-minute interview took ten minutes to send.

The new digital system changed everything. Recordings were captured on a much smaller bit of equipment, something that fitted in your hand. The audio was recorded as tracks or files. An audio file could be saved into the broadcast system in seconds regardless of how long the piece of audio was. When it came to editing, it was done on a computer screen. The audio was a continuous wave and you marked in and out points where it needed to be edited. The saved audio file was uploaded to the computer play-out system and it played out through the studio desk by pressing a button.

The change in the system was exceptional. It was like moving into a space age. There was a new modern newsroom with brand-spanking-new studios. The only problem was, I had to learn how to use the new system!

Clare Tompkins, a broadcast assistant, was assigned to teach me how everything worked. Thank goodness 'Claret' was highly knowledgeable and very patient. Day one came and went, and I was absolutely none the wiser as to how the system worked by the time I went home. Day two was a similar scenario. Clare explained in simple terms, but it wasn't sinking in. It was like a different language. I remember going home that evening and thinking, *What have I done? I'm unemployable. Should I give my mate Ollie a ring?* Then in an amazing development on day three it made sense; it fell into place. I could edit, I could upload audio. I could do it. I was employable – it was quite a relief.

Having got to grips with the technology, there were a few changes of my own I wanted to introduce. I was determined to make the sports coverage the best it could be. There were restrictions in terms of the budget and the number of staff I had. It was all about getting the best out of people. I knew my strength was my team – the people who worked for me. If I had motivated, happy staff, then the sports output would flourish.

I was the sports editor, who took on the role of presenter. Alistair Durden and Matt Pick, two excellent operators, were sports journalists. I did the rotas, which covered the sports shifts – two a day from Monday to Friday. Clare wasn't a broadcaster but was an incredible organiser and fixer. The rest of the Saturday team were part-time and worked elsewhere during the week.

On my return in 1997 I recognised an anomaly in the sports coverage. This was really important, and I knew I had to address it. Historically, Phil Tottle and Colin Howlett were the voices of City and Rovers, respectively. They were both part-time and did commentary of all the games – home and away. They even travelled on the team bus to away games. I really liked Colin and Phil. Colin had covered 99 per cent of my Rovers appearances. They were both really good operators, but I didn't like the idea of one person being assigned to a club. It was too close, and I felt that when the big questions had to be asked there was too much familiarity. Furthermore, the full-time sports journalists employed by Radio Bristol were working Monday to Friday and not on Saturdays. This made no sense to me whatsoever. My plan was to have a pool of voices, the full-time journalists plus Colin and Phil, and I would allocate who I thought was the best person for the match on a game-by-game basis.

Around that time, Mike Kay replaced Colin as the Rovers voice. This was unrelated to my thinking and was entirely Colin's decision. Colin was a glorious man and a fine commentator. One of my great regrets is missing Colin's funeral. I was misinformed about where it was being held. By the time I realised the error of my ways it was too late to make the service. I visited his widow Janet and son Martyn a few days after. The Howletts are a great clan.

I took my masterplan to Jenny Lacey, who by this time had taken over as the station's managing editor. She backed me but was concerned that people wouldn't like change. I acknowledged that this would be the case, but I also knew it was the right call as the coverage would be enhanced.

On the very day that I'd scheduled back-to-back meetings with Phil and Mike, Jenny panicked and tried to convince me to let things remain the same. I didn't waver, so she agreed to let me flick the switch on my plan. I met Phil and Mike separately but five minutes apart, so they were unable to meet and confer between meetings. To be fair, they took it really well and understood my rationale.

Radio Bristol now had a squad of voices that would be selected on merit and availability – a bit like a football team. This change of dynamic was a huge step in modernising and improving the station's sports coverage. Without this change of strategy, the likes of Alistair Bruce-Ball, Alistair Durden, John Bennett, Matt Pick and many others wouldn't have had the opportunity to shine and develop.

The new plan was going well. There was a fresh sound to the coverage. Nobody was under pressure, but everyone knew they had to be on top of their game. The managers also had to deal with a new dynamic in terms of not having the same reporter at every game. A few fans expressed their displeasure as they were used to the regular voices, but I asked everyone to give it time and get back to me in six months if they felt the same way. No one did.

One person who struggled with it was Scott Davidson, the Bristol City chairman at the time. Scott was and remains a great bloke. He never declined an interview and saw real value in the coverage afforded by Radio Bristol. I'm delighted that decades on we have a mutual respect and genuine friendship. I implemented the plan at the start of the 1998/99 season. City got off to a poor start, winning just one of their opening 13 games. During the iffy spell, Scott rang me: 'Geoff, I really think that taking Phil Tottle off our games has had an adverse effect on the results. Could you put him back on every game please?'

I've always liked Scott, so I had to be diplomatic with my reply: 'Scott, you're a very intelligent man, who runs a hugely successful business. Do you really think the outcome of a football match is affected by who is behind the microphone for the local BBC radio station?'

Scott's response was short and sharp: 'Geoff, I'm sorry for wasting your time. When do you want me to come on the Friday phone-in?'

Scott was very accountable and transparent. He liked my Friday night phone-in, *Twentyman Talks Back*, and looked upon it as a valuable way of communicating with the fanbase. He never ducked a question or subject. It's great that he's involved with the Former Players' Association and the Heritage and Archive Trust. Scott is a Top Man.

Another thing I introduced was that football phone-in on a Friday evening. *Twentyman Talks Back* was essential listening for football fans. Before social media it was the way fans communicated with their local radio station. Some of the callers, such as 'Terry from Shirehampton', became real Bristol characters through their appearances on the show. Managers and club officials listened to and appeared on the programme.

The recurring question that people used to ask me when I was out and about was, 'Geoff, how do you put up with those callers? They talk absolute rubbish!' The reality was that the callers were voicing their own opinions, it was what they thought. They were passionate enough to call in. I always respected that, because if we all thought and said the same things, then life would be bland.

As the sports editor I thought it was crucial to make my team feel valued and to invest in them both personally and professionally. Feedback was crucial. Commentary was the most important skill the guys had. I used to take a 30-minute chunk out of their commentaries and provide feedback in one-to-one sessions. How often do you mention the score? What colours are the teams wearing? Which end of the ground is our team attacking? Where's the ball on the pitch? How long has been played? These are the essential basics of radio commentary. It's a blank canvas on the easel, and your eyes, ears and voice provide the paintbrush. I'd bring in commentary experts such as Ron Jones, an outstanding commentator on BBC Radio 5 Live, and a commentary guru and predecessor of mine, Rob Nothman, for individual sessions. Ron and Rob were experts in the skill. This made everyone a better commentator, but the staff felt valued and invested in. Also, I never denied anyone a request for time off. Being told you can't be off when you need to be is both frustrating and annoying. It's not rocket science, but happy staff who feel valued will go the extra mile.

As well as managing your staff, another skill is managing upwards – managing your boss. One such example occurred when I'd been back at the BBC a couple of years and local 'rivals' HTV contacted me to see if I'd be interested in becoming the face of their sports coverage. I was happy at the BBC, but I did the honourable thing and told Jenny Lacey about their interest. I was just letting her know, not delivering an ultimatum. My boss told me she didn't want me to talk to HTV, so she asked me to give her some time to enable her to consult her boss.

Around that time, Des Lynam had left the BBC for ITV. I'm not putting myself on that level, I hasten to add, but I think the BBC felt vulnerable, even locally in Bristol. Jenny came back to me with an improved package, including a substantial rise and a weekly Friday slot on *Points West*, the regional BBC TV programme. I didn't meet HTV, so I have no idea what they had to offer. If I'm honest, I never wanted to leave. I had a great team, and I was proud to work for the Corporation.

Not long after this episode, Jenny rang me and put a proposition to me that would have a huge effect on my career and, to be specific, my presentation skills. I'm a great believer in stepping out of your comfort zone, and Jenny certainly presented such an opportunity. She asked whether I'd consider presenting the breakfast show the following week with Rachel Burden.

Rachel, who has presented the breakfast show on 5 Live for decades, co-presented the show with Nigel Dando. Nigel, a highly respected former journalist at the *Bristol Evening Post* and who'd made a great transition into the world of radio, was having a week off. My immediate instinct was to accept. Apart from getting up at stupid o'clock, there was huge kudos to presenting the station's flagship programme. It was also very flattering to follow in the footsteps of the great Roger Bennett. It was a huge compliment from the boss, who was a great presenter in her own right before she moved into management. Significantly, it was the first time that I'd stepped out of the relative comfort zone of presenting my core subject – sport. I have no doubts that moving into general programmes made me a better interviewer and more accomplished presenter.

So, to the Monday morning and, after getting up at 4.15am, it was *Breakfast with Rachel Burden and Geoff Twentyman*. Dual presentation basically works with one presenter starting off the first hour and you alternate the stories and items between you throughout the hour. Then the other presenter starts the second hour, etc.

Rachel was a dream to work with and nursed me through the three-hour all-spoken programme. I remember vividly on the first show, during the eight o'clock news with the audience at its peak, Rachel said, 'Are you okay to interview Liam Fox?' I confirmed it was fine, but my heart started to thump as I opened the running order and read the script to myself. These really were uncharted waters. At the time I didn't have a big interest in politics, although that did change in the ensuing years. It's not about having geek knowledge, but you must have a basic understanding.

Dr Liam Fox was the local MP for North Somerset. He was also chairman of the Conservative Party, who'd had a bad weekend in the European elections. The introduction into the interview was written by the programme producer but the questions were devised by the presenter. Keeping as calm as I could, thankfully I had a flash of inspiration. Rather than think of him as a politician who'd had a bad result, I thought of him as a football manager who'd had a bad weekend results-wise. So, I asked him the same questions that I'd ask a manager.

'What's your reaction to the European election results?'

'What's your take on how the Conservatives have done?'

'Are there any reasons why you've underperformed at the polls?'

I remember reading somewhere that there could be a Cabinet reshuffle, so my last question was, 'Is there going to be a Cabinet reshuffle?'

Job done and breathe. I got through it, and I enjoyed being out of my comfort zone. Rachel was a real star, and I'm so chuffed she's enjoying a hugely successful career. When she arrived from BBC Suffolk her football hero was Marcus Stewart from his Ipswich Town days. She couldn't believe I played in the same Rovers team as him! I took her to meet her hero. She was overjoyed when she met Marcus and blushed delightfully.

I covered on the breakfast show for a few years and always did my phone-in show on a Friday. This meant I was on air at 6am and then at 6pm. Doing time checks on the phone-in was confusing!

My role as a deputy presenter extended to include the afternoon drivetime show between 4pm and 7pm, which was far more sociable.

When Ben Prater, another great guy and talented, natural presenter, left the station for BBC Radio Wiltshire, I threw my hat in the ring to take on the slot on a full-time basis. Tim Pemberton, who was in charge of the station, offered me the gig as long as I kept doing Saturday afternoons. I agreed to a six-day working week but relinquished the role of sports editor as there were only so many hours in a working week.

Drive was a great programme to present – news, current affairs, weather, sport, travel – all topics and subject matter to get my teeth into. My producer, Lucy Tegg, came up with an incredibly popular interactive challenge for the audience called 'Geoff's Quest'. During the show I gave out three clues for a place in the region. The audience loved it and would phone in or get in touch by social media to guess the location. Sometimes we'd have over 120 entries, which for local radio was incredible.

I really enjoyed interviewing people from different walks of life. I have an inquisitive mind and was very attentive to what a guest said in response to my questions. Everyone has a tale to tell. One of the slightly stranger interviews was when I interviewed Matthew Barzun, the US ambassador to the UK. The Americans were on a bit of a charm offensive and had contacted various local radio stations across the country. The day before Matthew was due on the show his security team visited the radio station to check windows, doors and access to and from the studios. They really were the Men in Black.

On the day of his visit, Matthew travelled from North Somerset, but he couldn't come via the iconic Clifton Suspension Bridge, as his armoured car was too heavy! Police outriders were parked outside the BBC an hour before his arrival. Matthew was a great guest as he enlightened us about President Barack Obama. He'd done his homework on me, as he mentioned his favourite team was Liverpool and mentioned my dad. During the interview, I noticed there was a security guard donning a black coat in the operations area outside the studio. After the show we had a debrief and my producer, Jackie Coles, told me that she'd asked him if he was armed. He opened his coat to reveal a holster with a handgun. Hilarious. Jackie was a great producer and a real joy to work with.

Another amazing chat on *Drive* was in 2012 with a very special lady called Michelle Bresnahan, who'd lost her 16-year-old son Ryan to meningitis. In his memory they were attempting to raise a million pounds for Meningitis UK. They'd reached a significant landmark in the fundraising. They were a quarter of the way to their target and Michelle had come on to give it some well-deserved publicity. It was a phone chat, and she was talking openly and with real strength about her son. In sensitive circumstances as a presenter, you must gauge the strength of the guest as to how far you can probe with your questions. I felt Michelle was strong enough, so I took a breath and asked a simple but important question: 'Tell me about Ryan, what was he like?'

There was a pause, a silence, then she replied with genuine pride and total love in her voice, 'Oh Geoff, he was amazing. You'd have loved him. He loved his football, he loved rugby. He loved sport, you'd have loved him.' I thought, *Wow!* It was one of those moments that reminded me what a privilege my job was. It was a remarkable conversation. In the tragic circumstances, Michelle was so courageous, so inspirational. It remains one of the most memorable conversations I ever had on the radio.

I hosted political debates with the candidates for all ten constituency seats in the Radio Bristol broadcast area. Three of these were in front of a live audience. In the run-up to the general election in 2015 I did separate live interviews with the three main party leaders: David Cameron, Ed Miliband and Nick Clegg.

I was really enjoying the *Drive* show when an unexpected curveball came my way, and I was happy to catch it. Jess Rudkin was appointed as the new manging editor. I liked Jess. She was ambitious, creative and thought outside the box. She had a straight-to-the-point approach to most things and got things done. A few weeks after her appointment she called me into her office for a chat. Jess was complimentary about *Drive*, but she wanted me to deliver an important project. As a Big City station Jess wanted Radio Bristol to have a sports show each weekday evening. She wanted me to produce and present it. In simple terms she wanted me to make it happen. I agreed to do it and Jess asked me to go away and draft my proposal. This was an exciting opportunity.

The obvious and easy option was to do a general sports show every evening. This would gravitate towards football and rugby. The easiest option is rarely the right one. This was like when I had a free kick after 87 minutes of the Bristol derby on New Year's Day in 1987, and I had to decide whether to pass the ball back and get a point or stick it in the mixer and see what happened. Again, I was going to have some fun with this one.

Bristol and its surrounding area is blessed to have a massive variety of sports and leisure activities. This was Radio Bristol's opportunity to do it justice and showcase it. I thought outside the box and made the following proposal for an hour-long magazine programme each evening at 6pm:

Monday – The Sound of the City. A Bristol City-themed show.

Tuesday – The Scrum. All things rugby, from club rugby to international action.

Wednesday – The Sports Store. Grassroots sport; anything and everything away from football and rugby.

Thursday – Having a Gas. A Bristol Rovers-themed show.

Friday – Friday Night Sport. A preview of the weekend's action.

Jess was thrilled with the proposal. She questioned the duration of an hour – whether it was sustainable. I assured her it was. She gave it the green light. The press officers at the respective football and rugby clubs were great and bought into it from day one. I did emphasise that the programmes weren't an extension of the clubs' PR operation. I pointed out that the clubs' hierarchy would be held to account when it was appropriate.

The clubs played ball and were happy to put up their A-listers for live studio interviews. The first guest on the City show was Mark Ashton, the newly appointed chief operating officer. Bristol Rugby put up star winger Tom Varndell – only one player had scored more tries in the Premiership. The first Rovers guest was Lee Mansell, who scored the winning penalty at Wembley when Rovers were promoted back to the Football League. The shows worked from day one.

My favourite edition of *Having a Gas* was when Chris Lines, Stuart Sinclair and Tom Lockyer were all live in the studio. Linesy and Sincs had been released by the club, and Locks was leaving on a free transfer as his contract had expired. All too often footballers leave a club and they never get the opportunity to say goodbye.

I invited them in and they were delighted to come on the show and reminisce and talk about their time in the blue and white quarters. They were top drawer, were relaxed and there was some great banter and tales. They got the send-off they deserved. All three of them are Top Men.

Tom had rung me a couple of weeks earlier when he was on his way to his final home appearance. Only he knew it was his final one! The club hadn't announced on their media channels that this was his last game at the Memorial Stadium. I was on air but found an appropriate window to call him back. He asked me to say on air that this was his last home game; he wanted the fans to know. I announced it on the show at 2pm and the Rovers fans on their way to and around the ground were made aware of the situation. He got a great send-off. The club wasn't best pleased, but had they done their job properly it would never have been an issue. If you snooze you lose. Locks is a great guy. His recent health issue when playing for Luton was scary, and I wish him good health and happiness going forward.

The Sound of the City in February 2022 to mark the 'Ashton Gate Eight' was a show I'll always remember. It was approaching the 40th anniversary of when eight Bristol City players tore up their contracts to ensure the football club didn't go out of business. City had never treated the men with the respect that they deserved but, thanks to the efforts of Scott Davidson and Neil Palmer – yes, my partner in crime on this book – the process of respect, thanks, understanding and appreciation started for real around this time.

I was chuffed with the show. A colleague, Tom Ryan, who's a radio genius, produced a wonderful opening montage using powerful audio from our archives. Two of the players, Trevor Tainton and Julian Marshall, came on the phone together and spoke from the heart. The BBC commentator Jonathan Pearce, who's a passionate City fan, covered the story at the time for Radio Bristol. He delivered an exceptional account of what had happened. The hair stood up on the back of my neck listening to JP. Long-standing City fan, Tom Hopegood, and other Reds came on to share their memories. Finally, Scott Davidson joined me from an airport on the other side of the world. It was the perfect ending to a programme that I remain immensely proud of.

My favourite edition of *The Scrum* was when Bristol's Callum Sheedy co-presented the programme. This was seriously out of his comfort zone, but he did a stellar job. He had to introduce pre-recorded features and chat with live guests. He got his team-mates Harry Randall and Dan Thomas on, who were great value. I think he preferred taking conversions with the last kick of the game to win a match, but kudos to 'Sheeds' for giving it a go. Top Man.

These were programmes for the fans, who were given a platform to express their thoughts. The popularity of the shows was incredible. Amazingly, some weeks *The Sound of the City* or *Having a Gas* were the most listened to shows on the sports section on BBC Sounds, beating Five Live productions, other podcasts and local radio shows. *The Scrum* would also frequently top the rugby charts.

This told me two things. The products were good, and sport is exceptionally important to Bristolians. I'll always be proud of the daily sport programmes. On leaving the BBC, my legacy was giving the supporters and sports fans something they enjoyed and, more importantly, deserved.

Managing people – square pegs in square holes

Be forensic when you assess your staff's abilities and your business needs. I'm not saying people can't and won't develop in different directions but as a rule of thumb play to your strengths and employ people in the best roles.

When Jess Rudkin took over at Radio Bristol she knew where she wanted me to operate. I was presenting the drivetime show, but she planned to move me back to sport on a full-time basis. To entice me she had a plan to have a daily sports show. She told me I was the only person on the station who could deliver it. That was clever management. She empowered me to deliver it. Square pegs, square holes.

Chapter 16

At the Coal Face

BECAUSE SOMEONE excels at sport, manages a football or rugby club, is in charge of a political party or for that matter runs the country, it doesn't make them extra special. Everyone has a story to tell or has information to impart. I treated them all the same. There was never a 'wow' factor. It's a simple process: ask the questions and listen to the answers. Often, if you listen closely enough, your next planned question may be replaced by something more pertinent. If the interviewee doesn't answer the question, ask the question again. Probe, always be inquisitive. You're asking the questions for your audience, not for yourself.

For nigh on three decades, I had an amazing job. I met some fantastic people; I was present at some incredible occasions. I shared the emotions of the highs and lows as dreams were realised and hearts broken. Presenting the sport on BBC Radio Bristol and BBC Somerset was a privilege. I also loved my time on the breakfast and drivetime shows.

I had a few important principles and practices. I'd never said anything on the radio about a club owner, a manager, a director of rugby or a player that I wouldn't say to their face. They may not like it, but I'd happily explain it if I needed to. It was never in my remit to suggest a football manager should be sacked. The fans on a phone can demand change, but it was my job to challenge the caller on what they said. My loyalty was to my audience – they're a constant. Owners, managers and players come and go. My credibility with my listeners was paramount.

I never got too close to a manager. Inevitably they'd hit rocky times. If results were poor, then I'd have to make observations and offer constructive criticism. I'd never leave myself open to accusations of being two-faced. This was hard as some of the 23 City managers and 22 Rovers bosses during my time at Radio Bristol were top guys and I really liked them.

Danny Wilson was a brilliant interviewee during his time at City. Danny was totally transparent, always meeting me with a grin and an 'alright, pal'. He was open and honest and was very hospitable. We played against each other when he was at Sheffield Wednesday, which meant there was a mutual respect. It was interesting watching Danny on the training ground as he improved his players. Small-sided games evolved from 'all-in' (no limit on the number of touches) to two touches and on occasions just one touch. As the players improved on the training ground it was transferred to Saturday afternoons. Danny was very relaxed. Some callers used to criticise him because he stood and leaned against the dugout during games. That was Danny's way, he didn't rant and rave. A classy guy. I just wish he'd had Leroy Lita on the bench for the Brighton play-off final in Cardiff. I received a brilliant message from Danny when I left the BBC. Danny Wilson is a Top Man.

I first met Gary Johnson when he took over at Yeovil. We just clicked. I have total admiration for the way he took Yeovil to the Championship and City to the Championship play-off final. He was a no-nonsense manager who loved dropping self-titled 'hand grenades' in the dressing room. Gary was fun to interview and was prone to a bit of banter. He was in the studio once and I told him we had two callers on the line, and he blurted out that his presence had doubled my usual audience! I was chuffed to attend Gary's 60th birthday party, although he's gutted that I'm younger than he is. One of my hardest chats was when Gary left City. I'll share that one shortly.

Former City boss Sean O'Driscoll was a strange one. I remember doing a sit-down chat with him for *Points West* on TV. It was produced in a way that the room was blacked out and we were each under a bright spotlight. Very arty! It made a good visual effect on the screen, but it was hard to establish eye contact with Sean as the room was so dark and the lights were so bright! I found it staggering when Sean told me he didn't ever look at the league table. He was shocked when I asked him why. He emphasised his stance by asking me why he should look at the table. I told him it was the barometer that either kept him in a job or not. He also told me he hated three o'clock. I used the expression 'gladiatorial time'. Again, he wasn't in favour of pitting his wits against the guy in the opposing technical area. I asked him what he actually liked about football management, and he told me it was being on the training ground from Monday to Friday. It was a good chat and made for a healthy debate among the City fanbase.

At Rovers, Darrell Clarke was a great interviewee. DC oozed honesty and passion. I'd never heard of him until he arrived at Rovers as John Ward's assistant. Darrell was put in charge for the last seven games of the 2013/14 season and was distraught at being the manager when The Gas dropped into the Conference. The following Friday my phone-in was dedicated to the Rovers' demise. The chairman, Nick Higgs, 'wasn't available' to come into the studio so the club sent Darrell to face my cross-examination and to take calls from the fans. DC, the sacrificial lamb, was awesome. His passion for the club and the fans was powerful. He promised a return to the Football League or, at the very least, a group of players who'd give everything to the cause. The fans loved him for his honesty and his passion, and they were 100 per cent behind him. His words weren't a hollow promise, as Darrell delivered a squad that cared, a talented group who secured back-to-back promotions. He was a man of the people and connected passionately with the Gasheads. We've kept in touch since he left Rovers and I really hope that he's successful at his new club Barnsley.

Mark McGhee was a strange guy. I always felt he thought he was too good to manage Bristol Rovers. But he wasn't. I experienced something unique during his unspectacular tenure. When he was appointed, I asked the questions at the press conference, which was broadcast live on Radio Bristol. I remember him outlining his plan: keep Rovers in League Two, recruit well in the summer and aim to be in the play-offs, at least, the following season. I liked the cut of his jib. They were memorable words. McGhee kept Rovers up. He recruited in the summer.

Fast forward to a third of the way through the following season. Rovers were struggling and were too near the bottom of League Two for comfort. I went to see him on a Thursday to record a routine chat ahead of the upcoming game. There were a few other reporters present as we gathered round the Rovers manager. I thought it was a fair question: 'In light of what you said at the press conference when you were appointed, how disappointed are you with your league position?' He glared at me and asked me to qualify what I meant. I recited what I was sure he'd said to me on day one.

His glare intensified: 'I bet you £100 that's not what I said.' I paused for a few seconds to digest what he'd just said. I told him in no uncertain terms that I was not in the practice of placing bets with football managers. I told him I'd seen a lot of managers come and go and no one had ever been so ridiculous as to offer me a bet. He was livid and came back for more. He insisted that if I was so sure of myself then I should take the bet. Less experienced people may have crumbled, but his attempt to intimidate me was a waste of time. I'd played against McGhee when he came on as a sub for Newcastle at St James' Park. The watching journalists, who'd become uninvited spectators to an uncomfortable exchange, were very uneasy. I remained composed and told him that I'd go back to the BBC and would send him a copy of the press conference from the day he was appointed. I told him I'd return that day and offer an unreserved apology if I'd misquoted him in my question. We then recorded our pre-match preview chat.

Back at base, I went into the archives and was relieved, but not surprised, when I listened to the press conference: 'I want to keep Rovers in League Two, we'll recruit well in the summer and the aim then is to be at least in the play-offs next season.' I copied the press conference on to a CD, state of the art at the time, and posted it to him with a covering letter. I never heard a word back from him, not a syllable. I don't think I ever saw him again. He was sacked in December 2012 with Rovers second-bottom of the Football League.

Benny Lennartsson was brought in by City chairman Scott Davidson to work alongside John Ward. However, the Swede was given ultimate control as he picked the team. John was squeezed out and left City months after getting them promoted into the second tier. City struggled under Benny. At the time I was presenting the Saturday afternoon sports show on Radio Bristol as well as a football phone-in on Friday evenings. I did a football feature on Fridays on *Points West*. I also answered the letters in the *Green 'Un*, the Saturday evening Bristol sports paper. Around that time a listener wrote to the Director General of the BBC and complained that I had a monopoly on football coverage in the region! For some reason, the correspondent thought it was wrong. Nothing ever came of the complaint!

Benny was under siege after some heavy defeats. It was never my role to say a manager should be sacked. However, you can only play devil's advocate for so long. My credibility with the fanbase was crucial and ultimately it was impossible to defend the indefensible. I said and wrote some strong things about the fans deserving better and the need for results to improve asap.

One Thursday I walked into the training ground at Abbot's Leigh and Benny was waiting for me. He was wearing his trademark red cap. 'Can I speak with you?' he said. I thought, *Here we go*, as I walked towards him. 'I read your comments. I've heard about what you say on the radio and the television.'

I countered, 'Yes, and what's your problem?'

I was staggered by his next line: 'You are xenophobic. You criticise me because I am not English.' Wow. I struggled to remain composed. Here was a rookie coach making a dog's dinner of a job that he probably should never have had in the first place, accusing me of being xenophobic.

'Benny, you're lucky I've been restrained for a while, but don't you make such a dreadful accusation. You're out of order. To be honest, I think you're a shit coach, and if you don't sort things out soon, you'll be history. That's not an opinion of someone who's xenophobic, it's the assessment of a former footballer who made over 400 first-team appearances.'

I may have been over the top, but I felt violated, and I wasn't happy, clearly. Benny didn't last long.

The final two City and Rovers managers who I interviewed were challenging and stimulating. They were strong personalities and I was genuinely excited by their arrival. Nigel Pearson and Joe Barton were both appointed on 22 February 2021. I interviewed them at the beginning and end of the season and there was a catch-up at the midway point of the campaign.

Nigel arrived with a reputation for being feisty and difficult. This was a million miles from the truth. He really values local radio and the coverage it provides. But what you had to do with the big man was ask decent questions, strong questions. Anything that didn't stimulate his brain was worthless and was treated appropriately. He gave some of the other local journalists a tough time but when you've marked each other on corners I guess the dynamic is different. It was simple with Nigel – ask good questions and you got good answers. I was in the tunnel area at Ashton Gate before a game against Birmingham when I'd nipped down to see my mate Andy Reece, who's the Blues' kit man, and Nigel came over to say hello.

> NP: 'You're interviewing the chief exec [Richard Gould] aren't you, at two o'clock?'
>
> GT: 'Yes, Nige, I'm looking forward to it.'
>
> NP: 'Make sure you ask him the right questions, don't give him an easy ride … oh, hang on … why am I saying this? You always ask the tough questions, always.'

This was praise indeed. We had a highly valued exchange of texts when he left the City. I always enjoyed interviewing Nigel. I hope he gets another job, as football is a better product with Nigel Pearson in the mix.

'Always judge people as you find them yourself.' That was something Mum taught me. I know Joe Barton arrived at Rovers with baggage and his appointment split the fanbase, but Joe was brilliant with me during his time at Rovers. I always call him Joe after asking him what he preferred, Joey or Joe. Like Nigel Pearson, Joe was cliché-free and liked to be tested. He has an active mind, strong opinions and he welcomed a tough question. He showed me the utmost respect and was aware of my Rovers history as well as Dad's Liverpool connections.

Not long before I met Joe for the first time, he'd publicly criticised both of his predecessors. He said Ben Garner and Paul Tisdale shouldn't be allowed to manage ever again. In typical Joe Barton style, he didn't hold back as he tore into them. I did some research and number crunching before our first chat. Sometimes research is king.

> GT (looking JB in the eye): 'Joe, I don't want to go into the whys and the wherefores of your comments about your predecessors, but do you not regret what you said about two fellow managers?'
>
> JB (looking GT in the eye): 'No Geoff, not at all, they both left this football club in a mess, a total mess. I have no regrets whatsoever.'
>
> GT: 'But Joe, I've worked out the points per game ratio for the three of you and yours is the worst. You have fewer points than both of them …'

Joe took the supplementary on the chin. He looked at me for a second, had a little bit of a head wobble, then he told me that his record was a direct consequence of what he'd inherited. We then talked about referees, and I made the point that he'd developed a habit of blaming refs when his side lost. I explained my theory that good relationships with the officials will get you the majority of 50/50 decisions. It's called human nature. To be fair to Joe he accepted my point and seemed to ease off the men in the middle.

He enjoyed talking about his time at Marseille when I asked 'what was that French accent all about?' Joe was always good value. You had to listen intently to his answers as he'd invariably give you a new line of enquiry. It was a fascinating experience, one that I found very stimulating.

When Rovers beat Scunthorpe 7-0 to clinch promotion on the final day of the 2021/22 season, I knew I had to get Joe on one of the two final editions of *Having a Gas*. The first week was 'a week off', so that wasn't possible. The following week Joe was in Turkey on a family holiday, but he agreed to do a live chat on the show. When we connected the call, the signal was crystal clear. Joe was fresh off the golf course, sat with a beer, raring to go. He told me he'd stay on the call as long as I needed him.

Andy Downie, the Rovers press officer, said to me before the chat, 'I don't know what it is with you. Joe has declined every interview request from national broadcasters, the broadsheet journalists. He said no to everyone, except you.'

I always wanted to conduct a full chat with Joe. What made him tick, everything about him. His past, his future, his philosophies, the lot. Unfortunately, as he was the subject of active court cases for a lot of his time in charge at Rovers, that kind of interview had to be avoided. I didn't fancy being charged with contempt of court. Some broadcast laws are complicated, others are obvious.

Away from the managers, Steve Lansdown was an 'A-lister' when it came to interviews. As the owner of Bristol City, Steve never declined an interview request and always took a fair question on the chin. He's done an incredible job for Bristol City, Bristol Rugby and sport in Bristol. I dread to think where City would be without Steve Lansdown.

I used to enjoy the big interviews, holding people to account. It was a privileged job and I had to ask the questions the supporters would ask themselves if they could. It was imperative not to let the audience down. The sacking, and to a lesser extent the appointment, of a football manager caused the biggest interest as emotions and opinions were stirred.

Gary Johnson left City 'by mutual consent' in 2010. I knew there had been an incident in the away dressing room at Plymouth two nights before his departure was announced. One of the players who was in the dressing room told me there had been a serious incident at half-time between Gary Johnson and Ivan Sproule. I trusted my source implicitly. When managers leave football clubs they usually disappear into the ether. On the Thursday after the game at Home Park, City announced that Gary was leaving, and the club held a press conference. Gary Johnson and Steve Lansdown were on the top table. Radio Bristol broadcast the press conference live and I led proceedings. My first question was a full toss to Steve – I asked him to assess the job Gary had done at the football club. He hit it for six and delivered a well-deserved, glowing tribute. Then the conversation got more serious as I locked eyes with the owner. This wasn't easy. As you've been reading, I had and have a huge regard for Gary. The overriding fact was that I had a job to do. I had to be professional.

> GT: 'Stephen, did anything happen at Home Park on Tuesday that's brought about the decision for Gary to leave?'
>
> SL: 'No, Geoff, nothing happened at all.'
>
> GT: 'Okay, did anything happen at half-time in the away dressing room at Home Park on Tuesday that brought about the decision for Gary to leave?'
>
> SL: 'No, Geoff, nothing happened at all.'

At that point I moved the conversation on as it was clear that Steve wasn't going to tell me anything. It was important that I asked the question as the internet was awash with rumour and counter-rumour, some of which was accurate. It was also important for me to maintain a professional relationship with Steve Lansdown, so I didn't cross the proverbial line. Both men shook my hand after the press conference. Both men knew that I knew. Another example of staying true to yourself.

I was at Scotty Murray's evening wedding reception at Mendip Spring Golf Club in North Somerset. City striker Tony Thorpe was looking across the room at me. I noticed it repeatedly. We'd never met before, so I went over to say hello. His opening gambit was that he'd heard that I'd criticised him on the radio. He was frosty.

Hearing something through a third party is always an interesting one. Has their account been accurate? Have they reported it in its entirety? Has the context been correct? For clarity, I shared my thoughts on the matter and what I'd said, which was that if his application and attitude matched his ability, he'd be tearing it up at City or even playing at a higher level. I told him it was constructive criticism, and it should be taken in a positive way. 'Thorpey' is a great bloke and he mulled over what I'd said and admitted, or half-admitted, that I made sense, or some sense. I admired him for raising the issue. A genuine mutual respect was born that night.

I'm not taking any credit for what happened, but Thorpey definitely got his head down and his game was transformed. I think Danny Wilson helped his game and he played with a smile on his face as well as a determined commitment. His natural ability shone through. He was top drawer.

I had no qualms about telling him what I'd said on the radio. I had to back myself. 'Fletch', as he's also known, is a great bloke. I liked his 'cheeky chappie' confident approach. Not long afterwards we played golf at Chipping Sodbury. He was decent with a golf club in his hands too. I was thrilled to record a chat with him for *The Sound of the City* last year when he was back at Ashton Gate as a guest of the excellent Former Players' Association. Thorpey is a Top Man.

It's always great to chat directly with a player or manager about things that have come up from my radio show, but sometimes these incidents can appear when you don't expect it, and one Saturday afternoon springs to mind. City had conceded another late goal and drew 1-1 at home. I was presenting the show live from Ashton Gate and fans were calling in to moan about 'another two points dropped, Geoff … we can't see a game out, Geoff … we've dropped 14 points from winning positions, Geoff …' I felt my mobile phone vibrate in my pocket. As I maintained the conversation on air with a dissatisfied City fan, I retrieved my phone to see the caller was Bradley Orr. Just 25 minutes earlier,

Bradley had traipsed off down the tunnel at Ashton Gate in the No.2 shirt. I sent him a text.

GT: 'Are you ok m8?'

BO: 'Yes m8, I wanna come on the show and talk with you.'

These were uncharted waters. All player interviews were supposed to be sanctioned by the football club, but this wasn't a time for protocols.

GT: 'Are you sure about this?'

BO: 'Yes, defo m8.'

Minutes later Bradley Orr was live on the show talking with real passion. He explained that he'd been listening to the show in his car before he left for home, and he felt compelled to ring in. It was powerful radio and incredible accountability from Bradley. I had to make the point that some of the criticisms were justified. Bradley accepted this but it was clear that he cared passionately about the shirt he wore, he loved playing for the City. Bradley Orr is an absolute Top Man.

Some months later the same Bradley Orr and a few other players did collaborate to give me an extraordinary drivetime programme. It was a Friday, and four City players were due in court after a punch-up with some bouncers at a nightclub in Bristol. The intel was that the most David Partridge, Bradley Orr, Steve Brooker and Scott Brown would get was a suspended sentence. In terms of the programme running order, it was unlikely to be the lead story. Then an hour before going on air, news came through that three of the quartet had been sent to prison. Partridge, Orr and Brooker were to serve custodial sentences and Brown was given community service. Wow!

Suddenly this was a massive story, and the newsroom was on high alert as we chased guests from any and every angle to talk with me live on air. It was exciting and exhilarating to cover the story but, within the excitement, it was imperative to be professional, impartial and considered.

Broadcasting at the big venues was always enjoyable and a privilege. Wembley – old and new – Twickenham, The Principality, Villa Park when Yeovil beat Stevenage to win the FA Trophy will all live long in the memory. City's wins over Hartlepool and Crystal Palace in play-off semi-finals were breathtaking occasions. Similarly, Rovers beating Dagenham & Redbridge in added time and Scunthorpe 7-0 to gain promotion were equally spellbinding. The Rec was an amazing place to be in May 2015 when Bath hammered Leicester in the rugby union play-off semi-final. Matt Banahan scored a hat-trick as Bath ran in seven tries. Some days it all clicks in sport, and that was such an occasion for Bath.

Before the general election in 2015, when I chatted with the three main party leaders separately on Radio Bristol, David Cameron, Nick Clegg and Ed Miliband were well trained and machine-like in their knowledge and delivery on national issues. I have no political persuasion but I did enjoy bringing a local issue to Prime Minister Cameron's attention. Protocol deems that I called him Mr Prime Minister or Mr Cameron. David or Dave were off limits. After he'd talked about unemployment figures, the reason why he'd been made available, I asked Mr Cameron if we could talk about the NHS. 'Of course we can,' he replied.

> GT: 'Is the Conservative Party running down the NHS? There's a perception that so much of it is being contracted out to private companies.'

> PM: 'Not at all, Geoff. That could not be further from the truth. We are investing millions in the NHS. Here in Bristol you have one of our super hospitals.'
>
> GT: 'Southmead?'
>
> PM: 'Yes, Southmead.'
>
> GT: 'Super hospital is a bit of a misnomer though, isn't it Mr Prime Minister?'
>
> PM: 'What do you mean?'
>
> GT: 'Well, last week I had a lady, in tears, on this show. Her mother had spent 12 hours on a trolley outside A&E at Southmead, the super hospital, before she was treated.'
>
> PM: 'Well that's not right, Geoff, that shouldn't have happened.'
>
> GT: 'I agree, Mr Prime Minister, and I'm sure that everyone listening to our conversation agrees it's not right.'

The PM played his get-out-of-jail-free card: 'I'll tell you what I'll do, Geoff. I'll get this situation investigated and I'll get back to you by email as to what happened, and I'll find out what measures have been taken to ensure there's no repeat.'

The email didn't drop into my inbox.

Away from the arduous world of politics, George Ezra was performing in Bristol one evening. We managed to get him on the show. He was walking along the beautiful waterfront and chatted on his phone. He was a delight, very natural and totally engaging. We talked about how he'd evolved through *BBC Introducing*, which he was delighted to talk about. He was great value.

There have also been some really dark stories to cover over the years. In 2015, when I was presenting the drivetime show, I had to cover, on an almost daily basis for a long time, the murder of Bristol teenager Becky Watts. This was truly dreadful; her mutilated body was eventually found in a shed in the Barton Hill area of Bristol. For a long time it was a missing person's case, and the distraught family made public appeals for information. I remember her uncle coming on my show and talking live. He was beside himself with grief and desperate to find his niece. I conducted interviews with police officers dealing with the case; it was intense at times.

The perpetrators were caught and charged. The case went off the news agenda for months until it went to court. That's when the coverage restarts, and the gruesome facts are once again in the public domain. Eventually, the two despicable individuals who committed the heinous crime, the step-brother Nathan Matthews and his girlfriend Shauna Hoare, were brought to justice.

These are challenging stories to cover and there's no denying they get inside your body and your soul. You share the sadness, the grief and the heartbreak. It becomes almost personal.

Presenting the drivetime show was important in terms of my evolution behind the microphone. The variety of the subjects, the guests and the breaking news stories made me a better presenter. I'll be eternally grateful to Jenny Lacey for giving me the break on general programmes.

Away from the microphone, I always help charities when I can. In 1989, in the aftermath of Hillsborough, I felt compelled to organise a celebrity golf day at the excellent St Pierre Golf Club near Chepstow. Teams of three were joined by a celebrity guest from the world of sport or stage and screen. Despite being suspended by Rovers at the time, I pressed ahead with the day, which was hugely successful. Liverpool FC sent me a first-team shirt signed by Kenny Dalglish, which helped to raise money for the Hillsborough Disaster Fund. The former Coventry, Manchester City and Swansea footballer Tommy Hutchison was the celebrity in the winning team.

That day motivated me to host an annual golf day for BRACE (Bristol Research into Alzheimer's and Care for the Elderly). For years this became an annual event at Henbury Golf Club in Bristol. It raised good money for a great cause. In 2004, the year Dad passed away after suffering with Alzheimer's, my team won the golf day.

In 2014 the station manager Jenny Lacey made a bold promise that Radio Bristol would raise £1 million for 'Babe's Big Appeal'. The money was to go towards building a Children's Hospice in Wraxall, just outside Bristol, in North Somerset. I came up with an idea. 'The Twentyman Challenge' involved 19 BBC listeners or viewers joining me in playing three rounds of golf in a day. Each golfer had to raise a thousand pounds, so we'd raise £20,000 in all. The three courses we played on the longest day were Henbury, The Players and The Kendleshire. Pat Murphy, the director of golf at The Kendleshire, played a key role in making the event happen.

It was a great day for so many reasons. Matt Weeks played with the same ball on all 54 holes. Two of the courses have plenty of water features so that was highly impressive from Matt. A blind Radio Bristol listener, 'Les from Bath', was willing to sponsor me to the tune of £500 if I had a photograph taken with him before the big day. It was incredible to think Les Bowden paid so much money for a picture that he'd never see. It took pride of place in his lounge. He assured me that it was worth every penny as he derived so much pleasure from listening to the sport on Radio Bristol. Some of the golfers were competitive with their sponsorship and the day raised £28,000. Incredibly, Radio Bristol surpassed the £1 million target.

In 2019, I did a 24-hour broadcast with three other Radio Bristol presenters to raise money for the 'Live Appeal', which made a difference to older people in Bristol. Emma Britton, Joe Lemer and John Darvall were great company. We spun the wheel at the top of each hour to determine who'd be behind the mic for the ensuing 60 minutes, during which the other three presenters engaged in some activity or other. I'll never forget presenting one of the afternoon hours and *Points West*'s Alex Lovell walked towards the studio. I had to triple-take; she was carrying a crocodile. Yes, she was carrying a live crocodile into our studio. It was live radio, so I had to describe what was happening: 'Alex Lovell from *Points West* has just walked into the studio. She's carrying a crocodile. It's about five feet long and she's coming towards me!' Thankfully, the croc was well behaved and wasn't hungry. As its head rested on my shoulder, I did think 'one bite and I'm a goner'. I'd like to have seen the risk assessment form on that section of what was a brilliant show to be part of.

As I've said, I've met some incredible people along the way, and one person I must mention in this book is former player and Bristol City kit man Scott Murray. Scotty is an exceptional human being. I've never met anyone in my life who has done so much for so many. Bristol City have been exceptionally lucky to have him, and the city of Bristol is blessed that he's been in these parts for decades.

I first met him when I recorded a TV report the day after he scored a winning goal for City. Ella, his daughter, was a baby. She's now in her 20s. I'm proud that Scotty and I have been great mates ever since. I call him 'Scotty Boy', while he has labelled me 'Sir Geoff'.

I remember when Scotty suffered a loss of form. His confidence had taken a knock, and he was in and out of the team. One day at the training ground a chat developed between the two of us – not for the radio, just two mates talking footy – and I gave him some advice. I told him to simplify his game. Do the basics well. Don't go for the Hollywood pass but play it easy. Don't force it. Don't give the ball away. Pass to a red shirt, eliminate the errors and your confidence will soon return.

Form is temporary, as they say, and Scotty was soon back to his best. I'll never forget one Saturday when I was in the studio listening to a post-match chat he did on Radio Bristol. Scotty, who was back on track, referenced our chat and thanked me for helping him when he needed it. He said the advice had been a big help. It was a long time ago, but it remains a special memory – one I'll never forget.

Scott used to help me with a wonderful annual ruse involving my daughter Hannah. He was her favourite footballer. Obviously, our careers didn't overlap! For several years I'd pop down to Ashton Gate with a birthday card in early November. Scott would sign it and pen a lovely message to Hannah. He'd write her name and address on the envelope, and I'd post it. Obviously, he wouldn't pay for a stamp. Then, there it was, Postman Pat delivered the envelope on 5 November.

Hannah was overjoyed that *the* Scott Murray had remembered her birthday *again*, and he'd been kind enough to send a card, *again*. Brilliant. I think we stopped it when she got to 30! Only joking, but it was brilliant seeing her face when she opened it. She'd take it to school: 'Look who's sent me a birthday card again.' She was the envy of her mates. Class from an absolute Top Man.

Another legend who has crossed my path is John Motson. John is someone I first connected with before the Rovers/ Liverpool FA Cup matches in 1992. I was set to miss the tie as I broke my ankle in the previous round. There was a call to the house phone; it was as if a member of the royal family had called me. John wanted to gather some intel on the lads ahead of the game, which he was commentating on for BBC TV. He was a delightful man, interested and interesting. We must have chatted for an hour or more. It was a valuable lesson for me when I moved into broadcasting – preparation is key. For years we'd called David Mehew, David 'May-hew' but it transpired that John's research revealed the correct pronunciation was in fact 'Mee-hew'.

More recently I hosted a charity dinner with Motty at Ashton Gate, which was huge fun. He had some amazing tales to tell. He brought along a sheepskin coat, and I auctioned it to boost the coffers. Someone paid £5,000 for it. I asked the purchaser afterwards why he'd bought it; he simply shrugged his shoulders and stated the obvious: 'It was Motty's, Geoff. It was John Motson's.' Enough said.

In 2016, John and I had a brilliant chat on *Having a Gas* when we reminisced about the aforementioned Rovers/Liverpool FA Cup ties. It was a beautiful conversation, which we replayed on the day that he sadly passed away in 2023. John really was a Top Man.

While I'm naming names, during my Rovers days I met the great John Atyeo several times. John used to write a column in the local Sunday sports paper. He was an absolute gentleman. He had an aura of greatness. I could have talked football with 'Big John' for hours. It's a regret that we didn't do that, but he was so modest that he didn't like to talk about his career. I remember John publicly supported me in his column during the wedding business. That was incredibly important at the time.

There was also the time, prior to playing at Burnden Park, when I chatted with Bolton great Nat Lofthouse. He was also a delight; he knew the family name and it was a precious experience. Both John and Nat played against my dad. I met Jimmy Greaves at Ashton Gate and Sir Geoff Hurst at the then Swallow Royal Hotel in Bristol. I recorded a chat with Bobby Robson at a book launch in Bristol, and he was everything you'd have expected and much more. An absolute gentleman. All these men were incredibly humble. They all achieved so much but were the epitome of modesty. My life has been enriched by the experiences.

Talking of greatness, Marina Dolman, the president of Bristol City, is a remarkable lady. I relish every minute I spend in her company. She's elegant, graceful and a truly virtuous human being. Marina is the perfect figurehead for the football club. I can't think that any football club has a more fitting president.

As you're well aware, I've loved football at all levels of the game. Whether it be the top echelons or grassroots, bring it on, and one of the most popular places to play this wonderful game on a grassroots level in Bristol is on the Downs. The Bristol Downs League is a long-established, highly respected integral part of Bristol life. Dozens of pitches coexist, giving hundreds of amateur footballers a platform to enjoy the game. Apparently, only Hackney Marshes in London has more pitches in the UK.

In 2005, the Downs League celebrated its centenary. The management committee approached me to pull together a team to play a Downs XI in an exhibition match. Obviously, it was played on the Downs. I brought together a squad of BBC bods and some former pros. I was told the Downs squad would be made up of their longest-serving players. It turns out they picked their best players, who were all relatively young, fit, able and very keen to win.

My squad comprised: Tom Ryan (BBC), Mark Twentyman (captain's pick), Geoff Twentyman (BBC and ex-Rovers), Keith Millen (ex-City), John Bennett (BBC), Andy Howard (BBC), Gary Owers (ex-City and now BBC), Chris Spittles (BBC), Alan Walsh (ex-City), Tim McSweeney (BBC), David Mehew (ex-Rovers), Tom Burridge (BBC).

We turned up and played on pitch number 12. The grass, I use the word loosely, was yellow. It hadn't rained for weeks, maybe longer. The uneven surface and dry conditions were going to be a test. Not to mention the excited opposition! It finished 2-2. Tim McSweeney scored our first. It was a textbook header, powered back across the keeper. Tim resembled compatriot John Hartson and for a moment I thought we'd smuggled the Welsh international into our team. We were trailing 2-1 and Gary Owers, who played in an FA Cup Final for Sunderland during his illustrious career, was frantically urging our team to attack! Gal played to win, even on pitch 12 on the Downs. Cor, he lunged into some bone-jarring tackles as he drove us forward. Brilliant from another Top Man.

Former professionals may slow down with age, but they don't lose their touch and the desire to win. Who else but David 'Boris' Mehew should pop up to bag a late equaliser? It was a great match, very fitting of the occasion. Both squads and the Downs League hierarchy rehydrated in the Port of Call off Whiteladies Road in Clifton afterwards.

* * *

Bristol Rovers beat Sunderland 2-0 on 10 March 2020. At the time it was perceived as a good result, and I heard from within the club that the win kept manager Ben Garner in his job. No one had an inkling of what was going to follow three days later. On the Friday I was preparing for *Saturday Sport* and the news came through that the Premier League and Football League were suspended due to Covid-19. Strangely, non-league football was allowed to continue, and our focus was Bath City's game at Hungerford Town.

As sport ground to a dramatic standstill, we thought it was important to continue with *Saturday Sport* so that sports fans got their fix of what they needed. For 13 successive Saturdays I presented four hours of live sport … with no live sport. The local clubs at all levels were very helpful and made guests available for telephone chats about how the club and their staff were coping. I remember City's head coach, Lee Johnson, and Bath's director of rugby, Stuart Hooper, being really helpful and informative. There were no studio guests, and staffing levels were kept to a minimum. We were told we had to social distance.

The BBC was ultra-cautious and looked after the staff extremely well. You had to pass a temperature test before you were allowed on site. There were strict limits on the numbers allowed in the newsroom at any one time. One-way walking systems were introduced and screens were erected in the studio and operations areas. The production was creative and hopefully it was an engaging listen. I received emails from people who said the shows were vital for their well-being. As a regular on site, I had to test at least twice a week.

During the early stages of the pandemic I received news that a wonderful man, Dave Fear, was terminally ill. Dave was a massive Red and we'd known each other for decades. He did so much for so many people and raised a huge amount of money for charity over many years. We first met on the side of the pitch at Ashton Gate when his company sponsored a City/Rovers game. We chatted when I was on my way out to warm up. Dave told me some years later that he knew Rovers would win that night as he saw the fire and determination in my face and heard it in my voice. When Dave was ill, Hillie, his wife, contacted me and asked if I would visit him. Social distancing was a thing, and we were advised that we should only drive in emergencies. To me, seeing Dave was an emergency … well certainly a high priority. If the police had stopped me, then so be it. Some things in life must be done.

It was an incredible few hours. Richard Scudamore, the former CEO of the Premier League, who's also a big City fan, was there, as was Dave's son Tom. It was a glorious sunny day. We were sat in the courtyard reminiscing when the former City manager Russell Osman appeared – he was out on a road run and decided to venture to Dave's home. Russell's presence enhanced the wonderful occasion. I was honoured and humbled to present the celebration of Dave's life at Ashton Gate. Dave was without doubt a Top Man.

I was fortunate to have the Saturday programmes as my focal point in my life. I lived on my own and it was a lonely world. They were very weird times. I recall, about ten weeks in, thinking things need to change; this is all very negative. Then one day out walking I bumped into Lee Johnson. He'd just been informed that the top two tiers of English football were returning without spectators. This was positive news. For me it meant we'd have commentary matches back on the radio, but the protocols remained that I'd be studio-based. The BBC protocols allowed only two people inside the grounds – the commentator and summariser. Social distancing remained in place, but it was a small step in the right direction.

The first time I returned to a ground to present *Saturday Sport* was at the Rec for Bath v Bristol in the Premiership on 8 May 2021, 14 months after sport stopped. There were no spectators, but it felt liberating. Weirdly, I remember how green the grass was and how big the pitch looked. I could literally hear the players on the pitch shouting and expressing themselves. Later that month spectators returned for the first time to watch Bristol's home game with Gloucester, when 3,138 were dotted around Ashton Gate. The atmosphere was incredible as people expressed their excitement and genuine relief at watching live sport once again. It was amazing to be there and have live guests alongside me. It was almost a relief to see the whites of their eyes and interact fully. It had been a very long time.

The football and the rugby didn't restart at the same time, which meant the end-of-season recess was shorter than normal. Football ended and rugby continued. Then football came back, and rugby did likewise. The sports team and I remained very busy until both seasons got back into their normal schedules. They were very strange, challenging times. My grandchildren will study Covid-19 at school in years to come. It must be covered unequivocally and comprehensively.

I presented some reports on *BBC Inside Out West*, which was the investigative journalism arm of *Points West*. It was a bad decision by the BBC to do away with the strand as it delivered some excellent reports and addressed some important issues. I was flattered to front a 20-minute report on whether heading footballs causes dementia. A brilliant producer called Ben White was the driver of this one and we tackled the subject over a year before

Alan Shearer presented a similar report for the wider BBC. For me it was obviously a pertinent subject.

Our investigation included a chat with Dr Michael Grey at Birmingham University. Michael was researching the subject. I assumed that if there was a connection between heading footballs and dementia, it was a generational thing. The footballs that my dad headed in the 1950s were heavy on a dry day, but when it rained they absorbed water and the density and weight increased considerably. Was that a key factor? Michael Grey's answer was chilling. His research led him to believe that modern-day footballs are lighter, they fly considerably faster than the heavy ones of bygone days, therefore the impact is different, but just as damaging.

Our case study was a former Southampton centre-back called Kevin Moore. Kevin was a diamond of a guy and had a loan spell at Bristol Rovers at the back end of my playing days. Later in life, but at a terribly young age, Kevin developed Pick's disease, a variant of frontotemporal dementia. He died at the age of just 55. Because of my connection with Kevin, his wife Mandy agreed to chat with me. Gosh, she was courageous and so, so brave as she told me about his illness, the challenges, how he changed and how the love of her life and a former elite athlete deteriorated so much that he needed 24-hour care. Mandy, like my mum, was certain that repeated heading of a football led to Kevin's horrible death.

These are humbling chats, so tough when it relates to someone you've shared a dressing room with. It was very difficult as my dad had suffered a similar illness. I ended the report by calling for the football authorities, who are awash with money, to do more to establish the correlation between heading a football and dementia and its various strains and act accordingly. Rest easy Kevin, and thank you Mandy.

Chapter 17

The Fab Four

I DON'T know how many people I met and chatted with over the years – too many to count. Earlier chapters have included some of the memorable ones but here are four that I'll never forget.

On Monday, 10 August 2020, Bristol City were set to announce a new head coach. City embargoed the announcement until 6pm. This was perfect for *The Sound of the City*. The club had agreed that I could do phone chats with the new head coach and the CEO, Mark Ashton. The unconfirmed intelligence was that Dean Holden was to be the new man in charge. Dean had been in caretaker charge after head coach Lee Johnson was sacked. City were about to appoint the assistant to the head coach that they'd sacked. Dean is a brilliant bloke. He's very honest, very open and totally likeable. I like him a lot but, regardless, I had to do my job. I knew a lot of the fanbase would be underwhelmed by the appointment.

The official announcement was put back, and just after 6.15pm it was confirmed that Dean Holden was the new head coach and he appeared live on the show. Dean spoke with passion, pride and commitment. I told him that a large percentage of the fanbase wasn't pleased about his appointment. He took the comment on the chin and gave an inspirational reply in terms of his ambition for the club and his huge desire to succeed. The chat was followed by some fan reaction. I had to produce the programme while I presented it, as we were receiving messages from City telling us that Mark Ashton had been delayed but he should be on the show by 6.35pm. Then we received a further message to say it would be 6.45pm.

My gut feeling was that Mark Ashton had worked out that the later he came on the show the less time I'd have to cross-examine him. It didn't matter what time he appeared on the end of a phone, as I'd sorted a plan B. Some months previously I'd been told by a good source at Ashton Gate that the City CEO didn't like being interviewed by me. What Mark Ashton didn't know was that I'd had it sanctioned by my boss that I could extend the programme beyond 7pm so I could deliver a forensic interview. She told me to stay on air for as long as I needed to. Happy days. The conversation started just after 6.45pm and concluded at 7.15pm.

Mark explained why the club had appointed Dean Holden. It was far from convincing. He was a good human being – which was true – but it didn't mean the caretaker should have been given the job. The CEO assured me and the audience that Dean was first choice and no one else had been offered the job.

While the caretaker was in temporary charge, the club owner, Steve Lansdown, appeared on TalkSPORT in July and said the club needed a change in direction and new blood to inject a fresh impetus. That afternoon I did my homework. I listened to the interview on the TalkSPORT website. I wrote it down and read it out word for word: 'We need someone to take us to the next step, bring a breath of fresh air into the club, and we have a particular type of person that we want to come in.' I threw in my next question: 'Did that change after 9 July up to today in terms of the criteria?' Mark Ashton was flustered and struggled to explain a clear contradiction in policy. My Twitter account was in overdrive. The City fans were enjoying the listen. I've always maintained it was my job to ask the questions on behalf of the fans. If the answer was inadequate, I had to press until I felt it was at least reasonable. There was no finer example than this.

Mark Ashton wasn't willing to discuss the likes of Chris Hughton, Paul Cook or anyone who'd been linked with the job in the media. I asked him why. He claimed there were confidentiality issues. I was dismissive and reminded him there were tens of thousands of Bristol City fans listening to their CEO. He relented. Live radio is a pressure-cooker environment at times.

We talked about whether Dean Holden was the cheap option, together with Korey Smith and Jamie McAllister's departures from the club. The future of striker Famara Diédhiou was also discussed. As the conversation evolved, the messages supporting and thanking me for my efforts to hold their CEO to account on social media cascaded into the radio station.

Dean Holden had been appointed on a 12-month contract, so my final question was, 'Dean has got a 12-month rolling contract, what must he achieve in his first season positionally to make sure he is still in a job in 12 months' time?'

The response started, 'I'd ask that question slightly differently. I don't think we hold a gun to anyone's head, we've never done that—'

I rarely interrupted my guests, but I seized back control of the conversation: 'With respect, I'm asking the question, where do they have to finish in the league in 12 months' time to make sure he's doing the right job?'

Bristol Live transcribed the entire interview on their website. Ding, ding – round one! Strap yourselves in for the full interview between Mark Ashton and Geoff Twentyman following the announcement of Dean Holden as Bristol City manager:

> The pair were involved in an often-heated interview on BBC Radio Bristol's *Sound of the City* programme, with Twentyman grilling Ashton on everything from the interview process to Holden's lack of experience.
>
> Tensions and frustrations were rife, with Ashton's sighs audible and Twentyman's interruptions evident, but what transpired was an in-depth, detailed account of how Holden became the new Robins boss.
>
> The former Bristol Rovers player was praised for his tenacity when interviewing the City CEO, with Bristol City fans' favourite 'Gashead' not taking no for an answer on several questions.

City fans seemed to enjoy the exchange. The fans' focus shifted from Dean Holden being appointed to my interview with Mark Ashton. For weeks I'd receive messages or be stopped in the street and people thanked me for holding the club to account. You only get one chance to conduct these important interviews, so it's vital to get them right.

It wasn't always about holding people to account and confrontation. I was privileged to record chats with two remarkable human beings. Over a period of a few months, I met and chatted separately with the oldest former Bristol City and Bristol Rovers players. Sadly, both men have since passed away, but I'll never forget the time I spent with them both. It was an absolute privilege.

Con Sullivan and Josser Watling were both in their 90s when I recorded the chats. Con was City's keeper from 1950 to 1953 before he moved to Arsenal. Josser was a one-club man and played for The Gas from 1945 to 1963. Both men were a delight – so humble, so sharp, genuine characters – and were adorable. Both recounted some incredible stories. Con, when it started to rain, once borrowed a pair of leather gloves from a police officer who walked behind the goal at Ashton Gate. Cornelius had lived in the same house in Knowle West in south Bristol for 86 years. 86 years! He sat in a chair in the corner of his lounge. On the wall above him there was a black-and-white photograph of him making a save.

I said, 'Look at you diving like a cat to make a save.'

The response was razor sharp: 'That must be why I drinks lots of milk.'

I attended Con's funeral and it was humbling and emotional that the family played some of our chat from *The Sound of the City* during the service.

John Daniel Watling didn't know why he was called 'Josser', but he recalled great tales of travelling to Eastville on the bus. Fans would give up their seats to allow the players to sit down. Josser told me the secret to his longevity was the 'occasional' Bacardi and coke, and that Anfield was his favourite away ground.

Even in his 90s Josser used to go to the Mem to watch games. It warmed my heart when he told me he listened to my show on the way home: 'I listens to you on the way home, I likes you on the radio.' The family invited me to his funeral, but sadly I was away on holiday.

RIP Con, sleep easy Josser. My life was enhanced by meeting you both. Two absolute Top Men.

Where were you when the Queen passed away on 8 September 2022? I'll remember the day forever. It was a Thursday, which meant I was presenting *Having a Gas.* A very special guest was coming into the studio. Rovers defender Nick Anderton is one of the most inspirational people I've ever met. In his mid-20s Nick was diagnosed with a rare form of bone cancer. The football club, through their press officer, Andy Downie, allowed me to conduct interviews with Nick throughout his diagnosis and treatment. Nick and the club trusted me implicitly. Nick and I got on really well. Coincidentally, we both played for the same three clubs – Chorley, Preston and Rovers.

This was going to be a poignant show as it was the first time he'd come into the studio since his diagnosis. We'd done phone chats, but this was important, it was big. As the day evolved, news came into the radio station that there was going to be an announcement from Buckingham Palace. It was obvious what the news was going to be. All the presenters had been briefed on the procedure for when there's a 'category A' death in the royal family. It's a short sharp process of just 11 words: 'We now join our colleagues in the BBC newsroom in London.' You don't say why, it's a clinical, concise procedure. Every BBC radio station joins up as one at that point.

When we went on air, the intel was that an announcement was imminent. I'd explained the situation to Nick, who understood. My biggest worry was if the news broke just minutes into the show and I had to hand over to London, it would have been insensitive and frustrating, but these were extraordinary circumstances.

At 6.10pm, barely five minutes into the show, a message appeared on my monitor saying the announcement could be at 6.15pm. Nothing happened. Thankfully, we were able to have a decent chat and I played a music montage of Nick's best moments in the blue and white quarters. My bosses were in the operations area outside the studio looking hassled and uncertain of what was going on! It was my job just to keep talking with a sense of calm. Nick was amazing as he told the story of his diagnosis and how he and his amazing partner Isabel were dealing with the extreme adversity. It was totally humbling and inspirational. Eventually, just after 6.25pm, I was told to make the announcement and Radio Bristol joined the newsroom in London.

So, there it was. I was live on BBC Radio Bristol when her Majesty Queen Elizabeth II passed away. That was quite something, but to have had Nick Anderton live in the studio added to the enormity of the experience. Nick and I are still in regular contact. I made a road trip earlier this year to see him near his home in Lancashire. He's making a near miraculous recovery. Life is good for him; he has two young children, Grace and George, and is back in football as a coach at AFC Fylde. Nick Anderton really is a Top Man.

* * *

I'd been on leave in 2009 and came back to a message detailing some calls I had to return. The Bath City fan and revered film director Ken Loach was on the list. I'd heard that he was about to release a film starring Eric Cantona, and the former Manchester United player was going to be at Twerton Park for a question-and-answer session. I assumed Ken was looking for some publicity for *Looking for Eric* and the event at Twerton Park. Ken rang me before I had a chance to return his call. He was keen to chat. After we exchanged pleasantries, Ken got down to the nitty gritty.

> KL: 'Geoff, do you know Eric's coming to Twerton Park? I wonder if you'd do me a favour?'
>
> GT: 'Of course, Ken, if I can [expecting him to ask for some publicity].'

KL: 'Great, will you host the Q&A with Eric for me please?'

GT: 'I'd love to, Ken, yes, thanks for asking.'

KL: 'But, Geoff, you don't know when it is [good point].'

GT: 'It doesn't matter when it is, Ken, I'll clear the diary!'

This was an opportunity that I wouldn't miss. Eric Cantona at Twerton Park. Read the sentence slowly.

Cantona was top drawer. He found time for everyone. He looked slightly overwhelmed at times as everyone wanted a piece of him. He wore a Bath City scarf and wandered on to the hallowed turf to have some pictures taken with the Bath boss Adie Britton and the players, including club legend Jim Rollo.

Cantona had been on TV the night before with Jonathan Ross. A few people said he seemed to be difficult and prickly. When Ken Loach introduced me to Eric, he told him I'd played over 400 professional games. Eric smiled and nodded, a nod of approval, as we shook hands. It was firm and he looked me in the eyes. I knew from that point he'd be as good as gold. Stuart James joined us for the chat. Stuart is a great bloke, who played for Bath City back in the day and is forging an impressive career as a sports journalist with *The Athletic* and was previously at *The Guardian*.

Two of the things I admired about Cantona were his ability to converse in someone else's language and, even more impressive, being humorous. Charlie's bar at Twerton Park was packed. There was standing room only as people crammed in. I'm guessing there should have been about 200 people seated but there were nearer to 250, as people stood where they could. And before you think it, no, they weren't quite packed in like sardines.

Cantona was a joy. I don't know what Jonathan Ross had done to him, but Eric was very relaxed and totally open. A genuine giver. I'd watched the film in advance, which was my form of research. He picked up on this in the chat and, as a result, I sensed he trusted me even more and answered my questions more openly.

I've never seen a room so star-struck. He had the audience in the palm of his hand, as people listened to every syllable. Men, women, children were sitting and standing, eyes popping out of their heads, mouths ajar, motionless, listening to 'the king' in Charlie's bar.

It was time for the big question: 'Eric, Selhurst Park 1995, and Matthew Simmons comes running down the stairs and you kung-fu kicked him over the advertising board. Do you have any regrets?'

Cantona looked at me, our eyes locked: 'Yes, I have one regret, just one regret.'

I nodded and raised my eyebrows to accentuate my interest. 'And what is that regret, Eric?'

Cantona paused for a couple of seconds as the room held its breath, and with the perfect timing that he'd displayed a million times on a football pitch, he responded, 'I should have fucking killed him!' The room exploded into laughter and applause. This was classic Cantona. This is why I told Ken Loach I'd clear the diary to be at Twerton Park to experience another wonderful afternoon.

It really is the best non-league ground in the country.

Chapter 18

Talent Spotting

I DON'T know whether it was an attribute I picked up from my dad, or it's deeper rooted than that, but I always felt that I had a good ear for talent. I was delighted to give a helping hand to some exceptionally talented people on the radio. In a slightly embarrassing admission, I spend the first 30 seconds or so of any initial conversation with someone by assessing how they'd sound on the radio. To get together my radio team I adopted a football mindset. You had to have ability, talent and a desire to be the best version of yourself. You also had to be committed to the job and be a team player.

In 1996, when I was the assistant manager at Rovers, I heard a voice that jumped out of the radio at me. He was reporting from a Gloucestershire cricket match. The voice was strong, clear, warm, had authority and was very natural. Alistair Bruce-Ball had the X factor. This guy was a talent.

When I returned to the BBC one of the first things I did was to bring him in for a breakfast meeting. A full English is a good accompaniment to any meeting. I had a plan. Although I knew I was going to change the existing system of a reporter allocated to the same team every week, I wanted to increase Ali's involvement.

I wanted him to do more. His inclusion would improve the sound of the Saturday afternoon show. He'd be ideal in my master plan, where ultimately a pool of voices would cover the main clubs in the future.

I didn't disclose my long-term plan but when I told him I wanted him to be our Yeovil Town correspondent he was thrilled. Ali Bruce-Ball was going to be a top-drawer sports broadcaster. He was destined for bigger and better things, but in the meantime I planned to fully utilise his considerable abilities.

I felt that Radio Bristol had to secure ABB on a full-time contract. If we didn't, another local radio station in the region would have swooped. I convinced my boss Jenny Lacey to sort out a contract. Jenny was a brilliant boss, and I'll be forever grateful for the opportunities and huge support that she gave me. She was passionate about local radio and knew what it was all about. In this instance she played a blinder. Jenny created the job of 'Bristol Reporter' and appointed Ali to the post. Jenny kept a pot of money separate to her annual budget for special situations. This was one such example. Ali worked between news and sport and was a huge asset to the station.

He did a great job as the Yeovil Town correspondent, and when I introduced my new way of covering matches using a pool of reporters, I knew he was going to be a key figure. A few months into my new way of covering games I decided it was time for Ali to make the quantum leap and cover one of the Bristol clubs. This would involve doing a full match commentary – a new challenge for Ali. There was genuine kudos in doing one of the two Football League clubs that we covered.

I took him for a game of golf on the Wednesday before the Saturday he was going to be thrown in at the deep end covering

Rovers. On the 10th tee at Chipping Sodbury Golf Club, I told him. He looked at me with excitement and fear in equal proportions and the colour drained from his face. A minute or so later, after he'd digested the enormity of the situation, he thanked me and said he couldn't wait and wouldn't let me down. I knew he wouldn't let me down. He then teed his ball up and hit a baby draw down the middle.

Ali went from strength to strength and was a network commentator in waiting. He had all the prerequisites and possessed a desire and focus to fulfil and maximise his potential. He listened and took on board what he was told. Inevitably, ABB told me he was going to apply for a job as a football commentator at 5 Live. He submitted his demo tape, which was an extraordinary Bristol derby at Ashton Gate. Rovers scored after a matter of seconds through Marcus Bignot but City won 3-2, with goals from Keith Millen, Tony Thorpe and Peter Beadle. For the record, Martin Cameron scored the other Rovers goal. I was Ali's co-commentator, and the night before we'd enjoyed the Radio Bristol Christmas party, where the drinks flowed into the early hours! The adrenaline and excitement of the occasion got us through!

Ali got the job and had to advise his bosses at 5 Live about his 'second sport'. During the summer recess he needed to be utilised, so I suggested golf as they weren't blessed with lots of golf voices, and it was a sport he knew well and played to a decent standard. He got the nod to do golf, has evolved into an outstanding on-course commentator (the ones who whisper around the greens), and he's worked at the Ryder Cup, The Open Championship and The Masters countless times. The first time Ali worked at Augusta National he entered his name in the press/media ballot to play the course on the morning after the final round. People from the world's media entered the draw. Lo and behold, ABB's name was drawn out and he played the most famous and exclusive golf course in the world. He even had a caddy sporting the white boiler suit. As the former voice of BBC golf Tony Adamson said at Ali and Lucy's wedding, he probably put his name in the ballot twice, Ali Bruce and Ali Ball.

Ali was a wonderful part of my team, and it has been a joy watching him develop into one of 5 Live's prized assets. To this day, he's humble and modest. Ali is so much more than a former colleague; he's a valued and trusted friend. The BBs – Lucy, Ewan and Rory – are great people. ABB is a Top Man.

Not long into my tenure as sports editor at Radio Bristol I received a call from a producer in London. They had a young woman on a BBC trainee scheme. She came from a sporting background, she was rated and they wanted to see what she was made of. Apparently, Radio Bristol, with its rich portfolio of sport, was the perfect place for her to cut her teeth.

Clare Balding was an absolute joy to have as part of the team for a few months. She was so committed from day one. She had a huge desire to learn and develop. She was from horse racing stock, but she wanted to learn about football, she wanted to learn about rugby. She just wanted to learn and was like a sponge as she absorbed every minute and each experience with us. Clare did the early shifts, she did the late finishes, she did the long days. She was a natural and it has been fantastic to see how she's developed into an incredibly talented, confident and accomplished presenter. Hopefully, her time in Bristol taught her the fundamentals and gave her the foundations on which she's built her impressive career.

From afar, Radio Bristol sport seemed to be a respected place for nurturing talent. In more recent times, after 5 Live moved to Manchester, I received a call from a different senior sports producer. For clarity, at national radio a producer is someone who plans, organises and sets up programmes and outside broadcasts. A broadcaster is the on-air talent who delivers the producer's work.

'Geoff, I have a young guy who's talented. I don't know if he's going to be a broadcaster or a producer. Could you take him on board for a month or so and see what you think, please?'

This 'young guy' arrived in Bristol and quickly passed the 'Geoff Twentyman 30-second test'. It was clear to me straight away that he had a great voice – clear, concise, natural, good authority and gravitas. I rang the senior producer that afternoon and told him it was a no-brainer. This well-mannered, respectful young man had all the attributes to be a broadcaster. He stayed with Radio Bristol for several weeks and, like Ali Bruce-Ball and Clare Balding, he was keen and willing to do anything. If he'd been on an early shift, it was a challenge to get him to go home as he was so keen to stay on and learn. He passed the ultimate broadcasting test when we put him on air. He was a class act. Chris Jones is now the BBC's rugby union correspondent.

I remember listening to 5 Live not that long ago and ABB and CJ were both on the programme. I don't take huge credit as the individuals are the ones who seized their opportunities, but it was great to help them on their journeys. As I drove my car, I felt an inner contentment and pride, for obvious reasons.

As I take stock, in addition to Ali, Clare and Chris, there's been a wealth of wonderful talent that's worked on or evolved through Radio Bristol sport over the last 30 years or so. The hardest aspect of a career with the BBC is the first step – getting through the front door. Sport provides such an opportunity as a lot of the roles are part-time. If you can cut it on sport, the rest of the operation is easy by comparison.

Matthew Pick came on a six-week short-term contract. Matt soon proved he was worthy of a much longer deal. He was quick to understand my ideas and ambitions and helped me to deliver them. Matt would cover any sport, he wasn't fazed by anything. He was a highly valued member of the team. He moved on to HTV, returned as a freelancer and has been back at the BBC for decades.

Alistair Durden was a teenager when he rang me and introduced himself as someone who was keen to get involved in the football coverage. He'd done some reporting on BBC Somerset and promised me, 'I won't let you down.' Blimey, that's an understatement. Ali is the best local radio football operator I've known, heard or worked with who didn't go to national radio. He's a fantastic football commentator and was the eyes, ears and voice when Bristol City famously won 5-4 at Mansfield in 2002. City were 4-2 down with three minutes to go. It was a compelling listen. In more recent times he became the face of TV sport on *Points West*. Thankfully, he still commentates on Radio Bristol. I was touched by his comment on my card when I left the BBC: 'my friend, my mentor'.

Will Shindler was a talent. His strength was as a presenter or bulletin reader. Will has a sharp mind and clever way with words. He moved on to HTV and 5 Live and then diversified into the BBC TV Drama department. He's now making a great career as a crime thriller writer. I've read all four of his books and highly recommend them.

I hadn't been sports editor for very long when I contacted Bristol University and the University of the West of England to see whether there were any bright young things that I could use on Saturdays. Both unis ran sports media journalism courses, so it made perfect sense to tap into both establishments. Being proactive is important. I was delighted when Helen Blaby, a student from the University of the West of England, contacted me. She was interested in getting involved in the on-air production side of *Saturday Sport*.

I still remember her walking across the car park as I looked out of an office window. She was shy. She was keen. I liked her cherubic smile. I've never seen anyone blush so often! Although she hadn't expressed any interest in being a broadcaster, she had a fab voice. My 30-second test never failed.

Helen took on the role of driving the Saturday show. Essentially, she coordinated the reporters at the various grounds and opened and closed the faders to bring them into the programme. We had a great dynamic, which was essential.

'Bomber', as she was affectionately known, was brilliant, but she was paranoid about the reporters all being in place at the start of the programme. She took it almost personally if someone wasn't at a ground when I delivered my intro at two o'clock. Reporters travelled the length and breadth of the country and inevitably there were traffic delays. Helen would stomp up and down in the studio area: 'Phil Tottle isn't there yet, GT. Bloody Phil Tottle!! I bet he didn't leave Bristol early enough for the game!' I used to pacify her by saying it was fine. As long as he arrived for kick-off there was no problem.

I told her repeatedly that she had a fab voice and that she should be a broadcaster. I think she lacked self-belief, but I was delighted when she eventually heeded my advice. After she completed her studies, I was chuffed to bits when she became the travel voice on *5*

Live Breakfast. That was a big gig and she nailed it. Helen has since gravitated to her hometown of Northampton and as a presenter she's an integral part of BBC Radio Northampton.

Tim McSweeney, the scorer of *that* header in the Downs centenary game, came in and worked on the production team on Saturday afternoons when he was studying at Bristol University. 'Sweens' was talented behind the microphone. After he graduated, Tim secured a full-time position at Radio Bristol. A few years later he went left field and went to work with monkeys and gorillas! But the lure of the BBC proved to be too much, so he returned and now works on the production team on the breakfast show.

John Bennett is another talent who graduated into the BBC after sending me a demo tape. It was a cassette, which tells you it was a few years ago. JB was working on the little-known station, FM 102 The Bear. It shows that everyone starts somewhere. I liked what I heard. I invited John in for a meeting and I was impressed with his attitude and modesty. He was keen, and desperate to forge a career in broadcasting.

JB worked on Saturdays and as a result secured himself a full-time role, not in sport, but as a news journalist at Radio Bristol. I was able to strike an arrangement whereby he worked two Saturdays a month on sport and was given time off from the news rotas. A change of management saw the agreement scuppered by Tim Pemberton 'because it was not in writing'. This wasn't good news for me as I lost a talented football reporter. As a result, JB pursued opportunities away from Bristol. Bravo to him as he's enjoying an impressive career at BBC World Service Sport and 5 Live. I'm glad John sent me that cassette back in the day.

Paul Breen-Turner was an interesting guy. He ran a pub between Bath and Bristol and had all the attributes to excel. One of the frustrations of local radio sport was the fact it was a small team in terms of full-time staff. PBT did brilliant work covering Yeovil and helped to significantly raise the standard on Saturday afternoons. I couldn't offer him more than Saturdays, so it was no surprise that he went on to be a huge success as a football commentator on Spanish radio and worked at TalkSPORT. Paul is a great guy, and we keep in touch all these years on.

Robin Markwell is another person who started his excellent BBC career on Saturday afternoons as part of the production team. Robin, another Bristol University student, got his feet under the table with sport but secured a free transfer to news and politics. He does sterling work presenting and producing BBC's *Politics West* and other political coverage and programmes across the BBC.

Chris Spittles worked for the *Western Daily Press* and doubled up as our co-commentator on our Yeovil Town coverage. 'Spitts' knows his football and has a really strong journalistic nous. He could dig out a story and deliver some excellent interviews. He left the ailing newspaper industry and, as a freelancer, he transitioned from summariser to the main commentator. He was very good and had a deep desire to improve. He never sat still and constantly asked for feedback. If I'd been able to, I'd have offered Chris a full-time position in my team but there were no opportunities. He therefore made a life decision to give up Saturdays and doing commentaries so he could spend more quality time with his growing family. I'm delighted he's back in the industry doing some excellent work at ITV Westcountry.

Richard Hoskin was on a training course in Bristol and dropped me a line to see if he could record an interview about Marcus Stewart with me for a programme he was producing at BBC Suffolk. I was impressed by his enthusiasm and the way he conducted himself. He was the kind of person I'd have in my team. I made a mental note of his potential as I knew it might be relevant in the foreseeable future. Some months later, Ali Bruce-Ball moved to 5 Live. We advertised the job, Richard applied and was appointed. He has been an integral part of the sports team for over two decades and has evolved into an excellent football commentator.

Damian Derrick hadn't been at *Points West* very long when he asked for a chat as he was interested in doing rugby commentary. This was great news for me as my full-time sports journalists specialised in football. 'Damo' was keen. He knew his rugby inside out, back to front. A few off-air practice runs and he was up and running. He was a natural commentator and has the ability to ad lib and make you smile in among the cut and thrust of 15 v 15. He always wanted feedback, he always wanted to learn. It has been a joy watching him evolve. Alongside his commentaries he's an excellent interviewer. He asks strong questions and always holds people to account when it's appropriate.

Andy Howard is another huge talent. He had a quiet entry into the sports team but made a big impression. He did some sterling work when we covered Paulton Rovers and their historic run to the first round of the FA Cup in 2009. Andy worked in other areas of Radio Bristol and Radio Somerset but when he worked on a Saturday it was clear he had tons of potential. As you'll read shortly, I had to oversee a recruitment process when Alistair Durden moved to *Points West*. Andy delivered a brilliant interview but just missed out on the job as it was an incredibly competitive field of applicants. It was a real testament to the quality of the sports team when someone like Andy didn't get the gig. It was tough telling him that he hadn't been appointed but I promised him that I'd use him more on Saturday afternoons. He was a talent and I wanted to make him even better.

I only employed people who wanted to learn, people who wanted to get better, people who were team players. Andy embraced all my criteria and more. He has developed into a brilliant football commentator and sets himself high standards. It's a joy watching his career develop both on Saturdays and on *Points West*. His only failing is that he's a Blue Nose. On his 30th birthday I contacted the former City boss Jimmy Lumsden, who was assistant manager to David Moyes at Everton. Jimmy sorted out a training top, which 'Moyesy' signed with a personal message to Andy. When he opened it, his face was an absolute picture. Some people are worth going the extra mile for.

Ed Hadwin was based at BBC Wiltshire in Swindon but lived in Bristol. I knew about his ability. I'd met him a few times when our respective teams played each other. Again, I'd noted his potential and felt he'd fit into the team. I knew that day would ultimately come as Ali Durden was on the longest attachment (radio's version of a loan deal) I'd ever known. Ali was at *Points West* and for whatever reason the management wouldn't make the move permanent. Thankfully, the BBC rules state an attachment between departments can only be extended so many times. Ali's well-deserved permanent transfer was confirmed, and I oversaw the process to recruit his replacement. Ed Hadwin was appointed. Ed excels at football commentary and his finest hour and a half was when Rovers beat Scunthorpe 7-0 on the final day of the 2021/22 season to gain promotion to League One. It was an exceptional afternoon and Ed did it total justice.

When I left the BBC, I received hundreds of messages. One was from Tom Gale. Tom is learning his trade on 5 Live. He got into the BBC via an excellent eight-week training programme that I worked on as a tutor. Each local radio station took in one trainee, and the 40 or so wannabe sports journalists descended on Bristol for a two-day training programme. Tom wrote:

> Hi Geoff, apologies for the message out of the blue. I saw your recent BBC employment news. Not expecting you to remember, but we met in the summer of 2012, when I was part of the BBC Kick Off scheme which did some training in Bristol. I don't remember the specifics, but I do recall you were very warm, engaging, up for a laugh, and gave me the confidence boost that yeah, I can do this. It definitely played a part in me pursuing a career within the industry. Thank you. Enjoy retirement and spoiling those grandchildren.

It was a fab message. Remember the name, Tom Gale.

In terms of my full-time sports journalists during my tenure, Ali Bruce-Ball and Alistair Durden were imperious, an outstanding pairing, and when they moved on, Richard Hoskin and Ed Hadwin were top drawer. I was lucky to have such an impressive team. This was enhanced by a plethora of talented people, some of whom were part-time and only worked on Saturdays. These included Andrew Sheridan, Dave Alred, Andy Champion, Phil Tottle, Colin Howlett, Mike Kay, Stewart Gardner, Christina Boxer, Ben Orr, Mike Kay, Sheridan Robins, John Ford, Rob Scanlon, Dan Albutt, Nick Bull, Mark Williams, Mark Hoskins and Adam Whitty.

When I took over as sports editor in 1993, just six months after joining the BBC, I had a vision and was determined to improve the sports output. A huge thanks to everyone who helped me realise my ambition.

Managing people - give talent a chance

This is one of the most rewarding aspects of being a boss. Identifying talent and giving that person the chance to evolve and develop is supremely satisfying. Trust your judgement and back your gut feeling. Ability is key but attitude and application are equally important. When you give an individual an opportunity it's important to have a plan to maintain their development. They need time to find their feet but need direction and feedback. It's also important that you deliver what you promise; never pay lip service. When Andy Howard's application for a full-time role in my sports team was unsuccessful, I explained that a lack of experience was the main reason. I saw his potential and, to ensure he gained the experience he lacked, I promised he would get more opportunities on Saturday afternoons. I did this and he's developed into a fine commentator and is enjoying a great career. As a boss, it's imperative that you never promise what you can't deliver - something that happened to me, as you'll read about shortly.

Chapter 19

City v Rovers Fantasy Football

THERE HASN'T been a league derby in Bristol since 2001. So, I thought I'd create a showdown. In my fantasy football match, I've thought about the best players I've played against and seen in Bristol since I arrived in 1986.

So here it is, my City XI v Rovers XI. Players who were shortlisted are included in brackets. Picking City's left-back and the Rovers strikers was tough. Discuss and debate at your leisure. Have I called it right? Who wins and by how many?

CITY
4-4-2

Goalkeeper: **Keith Welch** – a sweeper keeper decades before the term was ever a thing. Great agility and very composed with the ball at his feet. May have lacked the height of a modern-day keeper but was outstanding. (Steve Phillips, Adriano Basso)

Right-back: **Bradley Orr** – excellent defender and a good athlete, which enabled him to get forward and add quality to the offensive side of the team. Cared passionately about the badge on his shirt. A polished footballer, converted from midfield to full-back. Top drawer. (Andy Llewellyn, Luke Ayling)

Centre-backs: **Louis Carey** (captain) – there are 646 reasons to pick Louis. Consistent, excellent reader of the game and could build from the back when in possession. A leader, unspectacular but highly consistent – essential attributes for a centre-back. **Aden Flint** – absolute warrior. Big in both boxes. Imposing and influential. Good reader of the game, which helped negate a lack of pace. Incredible goalscoring record. He's the first man I'd have in the trenches with me. (Mark Shail, Rob Newman, Matty Bryant, Shaun Taylor, Danny Coles, Steven Caulker, Adam Webster)

Left-back: A tough school this one. **Micky Bell** – I first saw Micky play in 1996 when I was assistant manager at Rovers. Micky was playing for Wycombe and was outstanding at Adams Park; he hardly gave the ball away all day and bombed forward to great effect. He could defend, was quick and fleet of foot. Wand of a left peg. Deadly on free kicks and penalties. (Martin Scott, John Bailey, Jim Brennan, Joe Bryan, Darren Barnard, Jamie McAllister)

Right midfield: **Scotty Murray** – archetypal wide man, stayed touchline wide and attacked whatever was in front of him – space or the opposition. Could go inside or outside and relished one v one situations. Quick and well balanced. Brilliant finisher. As honest as the day is long. (Mark Gavin, Albert Adomah, Junior Bent)

Central midfield: **Marvin Elliott** – an incredible engine but could play too. Box to box and could break the lines and take opposing midfielders into places they didn't want to go. Good in the air and combative. **Brian Tinnion** – incredible left foot and vision. Saw a pass, short or long, and delivered it in an instant. 'Tins' loved a diagonal pass into Scotty Murray's path. Scotty set off before the pass was delivered and so often scored or made a goal from the passage of play. Highly consistent performer, class footballer. (Tommy Doherty, Alex Scott, Dave Rennie, Bobby Hutchison, Josh Brownhill, David Noble, Marlon Pack, Gary Shelton)

Left midfield: **Alan Walsh** – famed for the 'Walshy shuffle', you knew what he was going to do but you couldn't stop it. Strong, powerful runner and never gave up. Blockbuster of a left peg. (Dave Smith, Greg Goodridge)

Strikers: **Bob Taylor** – Bob was a class act. Great first touch and happy to play in front of you or make runs in behind. Strong and powerful and could finish. Bob would give it and take it in terms of the physical battle. You couldn't relax for a second with Bob in the opposition. A top-drawer striker. **Shaun Goater** – absolute predator. One of those nightmare front men who the defender would keep quiet for 90 minutes and then he'd score the winner in added time. Modest and gracious but an assassin in front of goal. (Wayne Allison, Ade Akinbiyi, Andy Cole, Dariuz Dziekanowski, Steve Neville, Glynn Riley, Tony Thorpe, Antoine Semenyo)

Welch
Orr Carey Flint Bell
Murray Elliott Tinnion Walsh
Taylor Goater

Manager: Danny Wilson
Physio: Buster Footman
Kit man: Roger Barton

ROVERS
4-3-1-2

Goalkeeper: **Nigel Martyn** – the first £1m goalkeeper. 'Blazey' had everything, absolutely everything. (Brian Parkin, Steve Phillips)

Right-back: **Ian Alexander** – tenacious, quick and combative. Read the game well, was comfortable in possession and loved to transition defence into attack. (Dave Pritchard, Michael Smith)

Centre-backs: **Andy Tillson** – absolute model professional. Gave everything, every game. Strong in the air and read the game beautifully. 'Tilly' delivered some defence-splitting long passes. An inspirational leader. **Steve Yates** – my best-ever defensive partner. No-nonsense destroyer. Exceptionally quick, and good in the air for his size. An outstanding professional who loved every minute of every day of his football career. (Tom Lockyer, Steve Foster, Steve Elliott)

Left-back: **Vaughan Jones** (captain) – no-nonsense defender. Strong personality who ruffled feathers when needed and led by example. Read the game well, an excellent communicator and loved a tackle. (Lee Brown, Trevor Challis)

Right midfield: **David Mehew** – 'Boris' had an extraordinary knack of arriving in the penalty box at the right time and was a natural finisher. Worked hard out of possession and formed a strong link with Ian Alexander down the right. His goals were fundamental to the success under Gerry Francis. (Billy Bodin)

Central midfield: **Ian Holloway** – the heartbeat of the Championship-winning team. Not the best player I ever played with but the most influential. Ollie never gave up and always believed we could come back from losing positions. Excellent delivery on free kicks and corners. Showed great courage and technique to slot some crucial penalties during the run-in to the 1989/90 season. (Craig Disley, Andy Reece, Chris Lines, Stuart Campbell, Vitalijs Astafjevs)

Left midfield: **Elliot Anderson** – a cheat code! Too good for the level that he played at. Without doubt the single reason Rovers were promoted in 2022. Strong, fast, skilful, good in the air, high work rate and could score. Made the game look easy at times. Modest and understated off the pitch. (Phil Purnell, Mark Walters)

Strikers: Cor, this is a tough category! **Marcus Stewart** – the best outfield player I ever played with. Supremely balanced and had a velvet touch. 'Stewie' had an amazing appreciation of everything around him, he had great movement in the box and made goalscoring look ridiculously easy at times. **Rickie Lambert** – powerful and at times unplayable. Pure striker of the ball and could score from the most ridiculous situations and distances. **Gary Penrice** – a potent football brain allied with exceptional technique. 'Penny' played with a smile on his face and was a great finisher. We called him 'Lazarus' as he might not train until Friday morning then he'd invariably be outstanding on the Saturday. (Nathan Ellington, Jamie Cureton, Richard Walker, Barry Hayles, Jason Roberts, Devon White, Junior Agogo)

Martyn
Alexander Tillson Yates Jones
Mehew Holloway Anderson
Penrice
Lambert Stewart

Manager: Gerry Francis
Physio: Phil Kite
Kit man: Ray Kendall

Chapter 20

The Circle of Life

MY PARENTS' mortality is without doubt the most challenging thing I've ever had to deal with. As I said earlier, they shaped me, they taught me the values of life, they showed me love and affection. They taught me how to stand on my own two feet and what was right and what was wrong. They were two incredible people.

Dad passed away in 2004 at the age of 74. He suffered with Alzheimer's. He became forgetful in his mid-60s. For me, the start of this was when he gave up being a football talent scout. Dad had an amazing ability to remember players. If I mentioned the name of a footballer, he'd articulate his attributes and shortcomings immediately. This was before spreadsheets and computers. He kept a book and recorded some of the detail in writing, but most of it was in his head. Mum was convinced his situation was the result of heading footballs during his playing days. That definitely contributed to it and the football authorities need to get their act together in addressing this subject. I felt that Dad's brain slowed down when he no longer had to compute football information. He went from being exceptionally busy to not doing anything. The forgetfulness became more frequent, and

I guess it evolved into dementia. Then the gruesome diagnosis of Alzheimer's.

Mum had sheltered his situation from the family until she slipped on the stairs and broke her lower leg. The first night that my brother stayed with Dad the dreadful reality of his situation became painfully apparent. He wouldn't sleep, he walked round the house and wanted to go out for walks throughout the night. It was obvious he needed special care and was destined to live the rest of his life in a secure nursing home.

The care, love and kindness he received from the staff at the home in Southport was amazing. He was trapped in a world that no one should endure. It wasn't a life; it was an existence – a dire one at that. To be fair, my brother bore the burden of Dad's situation incredibly well. He took him out for walks and car journeys but inevitably there were problems as incontinence set in.

It was harrowing to shake hands with my dad. I'd look him in the eye, and he didn't have a clue who I was. Not a clue. I remember going to visit him after he'd been in the home a few years. He was sat motionless in a chair in the main lounge, just gazing into space. He heard my voice as I entered the room and from 25 feet away, he magically shouted, 'The big man's come to see me, the big man is here ...' I strode purposefully towards him, hoping for a proper welcome, but when I stood in front of him he'd reverted to type. He looked through me, he didn't know who I was. He was trapped in a cruel existence.

The only solace I took from his situation is that it seemed he was unaware of what was going on. I had no idea what went on inside his head, but it seemed that he didn't get anxious or upset when he didn't know who anyone was. He wasn't frustrated by his inability to live any form of a near normal life. He wasn't at pains with his situation. It was heart-breaking, it was my dad, my kids' granddad, a former elite athlete just trapped in his worthless world.

It was a relief when he was released from the existence. It was a Monday when I received a telephone call to tell me he'd taken a turn for the worse and that I needed to head from Bristol to the hospital in Southport. Dad had suffered some kind of major internal stomach trauma. The specialist felt that in the circumstances it wasn't a good idea to operate. When I arrived, Dad had passed away. I went into his room. He was sat up in his bed. He was in his pyjamas, his hair perfectly groomed. He looked peaceful, he looked younger than when I last saw him in the care home. I took his right hand and shook it firmly – the way he'd taught me. It was strange as he didn't grip me back, he didn't respond. I squeezed harder but to no effect. Dad had died, but I was relieved. He was free of an existence he didn't deserve, one he'd endured for way too long.

Alan Kennedy, a Liverpool great, dropped in to see Mum the next day. This was typical of the man that 'Barney' is. Liverpool manager Gérard Houllier sent Mum a beautiful letter.

The funeral at St Andrew's Church in Maghull was extraordinary. There were players from every decade of Liverpool Football Club's history from the 1950s when Dad wore the famous red shirt. I was on the back corner of the coffin and, as we entered the church, the first people I saw were Phil Thompson and Sammy Lee. Both were stood as if they had iron rods in their backs – upright, proud and respectful.

I spoke with obvious pride about Dad: 'Even in front of so many football luminaries and Liverpool greats, I have no hesitation in saying Dad was a football genius.'

As you read earlier, Graeme Souness was in the congregation; he loved my mum and dad. He was next to Emlyn Hughes. Ian St John was there, so was Ron Yeats. There were former team-mates and there were Liverpool supporters with red-and-white scarves draped on their shoulders. Emlyn, who passed away several months later, came back to the wake and told some fantastic tales about Dad and did a decent impression of Dad's Cumbrian accent.

I know I write this with an obvious bias, but Liverpool FC is a classy football club, it really is. Some years ago, a massive Red, Mark Platt, contacted me to see if I was aware of the tribute to Dad in one of the corporate lounges at Anfield. The 'Boot Room Boys' are remembered and paid permanent tribute to with a series of framed artwork highlighting their individual and unique abilities. They're amazing pieces of work. Mark sent me a photograph of the tribute to Dad, which is a pair of spectacles with his name and the words 'the best judge of character and eye for talent'. It's exceptional that Liverpool have remembered him and the key men from the club's history in such a spectacular and enduring way.

I sent a handwritten letter to the then CEO Ian Ayre and asked, with no expectation, whether I could pay for the production and shipping of a smaller version of Dad's artwork. A few weeks later I received a telephone call:

'Hello, is that Geoff?'

'Yes. Who's asking?'

'My name's Keith Watson from Liverpool Football Club. The chief executive has put your letter on my desk and told me to make it happen.'

Basically, Keith wanted the dimensions so he could 'make it happen'. He told me there would be no cost as Dad was held is such high regard at Anfield. When the piece of work was ready,

Liverpool showed their class by inviting me, Mark, Hannah and her fiancé Jon to Anfield for a game against Southampton. We were treated like royalty as we enjoyed food before and after the game in a corporate lounge. We watched from the directors' box. After the match, Alan Kennedy, who Dad scouted, made the presentation of the spectacular framed piece of work.

As if this wasn't enough, before the game something extraordinary occurred. In the week leading up to the Southampton game, Liverpool released an amazing piece of work called 'Liverpool FC Dream Scene'. This was a painting that depicted 19 key figures in the club's 125-year history inside of the home dressing room. It includes Paisley, Klopp, Shankly, Gerrard, Barnes, Dalglish, Liddell, Callaghan, Hughes, Hunt, Rush, Clemence and others. In the front right corner of the painting there's a book with 'Notes GT' on the cover.

On the Saturday we drove from Bristol and arrived in good time. Correction, our timing was absolute precision. We headed to the club's superstore where the original 'Dream Scene' was on display, and the artist Jamie Cooper was present to talk with fans and members of the public. There was a short queue, and we were soon at the front of the line. As we waited our turn, we heard the conversation between Jamie and two fans:

> JC: 'Yes, that's Roger Hunt and Ian Rush. There's Ian Callaghan and Ray Clemence.'
>
> Fan: 'It's an amazing piece of work, you've captured everyone so well, Mr Cooper. What's that book on the right with "Notes GT" on the front?'

Oh, my goodness. This was some form of outer-body experience. We were listening intently; they didn't have a clue who we were.

JC: 'Oh, that's Geoff Twentyman's book, the greatest football scout that ever lived. He discovered the likes of Ian Rush, Phil Neal, Alan Hansen and many others.'

Fan: 'Oh yes, of course, he was incredible, wasn't he?'

Mark and Hannah's faces were a joy to behold. This was their granddad who was being discussed and they were bursting with pride. So was I, obviously. The couple moved on, and I introduced myself and the family to Jamie, who found it extraordinary to meet Geoff Twentyman's immediate family. The whole episode was surreal. We'd travelled 175 miles, parked up and walked through Stanley Park to get to Anfield, and yet we arrived at the precise moment to hear this incredible conversation.

Liverpool FC continue to remember and respect the Boot Room Boys. In March of this year, I was thrilled to be at Anfield to witness the unveiling of a plaque to honour Ronnie Moran, Reuben Bennett, Joe Fagan, Roy Evans, Bob Paisley, Tom Saunders, John Benison and Dad. It was a class act from a classy football club. I also met Mark Platt and Keith Watson, which squared an important circle.

Mum passed away three years after Dad, in 2007. She was also deprived of any sense of a long, normal life as she had cancer for several years. I must say a huge thanks to my former mother-in-law Margaret Pollitt. She's a wonderful woman. I'd split up from her daughter, yet she took Mum into her nursing home and made sure she was afforded the best level of care possible. I know the family hugely appreciated her kindness.

Mum had withered away, which was a painful, sad sight to behold. She was bed-ridden and could only be fed water by using a teaspoon. She was incontinent and had to wear nappies. She was in a permanent sleep, and it was impossible to know if she was conscious. I don't know whether she was aware who was sat at her bedside.

I made a decision, a big call. I didn't want to sit and watch my mum die in front of me. It's a hugely personal thing but I opted not to be there. I asked the other family members for some privacy and was left alone with her. I moved in close and took her hand in mine. I spoke to her, not knowing if she could hear me, or if she could understand what I was saying: 'Mum, I'm going now, I'm going back to Bristol. I just want to thank you for everything that you've done for me. Thank you for making me the man that I am.' As I spoke, she gently squeezed my hand. She'd heard me. I squeezed her hand and kissed her on the cheek. As I did so, mini tears appeared and slowly trickled down her cheeks. It was a thing of beauty but broke my heart at the same time. I remained strong, kissed her for a final time and left. I know for sure that had I stayed and watched her die I wouldn't have had such a beautiful, intimate experience. I feel blessed to have said goodbye in such a glorious, ultra-personal way.

Mum died the next morning. She was some woman. Her legacy lives on as my daughter Hannah reminds me of her so much.

It's a strange feeling when both of your parents are no longer there. The ceiling has gone. There's no one to ask for advice, there's no one to run things by. There's a feeling of loneliness. I miss them every day, but I have so many amazing memories of two incredible people. I'm lucky to have had such wonderful parents.

The circle of life means when we lose, we gain. I'm blessed to be a father. Being a parent is a privilege. I was always close to Hannah and Mark, but our relationships gained an even greater level of closeness when their mother moved back to Liverpool after we divorced. I took on the exclusive responsibility of looking after them both.

Being a 'Pops' is an absolute joy. You must have experienced it to understand it. There's no saying 'no', there's just fun to be had and then you hand them back! Hannah and Jon have Ava, who's 13, Gigi's three and Teddy James is one. They're incredible, bright, funny, loving and entertaining. A quick word on Jon too. He's a fine man. When he asked for my permission to marry Hannah, I told him that I couldn't wish for a better man to look after my daughter for the rest of her life. Mark and Leanne have Mimi, who's three and is another delightful little human being.

It's important to surround yourself with people who bring value to your life. They could be family, they might be friends. Good, honest, positive people are uplifting. I'm not a fan of negativity. I know some situations must be approached with pragmatism but invariably I prefer a positive outlook.

I lost my best friend Dave Palmer in 2011. He was just 49, and a young 49 at that. Dave was on Rovers' books as a youngster and enjoyed a long and distinguished career at Bath City, where he made 445 appearances. 'Palmsey' was a brilliant bloke, an absolute Top Man. Tragically, he died of a heart condition. After various treatments didn't solve his problem, Dave was in Royal Papworth Hospital waiting for a heart transplant when he contracted a virus that caused his death. I was stunned. I always assumed he'd recover and would be back playing golf and living a normal life. It was numbing. Dave has two great kids in James and Ella. Ava was born and Dave passed away in the same week. My emotions were all over the place.

Dave and I played team golf at The Players. We were hugely competitive and were hard to beat. The year we lost Dave he won the nett club championship. Sadly, he wasn't well enough to attend the presentation evening that year and he didn't receive his trophy. The same year, Dave and I were drawn against each other in the semi-finals of the singles knockout competition. It was one of the toughest rounds of golf I've played. Coming up against your best mate and your team partner wasn't easy. I was two down with three holes to play. I managed to get it to one down as we teed it up on the 18th hole, which I won to take it into a sudden-death play-off. I won the match on the second extra hole. I felt totally underwhelmed. It's a tradition for the losing player to write the result on the competition sheet on the notice board in the clubhouse. Dave did the honourable thing and wrote my name in the slot for the final, and in brackets he wrote in capital letters (ONLY JUST). Typical Dave, brilliant.

We socialised with our partners at least once a month. My enduring memory of Dave is on our last night out (although I didn't know it at the time) in Bristol and it was last orders. He returned from the bar with a trademark big smile on his face, sparkling blue eyes, carrying four double gin and tonics – a perfect way to end the evening! I never saw him again. Life was for living as far as Dave Palmer was concerned. It was such an injustice that his was brought to such a tragically premature end. I think of Dave every day.

My golf buddies and big mates these days are two Top Men, Steve Colegate and Sam Clarke. I met Steve and Sam for the first time when I played in a charity golf day near Swindon over ten years ago. Sam, who ran a Jaguar dealership, had put a team in the event and I was assigned to his group, which included Steve. Cor, I was seriously hungover, having enjoyed the pre-event dinner until silly o'clock. My golf improved on the back nine after I'd had some sustenance at the halfway house. We got on well and Sam asked for my company the following year. We've been buddies ever since.

Steve is great fun and, despite stealing most of my banter, is brilliant company. He's a great confidant. He's a massive Red and loves the City. He tells me that the 1989/90 season simply didn't happen. With the considerable help of my mate Scotty Boy, I got Steve a signed City shirt for his 50th birthday with the number '50' and 'COLEGATE' on the back. I'll remember his reaction when he opened it forever; it was one of life's great moments for one of life's great guys.

Another great friend is Chris Bartlett. I've known 'Bartman' for decades. We met when he was the sports editor at the *Bristol Evening Post*. Chris took part in the Twentyman Challenge when we played three rounds in a day for Babe's Big Appeal. My enduring memory of 'Barts' that day is him scurrying to his car halfway round The Players to replenish his golf bag with more balls! To be fair, he did a brilliant two-page write-up of the event for the *Post* the following day. Chris was also the man behind my amazing 50th birthday gift. He loves telling the tale of when he rang Roger Hunt to arrange that game of golf for yours truly: 'Hello Roger, my name is Chris Barlett. You don't know me, but I'm after a favour …' Arranging it was a herculean effort, and I know Ali Bruce-Ball was also part of the process. It was an amazing day, one that I'll cherish for the rest of my life. Having mates who I can confide in and trust implicitly is a privilege.

Loyalty and friendships are important. In January 2000 I was listening to the radio in the kitchen and froze in my tracks as I heard that my former team-mate and good friend Dave Jones had been suspended by Southampton, where he was the manager. The report said Dave had been released on bail after being arrested for child abuse. The charges related to a time when he was a care worker on Merseyside, a role he took up after he finished playing football. Dave is married to Ann; he's a big family man and has four kids. Our families socialised together and, in my mind, Dave was a rock-solid bloke. I instinctively rang him. He answered straight away. He was devastated and in a state of shock. Without me asking, he told me he wasn't guilty and that he hadn't done anything. That was good enough for me.

A year or so later I received a call from a woman with a double-barrelled surname who worked for a London-based law firm with a triple-barrelled title. Having established that I knew Dave, she asked if she could send me a form to complete. It was to establish a character reference about Dave. It covered personality, anger, sexual tendencies, aggressive traits, interests and general behaviour. It was a comprehensive document. They wanted me to be as detailed as possible. I completed the form as diligently as I could. I cited an incident when Dave was manager of Stockport and I was assistant manager at Rovers. It all kicked off at Edgeley Park when at least six players from each side went at it in a mass brawl. Dave and I looked at each other, grinned, shrugged our shoulders, shook our heads and laughed. We let the referee sort it out. Dave rarely swore and hardly ever got annoyed. He's one of the most laid-back people I know.

A few days later the woman from the law firm rang back to advise me that the QC had determined that my reference was the strongest one that they'd gathered. She asked me if I'd be prepared to stand in the witness box in Liverpool Crown Court and articulate what I'd written in words under cross-examination. Instinctively, I replied, 'Yes, definitely.'

Dave faced more than a dozen charges. When the trial started, the red tops went for Dave and printed some horrendous allegations. It was written in a dreadful way – as if it was fact. It was grim and graphic. They had him bang to rights.

I prepared myself to be in court, but by the middle of the week the case was thrown out by the judge. All the charges were dropped. The prosecution case was flawed, and the prosecution witnesses were deemed unreliable. Some didn't even turn up to the court. As Dave had assured me at the start of his 18-month nightmare, he wasn't guilty, he hadn't done anything. It was a humbling experience when he called me that evening and thanked me for standing by him. Loyalty doesn't cost a penny.

Chapter 21

Joff Twentyman

OCTOBER 2022. There had been a lot of speculation about big changes in BBC local radio. In my decades at Radio Bristol 'change' had been effected a few times. However, this time the plans were going to have far-reaching effects on people's jobs, lives and livelihoods.

A series of Zoom calls were hosted by two senior BBC managers, Rhodri Talfan Davies and Jason Horton. The pair of BBC suits were going to overhaul local radio to deliver what was referred to as a 'better digital offering'. Inevitably this would come at a cost and there was a huge amount of opposition to the plans among staff. Managing editors were given new titles, and the majority were expected to run not one but two radio stations. It was going to be a very different new world. Just 12 months on from the big change, Radio Bristol had lost 40 per cent of its audience.

Shared programming, across several regions, in the weekday afternoons and evenings would potentially have a profound effect on me as I produced and presented my daily sport shows between 6pm and 7pm. Three strange days ensued that potentially had a major effect on my role:

> Day 1: On Monday to Friday all local radio stations were to have one regional, general programme from 6pm. This was bad.
>
> Day 2: The 6pm–7pm weekday sports programmes were to continue as before. This was good.
>
> Day 3: An email dropped to confirm that I was at risk of redundancy. This went to every local radio presenter. This was not good.

After 30 years it was a slap in the face. My themed football and rugby shows had often topped their respective charts on BBC Sounds. Being ahead of 5 Live programmes and podcasts counted for very little. Ironically, 12 months previously I'd been invited by Jonny Wall, the controller of BBC Sounds, to be part of a project to improve the profile of local radio sport on the BBC's listen-on-demand offering. Jonny is a great guy, and I was flattered to be part of the initiative.

The redundancy email sharply focused the mind but presented me with a wonderful opportunity. At 63 it was the perfect time to take voluntary redundancy. Two years' salary with some of it tax-free enabled me to sell my flat in Redland in Bristol and buy a new-build house in Magor in South Wales. Crucially, I'd be close to Hannah, Jon and my grandchildren. Seeing them growing up and being part of their lives was important to me. It was a priority. I could transition from seeing them once a week to enjoying their company as often as we wanted to. Perfect.

To be candid, I didn't want to have to apply for my own job. I didn't want to submit a show reel to display my apparent talent. I didn't want to go through an interview process. I wasn't being precious, but I had the option not to engage in the process.

In the same way as I left football and joined the BBC in 1993, I wanted to be in control of my own destiny. In November 2022 I clicked the option on the BBC website that submitted my expression of interest in voluntary redundancy. I received an acknowledgement with no timescale. This business was totally hush-hush. The only people who knew were Hannah, Jon and Mark. I told Jess Rudkin, my boss, and she said if that's what I wanted then she'd endorse my application. Jess was very supportive and gave me some great advice. Ironically, she'd also applied for voluntary redundancy and was a few months ahead of me in the process. My understanding was that if I didn't apply for my job, I'd be made redundant.

Until I heard back from HR it was business as usual. I felt sorry for colleagues who were worried about their futures. There was huge uncertainty for so many. There were lots of meetings, none of which I attended as I was confident that my future was elsewhere.

In February 2023 I messaged Jess for an update. She'd just had it confirmed that my voluntary redundancy had been sanctioned. Ironically, that week *Having a Gas* was the second most popular football show on BBC Sounds behind 5 Live's *Football Daily* – that show is not produced and presented by one person.

It was still totally confidential, but I had to action other important issues and put my flat on the market. The sales negotiator at the estate agent was a Radio Bristol listener and was interested in why I was moving and where I was moving to. Awkward.

I hadn't told any of my colleagues at this point. Jess left and was replaced by Gareth Roberts. Jess was a brilliant boss and was a modern-day Jenny Lacey. I'm not sure she'll thank me for that, but she also had a passion for radio, she was proactive and had an ability to get the best out of people.

When Jess introduced me to Gareth during their handover period, my opening gambit was, 'You've got big shoes to fill!' He accepted the comment in good faith. Gareth was brilliant in inheriting my situation and showed genuine empathy to my impending departure. It was still totally hush-hush while we worked out my final day at the BBC. I had quite a chunk of long-service leave and unused holidays outstanding. Gareth wanted me to stay until two weeks after the end of the football and rugby seasons so I could host the final editions of *The Sound of the City*, *The Scrum* and *Having a Gas*. My last day on air would be Monday, 22 May 2023, and my last day of service was 7 July.

On 11 April the genie was released from the bottle. In the morning Gareth sent an internal email to my colleagues at Radio Bristol and on *Points West* to let them know of my decision to leave the BBC. Everyone respected his request to not share the news until I'd told my audience that evening.

I announced my impending departure at around 6.20pm on *The Scrum*. Oh, my days. The response was incredible. I don't have the vocabulary to describe it, to be honest. Both Jess and Gareth had warned me there would be a huge reaction. I wasn't so sure, but the kindness and volume of messages way exceeded anything I'd anticipated. I was a million miles off the mark.

It was humbling, it was emotional, it was incessant. I'll remember the kindness forever. I didn't receive one adverse comment or message. For the next four weeks or so people stopped me for a chat. Life was far from normal. At times it was like I was living through an obituary, if that makes sense.

I was walking along Whiteladies Road in Bristol and a white van stopped. The driver got out and said nervously, 'It's Geoff Twentyman, isn't it?' He was a City fan in his mid-20s. He thanked me for my shows and *The Sound of the City* in particular. He listened on Saturdays on his way home from Ashton Gate. I admired his openness and the affection he showed. It's not easy for guys to express their emotions. We shook hands and he thanked me finally for being a huge part of his life. Extraordinary. Humbling.

I realised there were a huge number of people who listened to the shows, probably more than I'd previously appreciated. A guy messaged me on Twitter (now X) to say he used to listen to me in the back of his dad's car on their way to the City ground, and now he drove and his kids listened in the back of his car. That really is the circle of life. People were so kind.

A City fan called Matt Deane sent me a card containing a fabulous letter. He lives in Ringwood on the Hampshire/Dorset border and my shows were his way of keeping in touch with his club. He tuned in to *Saturday Sport* on the way to home games. On Mondays he listened to *The Sound of the City* with his eight-year-old daughter Charlotte. My sign-off at the end of each programme was always 'enjoy the rest of your Monday'. In his letter, which included a drawing from Charlotte, Matt told me that when she went to bed, she'd say to him, 'Dad, enjoy the rest of your Monday.' Incredible.

I presented *Saturday Sport* at the Memorial Stadium a week or so after announcing my departure, and Rovers fans literally queued to pass on their best wishes and thank me for my playing days and my time on the radio. It was a juggling act to chat with them while presenting live radio. People were incredibly kind.

I knew my last two Saturday outside broadcasts were at Ashton Gate for a City game and a Bristol Bears match. Rovers' final home game of the season was on a Sunday. I wasn't working. To be fair, the club invited me to be their guest but I declined the invite as I tried to avoid the public attention. It was all highly flattering but at times it was overwhelming.

I thought being live on air was a form of safe haven. It was my show, so I was in control. Think again Twentyman! I received an amazing reception before the City v Burnley game. I'll remember the applause reverberating around Ashton Gate for the rest of my life. The game went by, and afterwards two City fans, Paul Binning and Matt Withers, joined Gary Owers and me for some live analysis. It was always great to get fan opinion within minutes of the game ending. We were in full flow then something magical happened that I had absolutely no idea about. My show was hijacked. My programme, which I was in control of (allegedly), was railroaded by some incredible people.

Gary, Matt, Paul and I were chatting about the whys and the wherefores of the game when I heard a pop. You know that noise when a cork has been removed from a bottle of bubbly. No, surely not? Yes, absolutely, yes! I looked over my right shoulder and there was the smiling face of former City player Chris Honor, who also does some fantastic work on Radio Bristol covering City games. Chris was pouring champagne into some flutes. Alongside Chris was a group of Reds who were regular contributors to *The Sound of the City*. Rob Skeates, Ellie Jones, Nige Whittle, Lee Poole, Adam Gould, Leah Davis, Tony Wilkins and Mike Jones were representing a wider group of fans who'd commissioned and paid for an incredible framed caricature of yours truly. This was high-octane emotional stuff and I had to describe what was happening on the radio! It was an act of supreme kindness from a special group of people, some of whom have become valued friends.

During those 30 years on the radio, I had a theory that it was my job to deliver the news and not be the news. I think on this most special of special occasions it was permissible. That was some afternoon in BS3.

My final Saturday show was also at Ashton Gate as Bristol Bears hosted Gloucester. I thought everything was going to plan and I'd retained control of my show. Again, wrong. Towards the end of a pre-match interview with Bristol's chief operating officer, Tom Tainton, he told me that he'd gained permission from the BBC for the club to make a presentation to me on the pitch at half-time. This is obviously when I should have been behind the microphone, but I went along with it. The club presented me with a personalised Bears shirt with the number 20. They obviously didn't know I was a 15 in my pomp at Maghull Grammar! This was incredibly kind and hugely appreciated. Mark was in the mouth of the tunnel when I arrived pitch-side, which added to the surprise and emotion. I'm delighted that I'd helped to give the great game of rugby the coverage it deserves on Radio Bristol.

There were no further surprises as I got to 6pm and signed off. Pete Brealey and his colleagues from the excellent podcast *The Bears Beyond the Gate* were waiting to pass on their best wishes. This was my final Saturday show, which brought a feeling of sadness and pride. Sad because it was the last one, the end, but pride as I was happy with the quality of the shows and sports output that Radio Bristol was delivering.

So, there was a fortnight or so to go before my last programme on Monday, 22 May. Gareth Roberts told me not to over-produce the final edition of *The Sound of the City*, as 'we're going to take over halfway through'.

Walking into the BBC that final day was a strange feeling. I wasn't overly emotional. I think the sense of pride and satisfaction associated with my longevity overrode any sadness. This was my decision. I felt fulfilled and satisfied. I wanted to enjoy my final day. Enjoy my final day – now there's an understatement.

Hannah, Jon and the kids sent me a beautiful bouquet of flowers to mark my final day. I enjoyed an extended chat with John Darvall on his show. The plan was to go for food with Mark, Hannah and my partner Julie after *The Sound of the City*. The table was booked for 7.30pm.

For my final City show I was joined by three Top Men: Matt Withers, Del Bussey and Rob Blamey were live in the studio to talk about City's season that had ended a couple of weeks earlier. Like I said before, these guys were more than fans who came on my show. We got to know each other over the years and we enjoyed a beer on occasion. Friendships were formed and still prevail.

At 6.30pm, as advised, I switched chairs, and Richard Hoskin took over and presented an extraordinary sequence of messages and tributes. Several people had worked exceptionally hard to deliver highly polished, engaging and totally humbling radio. I'm indebted to Richard, Gareth, Tom Ryan and Kirsty Ward for making it happen. Every time I thought 'wow', the next guest was even more compelling.

Steve Lansdown, Joe Barton, Pat Lam, Caz May, the King of Southmead Joe Joyce, Lark Davies, Gary Johnson, Gary Owers, Bradley Orr and Keith Warmington got the ball rolling. Then, incredibly, Ian Holloway and Scotty Boy Murray arrived in the studio. Scott brought in a wonderful glass memento from City. There were further messages from Ali Bruce-Ball and Chris Jones.

Just as I thought the show had peaked, there was a mind-blowing sequence. It was seriously difficult not to get emotional and fall apart. Marcus Stewart sent an incredible message: 'My mate Geoff Twentyman …' it really tugged at my heartstrings. It was the only point of the show that I lost my composure and I just about managed to bring Scott into the conversation! Marcus is an inspiration to all of us in how to deal with adversity. His message was a thing of beauty. He's the best footballer I ever played with. He has a heart of gold. My heart aches for Marcus, Louise, Finlay and Kian.

Next up was a message from Jürgen Klopp. The video from the then Liverpool manager is mind-blowing. I struggled to compute what was going on. Jürgen Klopp had sent me a message. He was obviously briefed about the situation, but he delivered it with consummate poise and credibility:

> Joff. What can I say? The name Joff Twentyman is one that will always be associated with this wonderful football club. The achievements of your father speak for themselves and will always be celebrated. But today is about celebrating you and the incredible work you have done at the BBC. To spend 30 years at an organisation as well renowned as the BBC is remarkable in itself, but the fact this career only began after your previous one as a footballer makes it even more special. So, on behalf of everyone at Liverpool FC, I would like to wish you the very best for retirement. You have more than earned it so please enjoy it. You'll Never Walk Alone.

This was staggering, and just when I was thinking it was the perfect send-off there was the ultimate finale. Having listened to their recorded message, Hannah and Mark came into the studio. Sensational, absolutely sensational.

It was some send-off. I was humbled and flattered by the quality of the programme and the words expressed by so many great people. The 7.30pm table reservation had to be put back twice, to 8.15pm!

I'd wondered how I'd feel when I left the BBC for the final time. I was fine, and to walk out with my two kids felt absolutely perfect.

Manage people – be true to yourself

Although managing other people is your priority, you must be mindful that your well-being is paramount. If you're at peace with yourself, your chances of doing your job well will vastly improve.

It's essential that you're always true to yourself and keep regrets to a minimum. As a manager you'll have to make lots of decisions. You won't always get them right but make sure the majority are good calls. It can be useful to have someone outside of the business who you trust and can confide in. Having someone you can bounce ideas off and talk things through with is invaluable.

Career opportunities will come your way and it's important you make the right decisions at the right time. Have no regrets, you only live once!

Managing upwards is a skill. If you present your boss or manager with a problem, then offer a solution to the problem. Invariably they'll accept it.

You'll have situations when you and your boss see things differently and disagree. Don't expect to 'win' every argument. Allow your manager to win some, but make sure you succeed in the ones that really matter to you.

Chapter 22

Expect the Unexpected

'YOU'LL GET offers of work from people and businesses that you won't expect.' Jess Rudkin, my former boss, was astute. As usual she was on the money when we spoke about my life after my impending departure from the BBC.

On the day that I announced I was leaving, SGS College got in touch to sound me out about lecturing on their sport media journalism courses. Ian Holtby was the connection. I've known 'Holters' for decades, and the former stadium manager at Rovers, who's the site manager at the college's Wise Campus, was keen to get me involved. Ian set up a meeting with Alex Gaiger, a vice-principal at the college, and we sorted an agreement.

I'm delighted to be passing on my experience in small group sessions. The students are very bright and hugely committed. It's extremely stimulating to see them respond in a positive way. Max Baker, one of the tutors, has been brilliant in supporting me in the role. I helped to establish a collaboration with Bradley Stoke Radio. With considerable assistance from one of their presenters, John Lock, the SGS students now produce and present their own radio show. *The Friday Sports Club* is an excellent listen. The first academic year flew by and I'm looking forward to the sequel. Huge thanks to Holters for making the approach.

Carolyn Park is someone I've known for a few years. She owns a travel agency called C the World, in Thornbury in South Gloucestershire, and she contacted me soon after I left the BBC. She'd recently acquired a golf travel company called Golf to a Tee and asked me if I'd be interested in hosting some golf trips for her. When you put your name to something it's got to be a good product. Carolyn is top drawer and everything she does is of the highest quality. We had an amazing time in May when we took a group of golfers to the north coast of Northern Ireland. We played three amazing courses – Castlerock, Port Stewart and the 2025 Open venue Royal Portrush. The Harbour Bar in Portrush is well worth a visit if you're in the vicinity.

When I was at the BBC, Gary Owers asked me about doing a football roadshow. These are 'pie and a pint' nights to talk football at social clubs and pubs in and around Bristol. I wasn't allowed to do commercial ventures when I was a BBC employee. I've known Gary for decades, he's a brilliant bloke. We're enjoying the events, which are proving to be very popular. A massive thanks to my good friend Dave Willis from Heineken, who has been very supportive with our initiative. Dave is a Top Man.

Call it poacher turned gamekeeper if you like, but I'm also doing some media training with professional people. I know what makes a good interviewee as well as a good interviewer. This is very stimulating and really rewarding.

To be honest, the biggest challenge has been not to get too busy. The whole reason for leaving the BBC was to ease down, to see more of the family. I could easily have made the mistake of doing too much. It's all very flattering and it's fantastic to do things that I really want to do, some of which is new to me and I enjoy – things that stimulate me.

I nearly returned to the BBC not once but twice. When I was finalising my exit, the managing editor, Gareth Roberts, made an interesting comment: 'I hope it's not the end of your relationship with the BBC.' The rules state that you can return to the Corporation as a freelancer three months after taking a voluntary redundancy package.

Gareth and I met for a coffee in August 2023, just a few months after I'd left. He wanted me to go back to present *Saturday Sport*, the Saturday afternoon sports show. The earliest that I was allowed to return was 7 October – three months after my official leaving date. We agreed that I'd return on Saturday, 28 October. It was a busy day, with all five of the main teams in action. I was really looking forward to it. Then a few weeks later Gareth rang me to cancel the arrangement. Apparently, it was 'too sensitive', as some BBC presenters were being made redundant. This decision had come from people higher up the food chain. I emphasised that we were adhering to the BBC's own rules. Gareth shouldn't have made me an offer that he couldn't deliver.

He contacted me again in April 2024 and offered me the opportunity to return on the opening day of the 2024/25 football season. We once again agreed that I'd return; however, soon after, an unexpected opportunity came my way that made me change my mind. The reality is, had I gone back to the BBC on 28 October 2023, I'd still be there. Their indecision and reneging on our original agreement proved to be crucial. As Gareth said when I told him of my decision not to return, 'It wasn't meant to be.'

The three biggest things that have changed or affected broadcasting since I joined the BBC in 1993 are technology, social media and fan expectation. Technology has developed incredibly. Life is so much better, and having to broadcast via expensive permanent lines that had to be installed at the venue is a thing of the past. The cloud and the internet mean that you can pitch up and broadcast from almost anywhere. This is a hugely positive development.

Social media has its uses and is valuable in many ways. Huge numbers of people use it in a positive way, but it has unfortunately become a safe home for anonymous racists, homophobes and all-round abusers. The providers of the various platforms should be far more accountable and, in tandem with the government, far greater control should be exerted on 'keyboard warriors'.

As people know, I'm a huge advocate of giving supporters a platform to deliver their opinions. A fundamentally important element of my football- and rugby-themed programmes was to give the supporters of City, Rovers, Bath and Bristol an opportunity to praise and criticise objectively. It was my role to challenge and play devil's advocate to extend the discussion. Healthy discussions meant sometimes we'd agree to disagree. This was my idea of having constructive debates. Direct abuse on social media or a fans' forum isn't healthy. Some levels of abuse are simply unacceptable.

Football head coaches and managers seem to have less and less time to deliver success. We live in what I call an 'Amazon Society'. We can order something on Amazon in the morning and it will be delivered on the same day. We get used to instant, ultra-speedy processes. Football and rugby don't work that way. It takes time to build success but what managers must do is progress. Going backwards in terms of league positions season on season will always attract criticism. Some fans get carried away with short-termism. Three wins in a row and the manager is the best thing since sliced bread. Three defeats in succession and there are calls for a sacking. Realism and patience are two important qualities for fans to embrace.

Two aspects of player welfare in football and rugby concern me. Each sport gets one right and one wrong. Head injuries are dealt with really well in rugby. The need for an HIA (head injury assessment) might be obvious to the referee but it can also be ordered by an independent doctor. The player leaves the pitch and undergoes a series of tests to determine any level of concussion. The player can't return for ten minutes. If they fail the test, he or she has to be substituted and may be sidelined for up to two weeks. Football has no such process. I know the games are different, but footballers are still prone to head injuries. Football must learn from rugby.

The other thing I have an issue with is how injured players are removed from the field of play. Football gets this one right. Stretchers and trained medical staff are used. It takes time but the player may well have a serious injury and the period that the game is stopped for is simply added on. In rugby, all too often a player will hop off the field or be partly dragged off with their arms over the shoulders of two people who are invariably shorter than the injured player. I know rugby players are tough, but these are elite athletes and any chance of exacerbating the injury should be reduced by using a stretcher. Rugby must learn from football.

Football finances are out of kilter. The monetary value of TV deals for the Premier League continue to increase. Years ago, callers to my shows used to tell me the bubble would burst. The reality is the bubble is getting bigger. Multiple broadcasters and the global demand mean the current deals are worth more than £5 billion. Clubs in the Football League must maintain a responsibility to generate their own income and ensure they maintain financial stability, but I believe that some of the TV revenue should cascade or, realistically, trickle down to the Football League and the National League. The top clubs need the footballing infrastructure not only to find lower league gems but they need clubs to loan players out to so they can develop.

I'm not a fan of VAR (video assistant referee). It's wrong that a football fan can't celebrate a goal inside a stadium without the fear of it being disallowed after lines have been drawn on a screen for nearly five minutes to determine an offside call. VAR is here to stay but it must be defined to be more user-friendly. It must become much more efficient. There needs to be a maximum duration for a VAR check. Presently, the VAR official is making a subjective call, so why can't the responsibility remain with the match referee to make their own subjective decision? I wish the referee would back themselves more often when they review the incident on the pitch-side screen. I thought VAR was for 'clear and obvious mistakes'. It isn't being used that way. It's being employed as a forensic tool that's damaging the game's credibility. I worry that a significant number of fans will turn their backs on football. It's dangerous to suck the excitement out of a sport. Rugby and cricket have review systems that work or are certainly more functional and accepted than those in football. Football must sort VAR.

Rugby must find a way of reintroducing promotion and relegation to and from the Premiership. It's a false contest when there's no fear of being relegated. There must always be an incentive for the teams in the pyramid to be part of the top flight. Championship teams and their supporters must be allowed to be ambitious and dream of playing elite rugby. I'm a big rugby fan but feel the top level of the sport is too comfortable and the RFU and rugby hierarchy need to address this as a matter of some urgency.

'Health is wealth' is something really important that my daughter taught me in the last couple of years. Hannah was concerned about a mole on her leg that had changed shape. Typically, she looked the situation in the eye and sought medical attention straight away. The care she was afforded by the health service in Wales was incredible. It was a malignant melanoma. The specialist who removed it praised Hannah for addressing the situation with such immediacy. Had she delayed there was a high chance that the melanoma could have spread very quickly. I'll never forget Hannah and Jon going for an important hospital appointment after she'd been summoned at two days' notice. I looked after Gigi. Young and in love, they strode off into the sunshine. The next few hours were potentially life-changing, life-threatening.

For the first time in my adult life, I was scared. I couldn't affect the situation. As a dad you always think that you can look after your kids, there's always something you can do to help. Not this time. I was helpless. An hour or so later Hannah rang me from the hospital. I took a deep breath and answered. I could tell by the tone of her voice it was going to be good news. She'd had the all-clear. The relief was palpable. After we ended the call, I cried. Tears of joy, tears of relief.

I asked Hannah if I could share her experience with you. This was her reply: 'No problem. As I say, it may help one person and that's a good enough reason to include it.'

I know several people who are battling health issues. I have no idea how they and their families deal with the constant struggles.

I don't know how they cope. I can't relate to it, but I'm genuinely inspired and humbled by people such as Jazz Ellis, a big City fan; Sean Lewis, who I used to play golf with; Tony Morgan, who runs the Sartan Club in South Bristol; former Radio Bristol colleague Laura Rawlings; former City full-back Chris Honor; and my incredible mate Marcus Stewart. They're all in tough battles. I send them, and anyone in a similar situation, my love and every best wish possible.

My go-to man is Nick Anderton. The former Rovers player is a shining example that it's possible to recover, but fate must be your best friend. I hope that Jazz, Sean, Tony, Laura, Chris and Stewie win their battles. Hannah is so right: health really is wealth.

I've enjoyed putting my thoughts and experiences into print. It was an obsession at times. I'd read a chapter so many times and thought it was complete, then a memory or a thought would come to me at a strange time and place. It was a matter of scribbling it down in note form and then adding it to the main draft afterwards. It's been fun.

I'd deliberated about writing a book for quite a while. Several people had suggested that I should do it. I questioned it, wondering who'd want to read it. I guess I needed someone or something to give me that final bit of encouragement. That moment came after my extraordinary final show on 22 May 2023. I was in a state of semi-shock in the Radio Bristol studio after being the focal point of a programme with such an incredible cast list. I embraced my mate Ian Holloway, and Ollie said to me, 'If you don't do a book, I'll kill you … I mean it, you need to do a book …'

So, I did. I hope you've enjoyed it.